# myeconlab
### For Bade/Parkin Second Edition

**W9-AZZ-767**

## Great news!
## MyEconLab can help you improve your grades!

With your purchase of a new copy of this textbook, you received a Student Access Kit for **MyEconLab** for Bade/Parkin. Your Student Access Kit looks like this:

## DON'T THROW IT AWAY!

**If you did not purchase a new textbook or cannot locate the Student Access Kit** and would like to access the resources in **MyEconLab** for Bade/Parkin, you may purchase a subscription online with a major credit card at www.myeconlab.com/bade.

What is **MyEconLab** and how will it help you? **MyEconLab** is an extensive online learning environment with a variety of tools to help raise your test scores and increase your understanding of economics. **MyEconLab** includes the following resources:

- ***Foundations eText:*** Your textbook in an online interactive format, with animated graphs and audio narrations

- ***Foundations eStudy Guide:*** The Study Guide online, integrated with the eText

- ***Foundations Interactive:*** An online tutorial that allows you to manipulate variables, draw graphs, review concepts, and self-test

- ***Diagnostic Quizzes:*** Four levels of quizzes with instant grading and feedback

- ***Office Hours:*** A link that allows you to ask the textbook authors economics-related questions

- ***MathXL for Economics:*** A basic math skills tutorial with help on creating and interpreting graphs, solving applied problems using graphs, calculating ratios and percentages, and calculating average, median and mode

- Many other text-specific Web resources!

## To activate your prepaid subscription:

1. Locate the **MyEconLab** Student Access Kit that came bundled with your textbook.

2. Ask your instructor for your **MyEconLab** course ID.*

3. Go to www.myeconlab.com/bade. Follow the instructions on the screen and use the access code in your **MyEconLab** Student Access Kit to register as a new user.

\* If your instructor does not provide you with a Course ID, you can still access most of the online resources listed above. Go to www.myeconlab.com/bade to register.

JOBM

JobSatisfication

Emotional or Affective
Measure

| NATIONAL INCOME AND PRODUCT ACCOUNTS | 1968 | 1969 | 1970 | 1971 | 1972 | 1973 | 1974 | 1975 | 1976 | 1977 |
|---|---|---|---|---|---|---|---|---|---|---|
| **EXPENDITURES APPROACH** | | | | | | | | | | |
| the sum of — 1 Personal consumption expenditures | 558.7 | 605.5 | 648.9 | 702.4 | 770.7 | 852.5 | 932.4 | 1,030.3 | 1,149.8 | 1,278.4 |
| 2 Gross private domestic investment | 141.2 | 156.4 | 152.4 | 178.2 | 207.6 | 244.5 | 249.4 | 230.2 | 292.0 | 361.3 |
| 3 Government purchases | 212.8 | 224.6 | 237.1 | 251.0 | 270.1 | 287.9 | 322.4 | 361.1 | 384.5 | 415.3 |
| 4 Exports | 45.3 | 49.3 | 57.0 | 59.3 | 66.2 | 91.8 | 124.3 | 136.3 | 148.9 | 158.8 |
| less — 5 Imports | 46.6 | 50.5 | 55.8 | 62.3 | 74.2 | 91.2 | 127.5 | 122.7 | 151.1 | 182.4 |
| equals — 6 Gross domestic product | 911.5 | 985.3 | 1,039.7 | 1,128.6 | 1,240.4 | 1,385.5 | 1,501.0 | 1,635.2 | 1,823.9 | 2,031.4 |
| **INCOMES APPROACH** | | | | | | | | | | |
| the sum of — 7 Compensation of employees | 524.3 | 577.6 | 617.2 | 658.8 | 725.1 | 811.2 | 890.2 | 949.0 | 1,059.3 | 1,180.4 |
| 8 Proprietors' income | 75.4 | 78.9 | 79.8 | 86.1 | 97.7 | 115.2 | 115.5 | 121.6 | 134.3 | 148.3 |
| 9 Rental income of persons | 20.2 | 20.3 | 20.3 | 21.2 | 21.6 | 23.1 | 23.0 | 22.0 | 21.5 | 20.4 |
| 10 Corporate profits | 96.5 | 93.7 | 81.6 | 95.1 | 109.8 | 123.9 | 114.5 | 133.0 | 160.6 | 190.9 |
| 11 Net interest | 27.2 | 32.2 | 38.4 | 42.6 | 46.2 | 53.9 | 68.8 | 76.6 | 80.8 | 95.7 |
| equals — 12 National income | 743.6 | 802.7 | 837.5 | 903.9 | 1,000.4 | 1,127.4 | 1,211.9 | 1,302.2 | 1,456.4 | 1,635.8 |
| plus — 13 Indirect business tax minus subsidies | 70.8 | 76.7 | 86.7 | 98.1 | 100.4 | 102.5 | 108.6 | 128.8 | 141.3 | 143.3 |
| 14 Consumption of fixed capital | 90.9 | 99.8 | 109.1 | 118.9 | 130.9 | 142.9 | 164.8 | 190.9 | 209.0 | 231.6 |
| 15 Net factor incomes from rest of world | 6.2 | 6.1 | 6.4 | 7.7 | 8.7 | 12.7 | 15.7 | 13.3 | 17.2 | 20.7 |
| equals — 16 Gross domestic product | 911.5 | 985.3 | 1,039.7 | 1,128.6 | 1,240.4 | 1,385.5 | 1,501.0 | 1,635.2 | 1,823.9 | 2,031.4 |
| 17 Real GDP (billions of 1996 dollars) | 3,466.1 | 3,571.4 | 3,578.0 | 3,697.7 | 3,898.4 | 4,123.4 | 4,099.0 | 4,084.4 | 4,311.7 | 4,511.8 |
| 18 Real GDP growth (percent per year) | 4.8 | 3.0 | 0.2 | 3.3 | 5.4 | 5.8 | −0.6 | −0.4 | 5.6 | 4.6 |
| **OTHER DATA** | | | | | | | | | | |
| 19 Population (millions) | 200.7 | 202.7 | 205.1 | 207.7 | 209.9 | 211.9 | 213.9 | 216.0 | 218.0 | 220.2 |
| 20 Labor force (millions) | 78.7 | 80.7 | 82.8 | 84.4 | 87.0 | 89.4 | 91.9 | 93.8 | 96.2 | 99.0 |
| 21 Employment (millions) | 75.9 | 77.9 | 78.7 | 79.4 | 82.2 | 85.1 | 86.8 | 85.8 | 88.8 | 92.0 |
| 22 Unemployment (millions) | 2.8 | 2.8 | 4.1 | 5.0 | 4.9 | 4.4 | 5.2 | 7.9 | 7.4 | 7.0 |
| 23 Labor force participation rate (percent) | 59.6 | 60.1 | 60.4 | 60.2 | 60.4 | 60.8 | 61.3 | 61.2 | 61.6 | 62.3 |
| 24 Unemployment rate (percent of labor force) | 3.6 | 3.5 | 4.9 | 5.9 | 5.6 | 4.9 | 5.6 | 8.5 | 7.7 | 7.1 |
| 25 Real GDP per person (1996 dollars per year) | 17,270 | 17,621 | 17,449 | 17,806 | 18,573 | 19,458 | 19,167 | 18,912 | 19,775 | 20,486 |
| 26 Growth rate of real GDP per person (percent per year) | 3.7 | 2.0 | −1.0 | 2.0 | 4.3 | 4.8 | −1.5 | −1.3 | 4.6 | 3.6 |
| 27 Quantity of money (M2, billions of dollars) | 566.8 | 587.9 | 626.4 | 710.1 | 802.1 | 855.2 | 901.9 | 1,015.9 | 1,151.7 | 1,269.9 |
| 28 GDP deflator (1996 = 100) | 26.3 | 27.6 | 29.1 | 30.5 | 31.8 | 33.6 | 36.6 | 40.0 | 42.3 | 45.0 |
| 29 GDP deflator inflation rate (percent per year) | 4.3 | 4.9 | 5.3 | 5.0 | 4.2 | 5.6 | 9.0 | 9.3 | 5.7 | 6.4 |
| 30 Consumer price index (1982–1984 = 100) | 34.8 | 36.7 | 38.8 | 40.5 | 41.8 | 44.4 | 49.3 | 53.8 | 56.9 | 60.6 |
| 31 CPI inflation rate (percent per year) | 4.3 | 5.5 | 5.8 | 4.3 | 3.3 | 6.2 | 11.1 | 9.1 | 5.7 | 6.5 |
| 32 Current account balance (billions of dollars) | 0.6 | 0.4 | 2.3 | −1.4 | −5.8 | 7.1 | 2.0 | 18.1 | 4.3 | −14.3 |

# ESSENTIAL FOUNDATIONS *of* ECONOMICS

The challenge and thrill of learning a new subject is like the task of the explorers who first charted America's lakes and rivers. When we set out, we are unsure of the direction to take. Along the way, we often feel lost. But as we progress forward, we see ever more clearly the path we're taking, even the parts where we felt lost, and we see how our path fits into a bigger and broader picture.

Students, like explorers, benefit enormously from the experience of those who have traveled before them and from the maps that these earlier explorers have made. They also benefit from retracing their path. And they gain perspective by pausing and looking back at where they've been.

Our aims in *Essential Foundations of Economics* are to travel with you on a journey of discovery, to support you every step of the way so that you are never disoriented or lost, and to help you understand and appreciate the economic landscape that surrounds you.

The cover of this text symbolizes our aims. The lake is the terrain of economics that we're going to cover, understand, and appreciate. The rising sun and *Foundations* icon are our light sources—the clearest and most sharply focused explanations and illustrations of economic principles and ideas. The icon also emphasizes the idea of building blocks that fit one on top of another but that stand on a firm foundation. Each block is a small and easily handled object that can be understood on its own and then more keenly appreciated as part of a larger picture.

# ESSENTIAL FOUNDATIONS *of* ECONOMICS

## Second Edition

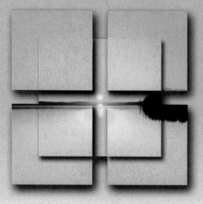

### Robin Bade

### Michael Parkin
*University of Western Ontario*

PEARSON

Addison
Wesley

Boston  San Francisco  New York
London  Toronto  Sydney  Tokyo  Singapore  Madrid
Mexico City  Munich  Paris  Cape Town  Hong Kong  Montreal

| | |
|---|---|
| *Editor-in-Chief* | Denise Clinton |
| *Senior Editor* | Victoria Warneck |
| *Editorial Assistant* | Catherine Bernstock |
| *Executive Development Manager* | Sylvia Mallory |
| *Senior Project Manager* | Mary Clare McEwing |
| *Supplements Editor* | Jason Miranda |
| *Senior Administrative Assistant* | Dottie Dennis |
| *Senior Media Producer* | Melissa Honig |
| *Senior Marketing Manager* | Stephen Frail |
| *Online Marketing Specialist* | Katherine Kwack |
| *Managing Editor* | James Rigney |
| *Senior Production Supervisor* | Nancy Fenton |
| *Senior Design Manager* | Regina Kolenda |
| *Technical Illustrator* | Richard Parkin |
| *Electronic Publisher* | Sally Simpson |
| *Electronic Publishing Specialist* | Laura Wiegleb |
| *Senior Manufacturing Buyer* | Hugh Crawford |
| *Copy Editor* | Barbara Willette |
| *Indexer* | Robin Bade |

Library of Congress Cataloging-in-Publication Data

Bade, Robin.
      Essential foundations of economics / Robin Bade, Michael Parkin.-- 2nd ed.
         p.    cm.
      Includes bibliographical references and index.
      ISBN 0-201-74880-0
      1. Economics.  I. Parkin, Michael, 1939–    II. Title

      HB171.5.B154 2004
      330—dc21                       2003050234

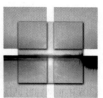

To Erin, Tessa, Jack, and Abby

## Robin Bade

**Robin Bade** was an undergraduate at the University of Queensland, Australia, where she earned degrees in mathematics and economics. After a spell teaching high school math and physics, she enrolled in the Ph.D. program at the Australian National University, from which she graduated in 1970. She has held faculty appointments at the University of Edinburgh in Scotland, at Bond University in Australia, and at the Universities of Manitoba, Toronto, and Western Ontario in Canada. Her research on international capital flows appears in the *International Economic Review* and the *Economic Record*.

Robin first taught the principles of economics course in 1970 and has taught it (alongside intermediate macroeconomics and international trade and finance) most years since then. She developed many of the ideas found in this text while conducting tutorials with her students at the University of Western Ontario.

## Michael Parkin

**Michael Parkin** studied economics in England and began his university teaching career immediately after graduating with a B.A. from the University of Leicester. He learned the subject on the job at the University of Essex, England's most exciting new university of the 1960s, and at the age of 30 became one of the youngest full professors. He is a past president of the Canadian Economics Association and has served on the editorial boards of the *American Economic Review* and the *Journal of Monetary Economics*. His research on macroeconomics, monetary economics, and international economics has resulted in more than 160 publications in journals and edited volumes, including the *American Economic Review*, the *Journal of Political Economy*, the *Review of Economic Studies*, the *Journal of Monetary Economics*, and the *Journal of Money, Credit, and Banking*. He is author of the best-selling textbook, *Economics* (Addison-Wesley), now in its Sixth Edition.

Robin and Michael are a wife-and-husband duo. Their most notable joint research created the Bade-Parkin Index of central bank independence and spawned a vast amount of research on that topic. They don't claim credit for the independence of the new European Central Bank, but its constitution and the movement toward greater independence of central banks around the world were aided by their pioneering work. Their joint textbooks include *Macroeconomics* (Prentice-Hall), *Modern Macroeconomics* (Pearson Education Canada), and *Economics: Canada in the Global Environment*, the Canadian adaptation of Parkin, *Economics* (Addison-Wesley). They are dedicated to the challenge of explaining economics ever more clearly to an ever-growing body of students.

Music, the theater, art, walking on the beach, and four fast-growing grandchildren provide their relaxation and fun.

# Economics

# Brief Contents

# Contents

**PART 3    PRICES, PROFITS, AND INDUSTRY PERFORMANCE                217**

## PART 5    UNDERSTANDING THE MACROECONOMY                 397

We began the preface to our first edition of *Foundations of Economics* by attempting to answer a question that we thought would be on many people's minds: *Why*? With Michael's book, *Economics*, Sixth Edition, an established, best-selling text, why on earth would we write a new book?

In retrospect, as we publish the Second Edition of *Foundations of Economics* and its companion volume, *Essential Foundations of Economics*, we find ourselves wondering more and more why we didn't write *Foundations* sooner. The response from the economics community has been tremendous. Clearly, many of you agree with our view that

- Most introductory economics textbooks try to do too much;
- Students too frequently get lost in a sea of detail; and
- Economics is a subject that can be learned only by doing it.

We have encountered this view from our own students, and we have heard it echoed by literally hundreds of colleagues across the United States and throughout the world. But creating a teaching and learning system that takes this view seriously is no easy task. *Foundations of Economics* is the result of our best effort to do so and to help students and teachers meet the challenges we all face.

## LOWERING THE BARRIERS TO ENTRY

Most economics professors want to teach a serious, analytical course that explains the core principles of our subject and helps students apply these principles in their lives and jobs. We are not content to teach "dumbed-down" economics. But most students drown rather than learn to swim when thrown into the deep end of the pool. In this book and its accompanying learning tools, we make painstaking efforts to lower the barriers to learning and to reach out to the beginning student.

We focus on core concepts. We steer a steady path between an overload of detail that swamps the students and a minimalist approach that leaves the student dangling with too much unsaid. We explain tough concepts with the simplest, most straightforward language possible, and we reinforce them with clear, fully explained graphs. And we offer students a rich array of active learning tools that provide alternative ways of accessing and mastering the material.

## ■ FOCUS ON CORE CONCEPTS

Each chapter of *Essential Foundations* concentrates on a manageable number of main ideas (most commonly three or four) and reinforces each idea several times throughout the chapter. This patient, confidence-building approach guides students through unfamiliar terrain and helps them to focus their efforts on the most important tools and concepts of our discipline.

## ■ DIAGRAMS THAT TELL THE WHOLE STORY

We developed the style of our diagrams with extensive feedback from faculty focus group participants and student reviewers. All figures make consistent use of color to show the direction of shifts and contain detailed, numbered captions designed to direct students' attention step by step through the action. Because beginning students of economics are often apprehensive about working with graphs, we have made a special effort to present material in as many as three ways—with graphs, words, and tables—in the same figure. And in an innovation that seems necessary but is to our knowledge unmatched, nearly all of the information supporting a figure appears on the same page as the figure itself. No more flipping pages back and forth!

## ■ MANY LEARNING TOOLS FOR MANY LEARNING STYLES

Our text and its integrated print and electronic learning package recognize that students have a variety of learning styles. Some learn easily by reading the textbook; others benefit from audio and visual reinforcement. All students can profit from an active learning approach. Your students' textbooks come with access to a suite of innovative learning tools, including tutorial software, an eText featuring animated graphs with audio voiceovers, interactive quizzes, and more.

### PRACTICE MAKES PERFECT

Everyone agrees that the only way to learn economics is to do it! Reading and remembering doesn't work. Active involvement, working problems, repeated self-testing: These are the ingredients to success in this subject. We have structured this text and its accompanying electronic and print tools to encourage learning by doing. The central device that accomplishes this goal is a tightly knit learning system based on our innovative *Checklist-Checkpoints* structure.

## ■ CHECKLISTS

Each chapter opens with a *Chapter Checklist*—a list of (usually) three or four tasks the student will be able to perform after completing the chapter. Each Checklist item corresponds to a section of the chapter that engages the student with a conversational writing style, well-chosen examples, and carefully designed illustrations.

## ■ CHECKPOINTS

A full-page *Checkpoint*—containing a Practice Problem with solution and a parallel Exercise—immediately follows each chapter section. The Checkpoints serve as stopping points and encourage students to review the concept and to practice using it before moving on to new ideas. Diagrams and tables bring added clarity to the Checkpoint problems and solutions.

Each Checkpoint also contains a page reference to the corresponding material in the Study Guide as well as a reference to the corresponding section of our online learning environment. We describe these learning tools more fully below.

## ■ CHAPTER CHECKPOINTS

At the end of each chapter, a *Chapter Checkpoint* summarizes what the student has just learned with a set of key points and a list of key terms. It also contains a further set of questions divided into three groups: exercises, critical thinking, and Web exercises.

## ■ CONVEYING THE EXCITEMENT

Students learn best when they can see the point of what they are studying. We show the point in a series of *Eye On...* features. Current and recent events appear in *Eye on the U.S. Economy* boxes. We place our present experience in global and historical perspectives with *Eye on the Global Economy* and *Eye on the Past* boxes. All of our *Eye On...* boxes connect theory with reality.

## ORGANIZATION

Our text focuses on core topics with maximum flexibility. We cover all the standard topics of the one-term principles of economics curriculum. And we do so in the order that is increasingly finding favor in the principles course. We believe that a powerful case can be made for teaching the subject in the order in which we present it here.

We introduce and explain the core ideas about efficiency and fairness early and then cover major policy issues using only the tools of demand and supply and the ideas of marginal benefit, marginal cost, and consumer and producer surplus. Topics such as cost curves, which are more technical, are covered later.

Deciding the order in which to teach the components of microeconomics involves a tradeoff between building all the foundations and getting to policy issues early in the course. There is little disagreement that the place to begin is with production possibilities and demand and supply. We provide a carefully paced and thoroughly modern treatment of these topics.

Following the order of this text, the course quickly gets to interesting policy issues. Two further chapters lay the foundation: elasticity in Chapter 5 and a discussion of the efficiency and fairness of markets in Chapter 6. Introducing students to both efficiency and fairness (equity) issues early in the course enables a more complete and engaging discussion of topics such as taxes, price floors, price ceilings, and externalities, all of which we cover in Chapters 7 and 8. Teaching this material early in the course maintains student interest, directly serves the role of the principles course as a foundation for citizenship, and provides an immediate payoff from learning the demand-supply and related tools. Only when these policy issues have been covered do we dig more deeply behind the consumption and production decisions.

Teachers who prefer to cover policy issues later in the course can skip Chapters 6 through 8 and move straight from elasticity to the economics of the firm. The policy-related chapters can be covered at any chosen point later in the course.

Our coverage of macroeconomics is organized in two parts: Monitoring the Macroeconomy and Understanding the Macroeconomy. We provide three solid chapters that deal respectively with measuring real GDP and the standard of living (Chapter 13); measuring the CPI and the cost of living (Chapter 14); and measuring the state of the labor market and fluctuations around full employment (Chapter 15).

The chapters that explain macroeconomic performance exploit the idea that at full employment, the real economy is influenced by only real variables and the price level is proportional to the quantity of money. So Chapter 16 explains economic growth and Chapters 17–19 explain the monetary system and long-term inflation trends. Away from full employment, real variables and nominal variables interact to bring the business cycle. Chapter 20 explains the cycle using the *AS-AD* model and Chapter 21 studies the use of monetary and fiscal policy to stabilize the business cycle.

By providing a firm understanding of the forces that determine potential GDP and long-term growth, the student better appreciates the more complex interactions of real and monetary factors that bring economic fluctuations. Further, the student sees that the long-term trends in our economy play a larger role in determining our standard of living and cost of living than do the fluctuations around those trends.

Extensive reviewing suggests that most teachers agree with our view on how to organize the course. But we recognize that there is a range of opinion about sequencing, and we have structured our text so that it works equally well if other sequences are preferred. Some teachers want to follow the measurement material with aggregate supply and aggregate demand, then money and the price level and finally economic growth. Our text supports this sequence. After Chapter 14, it is possible to jump to Chapter 20 (*AS-AD* and the Business Cycle). The money chapters (17, 18, and 19) can be covered next, followed by stabilization policy (Chapter 21).

## A RICH ARRAY OF SUPPORT MATERIALS FOR THE STUDENT

*Essential Foundations of Economics* is accompanied by the most comprehensive set of learning tools ever assembled. All the components of our package are organized by Checkpoint topic so that the student may move easily between the textbook, the Study Guide, eText, interactive tutorial, and online diagnostic quizzes, while mastering a single core concept.

The variety of tools that we provide enables students to select the path through the material that best suits their individual learning styles. The package is technology-enabled, not technology-dependent. Active learners will make extensive use of the *Foundations Interactive* tutorial and the animated graphics of eText, our online version of the textbook. Reflective learners may follow a print-only path if they prefer.

# ■ STUDY GUIDE

Tom Meyer of Patrick Henry Community College, Neil Garston and Tom Larson of California State University, Los Angeles, and Mark Rush of the University of Florida have prepared a Study Guide that is available in both print and electronic formats. The Study Guide provides an expanded Chapter Checklist that enables the student to break the learning tasks down into smaller, bite-sized pieces; self-test materials; expanded explanations of the solutions to the practice problems in the text; and additional practice problems. To ensure consistency across the entire package, the authors who wrote the questions for the Test Bank also wrote the self-test questions for the Study Guide.

# ■ FOUNDATIONS INTERACTIVE

A Java and JavaScript tutorial software program that runs in a Web browser, *Foundations Interactive* contains electronic interactive versions of most of the textbook figures. The student manipulates the figures by changing the conditions that lie behind them and observes how the economy responds to events. Quizzes that use five question types (fill-in-the-blank, true-or-false, multiple-choice, complete-the-graph, and numeric) can be worked with, or optionally without, detailed feedback. *Foundations Interactive* is available through the Foundations Web site, within the MyEconLab course, and on CD-ROM.

# ■ FOUNDATIONS WEB SITE

The Foundations Web site is a powerful and tightly integrated online learning environment. For students, the site includes

- eText—the entire textbook in PDF format with hyperlinks to all the other components of the Web site with video clips and animated figures accompanied by audio explanations prepared by us
- eStudy Guide—the entire Study Guide online
- *Foundations Interactive*—tutorials, quizzes, and graph tools that with a click of the mouse make curves shift and graphs come to life
- Diagnostic quizzes for every Checkpoint with feedback that includes hyperlinks to the e-text, e-Study Guide, and *Foundations Interactive*
- Economics in the News updated daily during the school year
- Online "Office Hours"—ask a question via email and one of us will respond within 24 hours!
- Economic links—links to sites that keep students up to date with what's going on in the economy and that enable them to work end-of-chapter Web exercises

# ■ MyEconLab COURSE

MyEconLab delivers the entire content of the Foundations Web site in a course management system. Students whose instructors use MyEconLab gain access not only to the resources of the Foundations Web site, but also to

- MathXL for Economics—a powerful tutorial to refresh students on the basics of creating and interpreting graphs, solving applied problems using graphs, calculating ratios and percentages, performing calculations, calculating average, median and mode, and finding areas.

- Research Navigator™—a one-stop research tool, with extensive help on the entire research process, including evaluating sources, drafting, and documentation, and access to a variety of scholarly journals and publications, a complete year of search for full-text articles from the *New York Times*, and a "Best of the Web" Link Library of peer-reviewed Web sites.
- eThemes of the Times—thematically related articles from the *New York Times* accompanied by critical thinking questions.

The Student Access Kit that arrives bundled with all new books walks students step-by-step through the registration process.

## ■ THE ECON TUTOR CENTER

Staffed by qualified, experienced college economics instructors, the Econ Tutor Center is open five days a week, seven hours a day. Tutors can be reached by phone, fax, and e-mail. The Econ Tutor Center hours are designed to meet your students' study schedules, with evening hours Sunday through Thursday. Students receive one-on-one tutoring on examples, related exercises, and problems. Please contact your Addison-Wesley representative for information on how to make this service available to your students.

## ■ ECONOMIST.COM EDITION

The premier online source of economic news analysis, economist.com provides your students with insight and opinion on current economic events. Through an agreement between Addison-Wesley and *The Economist*, your students can receive a low-cost subscription to this premium Web site for 3 months, including the complete text of the current issue of *The Economist* and access to *The Economist's* searchable archives. Other features include web-only weekly articles, news feeds with current world and business news, and stock market and currency data. Professors who adopt this special edition will receive a complimentary one-year subscription to economist.com.

## ■ THE WALL STREET JOURNAL EDITION

Addison-Wesley is also pleased to provide your students with access to *The Wall Street Journal*, the most respected and trusted daily source for information on business and economics. For a small additional charge, Addison-Wesley offers your students a 10-week subscription to *The Wall Street Journal* print edition and *The Wall Street Journal Interactive Edition*. Adopting professors will receive a complimentary one-year subscription of both the print and interactive versions.

## ■ FINANCIAL TIMES EDITION

Featuring international news and analysis from FT journalists in more than 50 countries, the *Financial Times* will provide your students with insights and perspectives on economic developments around the world. The *Financial Times Edition* provides your students with a 15-week subscription to one of the world's leading business publications. Adopting professors will receive a complimentary one-year subscription to the *Financial Times* as well as access to the Online Edition at FT.com.

## A QUALITY-ASSURED SUPPORT SYSTEM FOR THE INSTRUCTOR

Our instructor resource tools are the most comprehensive, carefully developed, and accurate materials ever made available. *Foundations Interactive*, the Study Guide, the diagnostic quizzes on the Foundations Web site, the PowerPoint lecture notes, the Instructor's Manual, and the Test Banks, all key off the Checkpoints in the textbook. The entire package has a tight integrity. We are the authors of *Foundations Interactive*, the diagnostic quizzes, and PowerPoint notes. We have paid close attention to the design, structure, and organization of the Web site. And we have helped in the reviewing and the revising of the Study Guide, Instructor's Manual, and Test Banks to ensure that every element of the package achieves the consistency that students and teachers need.

### ■ INSTRUCTOR'S MANUAL

The Instructor's Manual contains chapter outlines and road maps, answers to in-text exercises, additional exercises with solutions, and a virtual encyclopedia of suggestions on how to enrich class presentation and use class time efficiently. The micro portion has been written by Carol Dole (State University of West Georgia) and Mark Rush, and the macro portion has been written by Richard Gosselin (Houston Community College) and Mark Rush.

### ■ THREE TEST BANKS

Three separate Test Banks are available for *Essential Foundations of Economics*, with more than 5,000 multiple-choice, true-false, numerical, fill-in-the-blank, short-answer, and essay questions. New to this edition, integrative questions build on material from more than one Checkpoint or more than one chapter. Mark Rush reviewed and edited questions from seven dedicated principles instructors  for microeconomics and six for macroeconomics to form one of the most comprehensive testing systems on the market. Our questions authors on the micro side are Seemi Ahmad (Dutchess Community College), Sue Bartlett (University of South Florida), Jack Chambless (Valencia Community College), Carol Dole (State University of West Georgia), Paul Harris (Camden County Community College), William Mosher (Assumption College), and Terry Sutton (Southeast Missouri State University). Our questions authors on the macro side are Ali Ataiifar (Delaware County Community College), Diego Mendez-Carbajo (Illinois Wesleyan University), William Mosher (Assumption College), Terry Sutton (Southeast Missouri State University), Cindy Tori (Valdosta State University), and Nora Underwood (University of California-Davis). These Test Bank authors also wrote questions for the Study Guide to ensure consistency.

### ■ POWERPOINT RESOURCES

We have created the PowerPoint resources based on our 10 years of experience using this tool in our own classrooms. Every figure and table—every single one, even those used in Checkpoint questions and solutions—is included in the PowerPoint lecture notes, many of them animated so that you can build them gradually in the classroom. Key figures can be expanded to full screen size or shrunk to make space for text explanations at a single mouse click during a lecture. We have determined the optimal build sequence for the animated figures and produced them with the same degree of clarity and precision as the figures in the text.

The speaking notes sections of the PowerPoint files provide material from the Instructor's Manual on teaching tips and suggestions.

### ■ MyEconLab

Custom built for *Essential Foundations*, MyEconLab delivers all of the interactive resources available on the Foundations Web site in a comprehensive online course. With MyEconLab, instructors can customize existing content and add their own. They can manage, create, and assign tests to students, choosing from our extensive test bank, or upload tests they've written themselves. MyEconLab also includes advanced tracking features that record students' usage and performance, and a Gradebook feature to see students' test results. In addition, the instructor will find short video clips for each chapter—ideal for sparking classroom discussion or motivating lectures. Please refer to the Instructor Quick Start Guide or contact your Addison-Wesley sales representative to set up your course.

### ■ VIDEOS

In addition to the short video clips mentioned above, a comprehensive series of lecture videos accompanies the text. The videos follow the same Checklist-Checkpoint format as the book itself, and feature presentations by Robin Bade, Michael Parkin, Kaya Ford (Northern Virginia Community College), Gary Latanich (Arkansas State University), Kirk Gifford (Brigham Young University, Idaho), and Carol Dole (State University of West Georgia). The videos are available on VHS tapes and on CD-ROM.

### ■ OVERHEAD TRANSPARENCIES

Full-color overhead transparencies of *all* figures from the text will improve the clarity of your lectures. They are available to qualified adopters of the text (contact your Addison-Wesley sales representative).

### ■ INSTRUCTOR'S RESOURCE DISK WITH COMPUTERIZED TEST BANKS

This CD-ROM contains Computerized Test Bank files, Test Bank and Instructor's Manual files in Microsoft Word, and PowerPoint files. All three Test Banks are available in Test Generator Software (TestGen-EQ with QuizMaster-EQ). Fully networkable, it is available for Windows and Macintosh. TestGen-EQ's graphical interface enables instructors to view, edit, and add questions, transfer questions to tests, and print different forms of tests. Tests can be formatted by varying fonts and styles, margins, and headers and footers, as in any word-processing document. Search and sort features let the instructor quickly locate questions and arrange them in a preferred order. QuizMaster-EQ, working with your school's computer network, automatically grades the exams, stores the results on disk, and allows the instructor to view and print a variety of reports.

## ■ FASTFAX TESTING

FastFax Testing is designed for instructors who do not have access to a computer or an assistant who can help prepare tests for students. Simply choose from a large pool of questions in the print test bank and include custom headers, if you like. Fill out the test information sheet that lists instructor-selected questions and test preferences that describe how the test should be generated. You may even request multiple forms of a test and receive answer keys for each one.

Turnaround time is usually 48 hours or less and test pages can be mailed or faxed back to you by the date the test is needed. FastFax Testing is fast, reliable, and free to qualified adopters of this text.

## ACKNOWLEDGMENTS

Working on a project such as this generates many debts that can never be repaid. But they can be acknowledged, and it is a special pleasure to be able to do so here and to express our heartfelt thanks to each and every one of the following long list, without whose contributions we could not have produced *Essential Foundations*.

Mark Rush is our Study Guide, Instructor's Manual, and Test Bank coordinator and manager. He assembled, polished, wrote, and rewrote these materials to ensure their close consistency with the text. He and we were in constant contact as all the elements of our text and package came together. Mark also made many valuable suggestions for improving the text and the Checkpoints. His contribution went well beyond that of a reviewer. And his effervescent sense of humor kept us all in good spirits along the way. Working closely with Mark, Tom Meyer, Neil Garston, and Tom Larson wrote content for the Study Guide and Carol Dole and Richard Gosselin wrote content for the Instructor's Manual. Seemi Ahmad, Ali Ataiifar, Sue Bartlett, Jack Chambless, Carol Dole, Paul Harris, Diego Mendez-Carbajo, William Mosher, Terry Sutton, Cindy Tori, and Nora Underwood provided questions for the Study Guide and Test Banks.

The ideas that ultimately became *Foundations* began to form over dinner at the Andover Inn in Andover, Massachusetts, with Denise Clinton and Sylvia Mallory. We gratefully acknowledge Sylvia's role not only at the birth of this project but also in managing the entire development team. Denise has been our ongoing inspiration for almost ten years. She is the most knowledgeable economics editor in the business, and we are privileged to have the benefit of her enormous experience.

The success of *Foundations* owes much to Victoria Richardson Warneck, our outstanding sponsoring editor. We are in awe of Victoria's extraordinary editorial craft. It has been, and we hope it will for many future editions remain, a joy to work with her.

Mary Clare McEwing has been our indomitable development editor, ably assisted by Dottie Dennis. We said in the preface to the first edition that Mary Clare had rounded up the best group of reviewers we'd ever worked with. We are astounded to report that for this edition, she has surpassed even the high standards she previously achieved. Mary Clare has steered the revision along through several redrafts and polishes. And she began the design process with focus groups that told us what teachers and students look for in the design of a textbook.

Gina Kolenda converted the raw ideas into this outstandingly designed text. Meredith Nightingale provided the detailed figure designs.

Jason Miranda did an incredible job as editor of our print supplements and coordinated the work of our large team of coauthors.

Michelle Neil, Executive Media Producer, and Melissa Honig, our technology gurus, have brought much to this project. Michelle spearheaded the effort to set up MyEconLab, worked creatively to improve our technology systems, and worked with our editors and us to develop our media strategy. Melissa built our Web site and worked tirelessly to help develop the engine that drives *Foundations Interactive*. They have both been sources of high energy, good sense, and level-headed advice, and have quickly found creative solutions to all our technology problems.

Nancy Fenton, our ever cheerful, never stressed production supervisor, ensured that all the elements eventually came together to bring our text out on schedule. Sally Simpson, our electronic publisher, and Laura Wiegleb, electronic production specialist, performed their magic to make our pages look beautiful. And Hugh Crawford oversaw the manufacturing process and worked with the printers and binders to produce beautiful, on-time books.

Our marketing manager, Adrienne D'Ambrosio, added enormous value, not only by being acutely intelligent and having a sensitive understanding of the market, but also by sharpening our vision of our text and package. As this book was in progress, Adrienne moved on to become an economics acquisitions editor and Stephen Frail joined us as marketing manager. Jit Teo and Catherine Bernstock stayed late many nights fielding requests from the sales force, and Kathy Kwack managed our online marketing efforts.

Our copy editor, Barbara Willette, and supplements copy editor, Sheryl Nelson, gave our work a thorough review and helpful polish.

Richard Parkin, our technical illustrator, created the figures in the text, the dynamic figures in the online version of the text, the illustrations in *Foundations Interactive*, and the animated versions of the figures in the PowerPoint presentations and contributed many ideas to improve the clarity of our illustrations. Laurel Davies created and edited the *Foundations Interactive* database and acted as its accuracy checker and reviewer.

Jeannie Gillmore, our personal assistant, worked closely with us in creating *Foundations Interactive* and the diagnostic Web quizzes and served as a meticulous accuracy checker on the text, Study Guide, and Instructor's Manual. John Graham of Rutgers University, Stephen McCafferty of Ohio State University, Harry Ellis of the University of North Texas, Paul Poast of Ohio State University, and Kate Krause of the University of New Mexico also provided careful accuracy reviews.

Jane McAndrew, economics librarian at the University of Western Ontario, went the extra mile on many occasions to help us track down the data and references we needed.

Finally, our reviewers, whose names appear on the following pages, have made an enormous contribution to this text. In the many texts that we've now written, we've never seen reviewing of the quality that we enjoyed on this project. It has been a pleasure (if at times a challenge) to respond constructively to their many excellent suggestions.

Robin Bade
Michael Parkin
London, Ontario, Canada
robin@econ100.com
michael.parkin@uwo.ca

Charles Aguilar, El Paso Community College
Seemi Ahmad, Dutchess Community College
William Aldridge, Shelton State Community College
Ali Ataiifar, Delaware County Community College
John Baffoe-Bonnie, Pennsylvania State University, Delaware County Campus
Kenneth Baker, University of Tennessee, Knoxville
A. Paul Ballantyne, University of Colorado
Sue Bartlett, University of South Florida
Klaus Becker, Texas Tech University
Daniel Bernhofen, Clark University
John Bethune, Barton College
David Bivin, Indiana University–Purdue University at Indianapolis
Geoffrey Black, Boise State University
Barbara Brogan, Northern Virginia Community College
Christopher Brown, Arkansas State University
Donna Bueckman, University of Tennessee, Knoxville
Nancy Burnett, University of Wisconsin at Oshkosh
Barbara Caldwell, University of South Florida
Bruce Caldwell, University of North Carolina, Greensboro
Robert Carlsson, University of South Carolina
Shawn Carter, Jacksonville State University
Jack Chambless, Valencia Community College
Joni Charles, Southwest Texas State University
Robert Cherry, Brooklyn College
Paul Cichello, Xavier University
Quentin Ciolfi, Brevard Community College
Jim Cobbe, Florida State University
John Cochran, Metropolitan State College
Ludovic Comeau, De Paul University
Carol Conrad, Cerro Coso Community College
Christopher Cornell, Fordham University
Richard Cornwall, University of California, Davis
Kevin Cotter, Wayne State University
Tom Creahan, Morehead State University
Elizabeth Crowell, University of Michigan at Dearborn
Susan Dadres, Southern Methodist University
Jeffrey Davis, ITT Technical Institute (Utah)
Dennis Debrecht, Carroll College
Al DeCooke, Broward Community College
Vince DiMartino, University of Texas at San Antonio
Carol Dole, State University of West Georgia
John Dorsey, University of Maryland, College Park
Marie Duggan, Keene State College

David Eaton, Murray State University
Harry Ellis, University of North Texas
Stephen Ellis, North Central Texas College
Carl Enomoto, New Mexico State University
Gary Ferrier, University of Arkansas
Rudy Fichtenbaum, Wright State University
Kaya Ford, Northern Virginia Community College
Robert Francis, Shoreline Community College
Roger Frantz, San Diego State University
Arthur Friedberg, Mohawk Valley Community College
Todd Gabe, University of Maine
James Gale, Michigan Technological University
Julie Gallaway, Southwest Missouri State University
Neil Garston, California State University at Los Angeles
Lisa Geib-Gunderson, University of Maryland
Linda Ghent, Eastern Illinois University
Kirk Gifford, Ricks College
Maria Giuili, Diablo Valley Community College
Mark Gius, Quinnipiac College
Randall Glover, Brevard Community College
Stephan Gohmann, University of Louisville
Richard Gosselin, Houston Community College
John Graham, Rutgers University
Warren Graham, Tulsa Community College
Jang-Ting Guo, University of California, Riverside
Dennis Hammett, University of Texas at El Paso
Leo Hardwick, Macomb Community College
Mehdi Haririan, Bloomsburg University
Paul Harris, Camden County Community College
Gus Herring, Brookhaven College
Michael Heslop, Northern Virginia Community College
Steven Hickerson, Mankato State University
Andy Howard, Rio Hondo College
Yu Hsing, Southeastern Louisiana University
Matthew Hyle, Winona State University
Harvey James, University of Hartford
Russell Janis, University of Massachusetts at Amherst
Philip N. Jefferson, Swarthmore College
Ted Joyce, City University of New York, Baruch College
Arthur Kartman, San Diego State University
Chris Kauffman, University of Tennessee
Diane Keenan, Cerritos College
Brian Kench, University of Tampa
John Keith, Utah State University
Douglas Kinnear, Colorado State University
Morris Knapp, Miami-Dade Community College
Steven Koch, Georgia Southern University
Kate Krause, University of New Mexico

Stephan Kroll, St. Lawrence University
Charles Krusekopf, Austin College
Joyce Lapping, University of Southern Maine
Tom Larson, California State University, Los Angeles
Robert Lemke, Florida International University
Tony Lima, California State University at Hayward
Kenneth Long, New River Community College
Marty Ludlum, Oklahoma City Community College
Zachary B. Machunda, Minnesota State University, Moorhead
Roger Mack, De Anza College
Michael Magura, University of Toledo
Mark Maier, Glendale College
Paula Manns, Atlantic Cape Community College
Kathryn Marshall, Ohio State University
Drew E. Mattson, Anoka-Ramsey Community College
Stephen McCafferty, Ohio State University
Thomas McCaleb, Florida State University
Diego Mendez-Carbajo, Illinois Wesleyan University
Thomas Meyer, Patrick Henry Community College
Meghan Millea, Mississippi State University
Michael Milligan, Front Range Community College
Jenny Minier, University of Miami
David Mitchell, Valdosta State University
William Mosher, Assumption College
Ronald Nate, Brigham Young University, Idaho
Michael Nelson, Texas A&M University
Charles Newton, Houston Community College Southwest
Melinda Nish, Salt Lake Community College
Lee Nordgren, Indiana University at Bloomington
William C. O'Connor, Western Montana College–University of Montana
Charles Okeke, College of Southern Nevada
Kathy Parkison, Indiana University, Kokomo
Sanjay Paul, Elizabethtown College
Ken Peterson, Furman University
Tim Petry, North Dakota State University
Charles Pflanz, Scottsdale Community College
Paul Poast, Ohio State University
Greg Pratt, Mesa Community College
Fernando Quijano, Dickinson State University
Karen Reid, University of Wisconsin, Parkside
Mary Rigdon, University of Texas, Austin
Helen Roberts, University of Illinois, Chicago
Barbara Ross-Pfeiffer, Kapiolani Community College
Jeffrey Rous, University of North Texas
Udayan Roy, Long Island University
Mark Rush, University of Florida
Joseph Santos, South Dakota State University
Roland Santos, Lakeland Community College

Ted Scheinman, Mount Hood Community College
Jerry Schwartz, Broward Community College
Sharmistha Self, College of St. Benedict/St. John's University
Gautam Sethi, Bard College
Martin Spechler, Indiana University
John Stiver, University of Connecticut
Terry Sutton, Southeast Missouri State University
Vera Tabakova, Louisiana State University
Donna Thompson, Brookdale Community College
James Thorson, Southern Connecticut State University
Marc Tomljanovich, Colgate University
Cynthia Royal Tori, Valdosta State University
Ngoc-Bich Tran, San Jacinto College South
Nora Underwood, University of California, Davis
Christian Weber, Seattle University
Jack Wegman, Santa Rosa Junior College
Jason White, Northwest Missouri State University
Benjamin Widner, Colorado State University
Barbara Wiens-Tuers, Pennsylvania State University, Altoona
William Wood, James Madison University
Ben Young, University of Missouri, Kansas City
Michael Youngblood, Rock Valley College
Joachim Zietz, Middle Tennessee State University
Armand Zottola, Central Connecticut State University

# Getting Started

## CHAPTER CHECKLIST

When you have completed your study of this chapter,
you will be able to

**1** Define economics, distinguish between microeconomics and macroeconomics, and explain the questions economics tries to answer.

**2** Describe the work of economists as social scientists.

**3** Explain five core ideas that define the economic way of thinking.

**4** Explain why economics is worth studying.

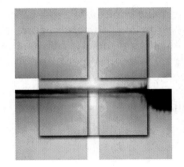

You are studying economics at a time of enormous change. After a decade of technological change that brought MP3 music, DVD movies, cell phones, Palm Pilots, and a host of other gadgets and toys that have transformed the way we work and play, our lives were changed by the terrorist attacks of September 11, 2001. The shock waves from that day will pulsate through our economy for many years. They have shrunk our airlines, expanded our security and defense industries, and created huge uncertainty about the future.

Outside the United States, more than 1 billion of the world's 6.3 billion people survive on $1 a day or less. Disturbed by the combination of increasing wealth and persistent poverty, some people are pointing to globalization as the source of growing economic inequality.

Your course in economics will help you to understand the powerful forces that are shaping our economic world and help you to navigate it in your everyday life and work.

## 1.1 DEFINITIONS AND QUESTIONS

All economic questions and problems arise because human wants exceed the resources available to satisfy them. We want good health and long lives. We want spacious and comfortable homes. We want a huge range of sports and recreational equipment from running shoes to jet skis. We want the time to enjoy our favorite sports, video games, novels, music, and movies; to travel to exotic places; and just to hang out with friends.

In the world of politics, it is easy to get carried away with the idea that we can have it all. Politicians tell us they will provide all the extra public services that we want, and at the same time, they will cut our taxes so that we can spend more on the things that we enjoy.

Despite the promises of politicians, we cannot have it all. The ability of each of us to satisfy our wants is limited by time and by the incomes we earn and the prices we pay for the things we buy. These limits mean that everyone has unsatisfied wants. Our ability as a society to satisfy our wants is limited by the productive resources that exist. These resources include the gifts of nature, our own labor and ingenuity, and tools and equipment that we have produced.

**Scarcity**
The condition that arises because the available resources are insufficient to satisfy wants.

Our inability to satisfy all our wants is called **scarcity**. The poor and the rich alike face scarcity. A child wants a $1.00 can of soda and two 50¢ packs of gum but has only $1.00 in his pocket. He faces scarcity. A millionaire wants to spend the weekend playing golf *and* spend the same weekend at the office attending a business strategy meeting. She faces scarcity. A society wants to provide vastly improved health care, install an Internet connection in every classroom, explore space, clean polluted lakes and rivers, and so on. Society also faces scarcity.

Faced with scarcity, we must make choices. We must *choose* among the available alternatives. The child must *choose* the soda *or* the gum. The millionaire must *choose* the golf game *or* the meeting. As a society, we must *choose* among health care, computers, space exploration, the environment, and so on.

**Incentive**
A reward or a penalty—a "carrot" or a "stick"—that encourages or discourages an action.

The choices we make depend on the incentives we face. An **incentive** is a reward or a penalty—a "carrot" or a "stick"—that encourages or discourages an action. If the price of gum rises and the price of soda falls, the child has an *incentive*

*Even parrots face scarcity!*

Not only do <u>I</u> want a cracker—we <u>all</u> want a cracker!

©The New Yorker Collection 1985
Frank Modell from cartoonbank.com. All Rights Reserved.

to choose less gum and more soda. If a profit of $10 million is at stake, the millionaire has an *incentive* to attend the meeting and skip the golf game. As computer prices tumble, school boards have a stronger *incentive* to connect more classrooms to the Internet.

**Economics** is the social science that studies the choices that we make as we cope with *scarcity* and the *incentives* that influence and reconcile our choices. The subject divides into two main parts:

- Microeconomics
- Macroeconomics

**Economics**
The social science that studies the choices that we make as we cope with *scarcity* and the *incentives* that influence and reconcile our choices.

## ■ Microeconomics

**Microeconomics** is the study of the choices that individuals and businesses make and the way these choices respond to incentives, interact, and are influenced by governments. Some examples of microeconomic questions are: Why are more people buying SUVs and fewer people buying minivans? How will a cut in the price of the Sony PlayStation and Microsoft Xbox affect the quantities of these items that people buy?

**Microeconomics**
The study of the choices that individuals and businesses make and the way these choices respond to incentives, interact, and are influenced by governments.

## ■ Macroeconomics

**Macroeconomics** is the study of the aggregate (or total) effects on the national economy and the global economy of the choices that individuals, businesses, and governments make. Some examples of macroeconomic questions are: Why did production and jobs expand so rapidly in the United States during the 1990s? Why has Japan been in a long period of economic stagnation? Why did the Federal Reserve cut interest rates during 2001 and keep them low through 2002?

**Macroeconomics**
The study of the aggregate (or total) effects on the national economy and the global economy of the choices that individuals, businesses, and governments make.

## ■ Microeconomic Questions

The economic choices that individuals, businesses, and governments make and the interactions of those choices answer the three major questions:

- What?
- How?
- For whom?

*The distinction between microeconomics and macroeconomics is similar to the distinction between two views of a display of national flags in an Olympic stadium. The micro view (left) is of a single participant and the actions he or she is taking. The macro view (right) is the patterns formed by the joint actions of all the people participating in the entire display.*

## What?

*What* goods and services get produced and in what quantities? **Goods and services** are the objects that people value and produce to satisfy human wants. Goods are physical objects such as golf balls. Services are tasks performed for people such as haircuts. The nation's farms, factories, construction sites, shops, and offices produce a dazzling array of goods and services that range from necessities such as food, houses, and apartments to leisure items such ocean cruises, SUVs, and DVD players.

What determines the quantities of corn we grow, homes we build, and DVD players we produce? How do these quantities change over time? And how are they affected by the ongoing changes in technology that make an ever-wider array of goods and services available to us?

## How?

*How* are goods and services produced? In a vineyard in France, basket-carrying workers pick the annual grape crop by hand. In a vineyard in California, a huge machine and a few workers do the same job that a hundred French grape pickers do. Look around you and you will see many examples of this phenomenon—the same job being done in different ways. In some supermarkets, checkout clerks key in prices. In others, they use a laser scanner. One farmer keeps track of his livestock feeding schedules and inventories by using paper-and-pencil records, while another uses a personal computer. GM hires workers to weld auto bodies in some of its plants and uses robots to do the job in others.

Why do we use machines in some cases and people in others? Do mechanization and technological change destroy more jobs than they create? Do they make us better off or worse off?

## For Whom?

*For whom* are goods and services produced? The answer to this question depends on the incomes that people earn and the prices they pay for the goods and services they buy. At given prices, a person who has a high income is able to buy more goods and services than a person who has a low income. Doctors earn much higher incomes than do nurses and medical assistants. So doctors get more of the goods and services produced than nurses and medical assistants get.

You probably know about many other persistent differences in incomes. Men, on the average, earn more than women. Whites, on the average, earn more than minorities. College graduates, on the average, earn more than high school graduates. Americans, on the average, earn more than Europeans, who in turn earn more, on the average, than Asians and Africans earn. But there are some significant exceptions. The people of Japan and Hong Kong now earn an average income similar to that of Americans. And there is a lot of income inequality throughout the world.

What determines the incomes we earn? Why do doctors earn larger incomes than nurses? Why do white male college graduates earn more than minority female high school graduates? Why do Americans earn more, on the average, than Africans?

Microeconomics explains how the economic choices that individuals, businesses, and governments make and the interactions of those choices end up determining *what*, *how*, and *for whom* goods and services get produced.

**Goods and services**
The objects that people value and produce to satisfy human wants. Goods are physical objects and services are tasks performed for people.

*In a California vineyard a machine and a few workers do the same job as a hundred French grape pickers.*

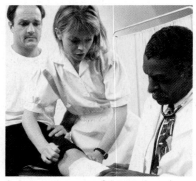

*A doctor gets more of the goods and services produced than a nurse or a medical assistant gets.*

**Standard of living**
The level of consumption of goods and services that people enjoy, on the average; it is measured by average income per person.

*Rising living standards have transformed working in the home from drudgery to a form of leisure.*

**Unemployment**
The state of being available and willing to work but unable to find an acceptable job.

**Cost of living**
The number of dollars it takes to buy the goods and services that achieve a given standard of living.

**Inflation**
A situation in which the cost of living is rising and the value of money is shrinking.

**Deflation**
A situation in which the cost of living is falling and the value of money is rising.

## ■ Macroeconomic Questions

The three big issues that macroeconomics tries to understand are

- The standard of living
- The cost of living
- Economic fluctuations—recessions and expansions

### The Standard of Living

The **standard of living** is the level of consumption of goods and services that people enjoy, on the average, and is measured by average income per person. In 2003, the quantity of goods and services produced by the nation's farms, factories, shops, and offices, measured by their value in today's prices, was 20 times greater than that in 1903. But over that same 100 years, the population of the United States has increased to not quite four times its 1903 level. Because we now produce more goods and services per person, we have a much higher standard of living than our grandparents had.

For most of us, achieving a high standard of living means finding a good job. And if we lose our job, it means spending some time being unemployed while we search for the right new job. **Unemployment** is the state of being available and willing to work but unable to find an acceptable job. In the United States in 2003, employment was high and unemployment low. In January 2003, 63 percent of adults had jobs and 6 percent of people who think of themselves as being in the labor force were looking for jobs but unable to find them. Some other countries—for example, Canada, France, and Germany—experience higher unemployment rates than does the United States.

Will our standard of living continue rise? Will your world and the world of your children be more prosperous than today's? Your study of macroeconomics will help you to understand the progress that economists have made in seeking answers to these questions.

### The Cost of Living

The **cost of living** is the number of dollars it takes to buy the goods and services that achieve a given standard of living. A rising cost of living, which is called **inflation**, means a shrinking value of the dollar. A falling cost of living, which is called **deflation**, means a rising value of the dollar.

Has the cost of living increased or decreased? If we look back over the past 100 years, we see that it has increased and the value of the dollar has shrunk. In your great-grandparents' youth, when the electric light bulb was the latest big thing, the average American earned a wage of $1 a day. But your great-grandparents' dime would buy what you need a dollar to buy today. So the dollar of 2003 is worth only one tenth of the dollar of 1903. If the value of the dollar continues to shrink at its average rate of loss since 1903, by the time you retire (sure, that's a long time in the future), you'll need $3.30 to buy what $1 buys today. The dollar of 2053 will be worth about one third of the value of the dollar of 2003. But during the past few years, the cost of living has increased slowly and some people even talk about the possibility of deflation. Can we avoid the extremes of deflation and rapid inflation and keep our cost of living stable? Your study of macroeconomics will answer questions like these.

### Economic Fluctuations: Recessions and Expansions

**Business cycle**
A periodic but irregular up-and-down movement in production and jobs.

Over long periods, both the standard of living and the cost of living have increased. But these increases have not been smooth and continuous. Our economy fluctuates in a **business cycle**, a periodic but irregular up-and-down movement in production and jobs.

When production and jobs increase the economy is in a business cycle *expansion*. When production and jobs shrink, the economy is in a *recession*.

Figure 1.1 illustrates the phases and turning points of a business cycle. The economy in this figure has a recession from year 2 to year 4, then an expansion through year 8, followed by another recession through year 10. An expansion ends at a peak, and a recession ends at a trough.

The last recession in the United States occurred in 2001. The U.S. economy had an unusually long expansion that ran from the trough of the 1991 recession until early 2001.

**Great Depression**
A period during the 1930s in which the economy experienced its worst-ever recession.

The worst recession ever experienced occurred during the 1930s in an episode called the **Great Depression**. During this period, production shrank by more than 20 percent.

Jobs also fluctuate over the business cycle. During the Great Depression, a quarter of the U.S. labor force was unable to find jobs. During the early 1980s, a recession saw the U.S. unemployment rate climb to 10 percent of the labor force. But in the 2001 recession, the U.S. unemployment rate peaked at only 6 percent.

What kind of job market will you find when you graduate? Will you have lots of choices, or will you face a labor market with a high level of unemployment in which jobs are hard to find? Macroeconomics helps to answer these questions.

---

■ **FIGURE 1.1**
Business Cycle Phases and Turning Points

**Practice Online**

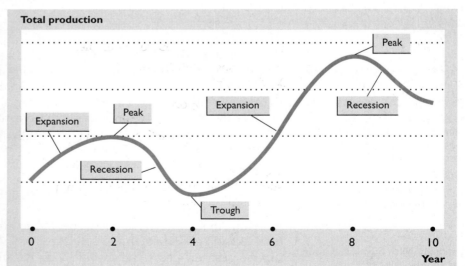

In a business cycle expansion, production increases, construction booms, and jobs are plentiful. In a recession, production and jobs shrink and unemployment lines lengthen. An expansion ends at a peak, and a recession ends at a trough.

# CHECKPOINT 1.1

**1** Define economics, distinguish between microeconomics and macroeconomics, and explain the questions economics tries to answer.

**Study Guide pp. 2–5**

**Practice Online 1.1**

## Practice Problems 1.1

1. Economics studies choices that arise from one fact. What is that fact?

2. Provide three examples of wants in the United States today that are especially pressing but not satisfied.

3. Provide an example of an incentive that is like a carrot and one that is like a stick.

4. Match the following headlines with the What, How, and For whom questions:
   a. With more research, we will cure cancer.
   b. A good education is the right of every child.
   c. What will the government do with its budget surplus?

5. Sort the following headlines into those that deal with (i) the standard of living, (ii) the cost of living, and (iii) the business cycle:
   a. Production per worker has grown for the tenth straight year.
   b. Firms lay off more workers as orders decline.
   c. New robots boost production across a wide range of industries.
   d. Money doesn't buy what it used to.

## Exercise 1.1

1. Every day, we make many choices. Why can't we avoid having to make choices?
2. Look at today's newspaper and find an example of a want that is not satisfied.
3. What is the incentive that Venus Williams and Tiger Woods face each day?
4. Check your local media for headlines that concern three microeconomic issues and three macroeconomic issues.

## Solution to Practice Problems 1.1

1. The fact is scarcity—human wants exceed the resources available.

2. Security from international terrorism, cleaner air in our cities, better public schools. (You can perhaps think of some more.)

3. If your economics instructor offers you an opportunity to earn 5 bonus points by completing an assignment on time, your incentive is a carrot. If your economics instructor warns you that there is a 5-point penalty for a late assignment, your incentive is a stick.

4a. More research is a How question, and a cure for cancer is a What question.
4b. Good education is a What question, and every child is a For whom question.
4c. Who will get the budget surplus is a For whom question.

5a. Deals with the standard of living because when production per worker grows, income per person, which measures the standard of living, increases.
5b. Deals with unemployment and the business cycle because as orders decline, production decreases and more workers become unemployed.
5c. Deals with the standard of living because robots that increase production across a wide range of industries increases production per worker.
5d. Deals with the cost of living because the value of money has fallen.

## 1.2 ECONOMICS: A SOCIAL SCIENCE

We've defined economics as the *social science* that studies the choices that individuals and societies make as they cope with scarcity. We're now going to look at the way economists go about their work as social scientists and at some of the problems they encounter.

The major goal of economists is to discover how the economic world works. In pursuit of this goal, economists (like all scientists) distinguish between two types of statements:

- What *is*
- What *ought to be*

Statements about what *is* are called *positive* statements. They say what is currently understood about the way the world operates. A positive statement might be right or wrong. And we can test a positive statement by checking it against the data. When a chemist does an experiment in her laboratory, she is attempting to check a positive statement against the facts.

Statements about what *ought to be* are called *normative* statements. These statements depend on values and cannot be tested. When Congress debates a motion, it is ultimately trying to decide what ought to be. It is making a normative statement.

To see the distinction between positive and normative statements, consider the controversy about global warming. Some scientists believe that 200 years of industrial activity and the large quantities of coal and oil that we burn are increasing the carbon dioxide content of the earth's atmosphere with devastating consequences for life on this planet. Other scientists disagree. The statement "Our planet is warming because of an increased carbon dioxide buildup in the atmosphere" is a positive statement. It can (in principle and with sufficient data) be tested. The statement "We should cut back on our use of carbon-based fuels such as coal and oil" is a normative statement. You may agree with or disagree with this statement, but you can't test it. It is based on values. Health-care reform provides another economic example of the distinction. "Universal health care will cut the amount of work time lost to illness" is a positive statement. "Every American should have equal access to health care" is a normative statement.

The task of economic science is to discover and catalog positive statements that are consistent with what we observe in the world and that enable us to understand how the economic world works. This task is a large one that can be broken into three steps:

- Observing and measuring
- Model building
- Testing

### ■ Observing and Measuring

The first step toward understanding how the economic world works is to observe and measure it. Economists keep track of huge amounts of economic data. Some examples are the amounts and locations of natural and human resources; wages and work hours; the prices and quantities of the different goods and services produced; taxes and government spending; and the volume of international trade.

## ■ Model Building

The second step is to build models. An **economic model** is a description of some aspect of the economic world that includes only those features of the world that are needed for the purpose at hand. A model is simpler than the reality it describes. What a model includes and what it leaves out result from *assumptions* about what are essential and what are inessential details.

You can see how ignoring details is useful—even essential—to our understanding by thinking about a model that you see every day: the TV weather map. The weather map is a model that helps to predict the temperature, wind speed and direction, and precipitation over a future period. The weather map shows lines called isobars—lines of equal barometric pressure. It doesn't show the interstate highways. The reason is that we think the location of the highways has no influence on the weather but the air pressure patterns do have an influence.

An economic model is similar to a weather map. It tells us how a number of variables are determined by a number of other variables. For example, an economic model of Boston's "Big Dig"—a $15 billion project to place the city's major highways underground—might tell us the impact of the project on house prices, apartment rents, jobs, and commuting times.

Economists use a variety of methods to describe their economic models. Most commonly, the method is mathematical. And if you plan on a career in economics, you will study a good deal of math. But the basic ideas of all economic models can be described using words and pictures or diagrams. That is how economic models are described in this text.

A rare exception is a model called the Phillips Economic Hydraulic Computer, shown here. Bill Phillips, a New Zealand-born engineer-turned-economist, created this model using plastic tubes and Plexiglas tanks at the London School of Economics in 1949. The model still works today in a London museum.

## ■ Testing

The third step is testing models. A model's predictions might correspond to or conflict with the data. If there is a conflict, the model needs to be modified or rejected. A model that has repeatedly passed the test of corresponding well with real-world data is the basis of an economic theory. An **economic theory** is a generalization that summarizes what we understand about the economic choices that people make and the economic performance of industries and nations.

The process of building and testing models creates theories. For example, meteorologists have a theory that if the isobars form a particular pattern at a particular time of the year (a model), then it will snow (reality). They have developed this theory by repeated observation and by carefully recording the weather that follows specific patterns of isobars.

Economics is a young science. Although philosophers have written about economic issues since the time of the ancient Greeks, it is generally agreed that as a modern social science, economics was born in 1776 with the publication of Adam Smith's *The Wealth of Nations*. Over the years since then, economists have discovered many useful theories. But in many areas, economists are still looking for answers. The gradual accumulation of economic knowledge gives most economists some faith that their methods will eventually provide usable answers.

But progress in economics comes slowly. A major reason is that it is difficult in economics to unscramble cause and effect.

**Economic model**
A description of some aspect of the economic world that includes only those features of the world that are needed for the purpose at hand.

*The Phillips Economic Hydraulic Computer: Colored water in plastic tubes and Plexiglas tanks illustrates the effects of government actions on incomes and expenditures. This model economy is in a London museum.*

**Economic theory**
A generalization that summarizes what we understand about the economic choices that people make and the economic performance of industries and nations based on models that have repeatedly passed the test of corresponding well with real-world data.

## Adam Smith and the Birth of Economics as a Modern Social Science

Many people had written about economics before Adam Smith, but he made economics a social science.

Born in 1723 in Kirkcaldy, a small fishing town near Edinburgh, Scotland, Smith was the only child of the town's customs officer. Lured from his professorship (he was a full professor at 28) by a wealthy Scottish duke who gave him a pension of £300 a year—ten times the average income at that time—he devoted ten years to writing his masterpiece, *An Inquiry into the Nature and Causes of the Wealth of Nations*, published in 1776.

Why, Adam Smith asked in that book, are some nations wealthy while others are poor? He was pondering these questions at the height of the Industrial Revolution. During these years, new technologies were applied to the manufacture of textiles, iron, transportation, and agriculture.

Adam Smith answered his questions by emphasizing the role of the division of labor and free markets. To illustrate his argument, he used the example of a pin factory. He guessed that one person, using the hand tools available in the 1770s, might make 20 pins a day. Yet, he observed, by using those same hand tools but breaking the process into a number of individually small operations in which people specialize—by the division of labor—ten people could make a staggering 48,000 pins a day. One draws out the wire, another straightens it, a third cuts it, a fourth points it, a fifth grinds it. Three specialists make the head, and a fourth attaches it. Finally, the pin is polished and packaged.

But a large market is needed to support the division of labor: One factory employing ten workers would need to sell more than 15 million pins a year to stay in business!

## ■ Unscrambling Cause and Effect

Are computers getting cheaper because people are buying them in greater quantities? Or are people buying computers in greater quantities because they are getting cheaper? Or is some third factor causing both the price of a computer to fall and the quantity of computers to increase? Economists want to answer questions like these, but doing so is often difficult. The central idea that economists (and all scientists) use to unscramble cause and effect is *ceteris paribus*.

### Ceteris Paribus

**Ceteris paribus**
Other things remaining the same (often abbreviated as *cet. par.*).

**Ceteris paribus** is a Latin term (often abbreviated as *cet. par.*) that means "other things being equal" or "if all other relevant things remain the same." Ensuring that other things are equal is crucial in many activities and all successful attempts to make scientific progress use this device. By changing one factor at a time and holding all the other relevant factors constant, we isolate the factor of interest and are able to investigate its effects in the clearest possible way.

Economic models, like the models in all other sciences, enable the influence of one factor at a time to be isolated in the imaginary world of the model. When we use a model, we are able to imagine what would happen if only one factor changed. But *ceteris paribus* can be a problem in economics when we try to test a model.

Laboratory scientists, such as chemists and physicists, perform controlled experiments by holding all the relevant factors constant except for the one under investigation. In economics, we observe the outcomes of the *simultaneous* operation of many factors. Consequently, it is hard to sort out the effects of each individual factor and to compare the effects with what a model predicts. To cope with this problem, economists take three complementary approaches:

- Natural experiments
- Statistical investigations
- Economic experiments

## Natural Experiments

A natural experiment is a situation that arises in the ordinary course of economic life in which the one factor of interest is different and other things are equal (or similar). For example, Canada has higher unemployment benefits than the United States, but the people in the two nations are similar. So to study the effects of unemployment benefits on the unemployment rate, economists might compare the United States with Canada.

## Statistical Investigations

Statistical investigations look for correlations. **Correlation** is the tendency for the values of two variables to move in a predictable and related way. For example, there is a correlation between the amount of cigarette smoking and the incidence of lung cancer. There is also a correlation between the size of a city's police force and the city's crime rate. Two economic examples are the correlation between household income and spending and the correlation between the price of a telephone call and the number of calls made. We must be careful to interpret a correlation correctly. Sometimes a correlation shows the strength of a *causal* influence of one variable on the other. For example, smoking causes lung cancer, and higher incomes cause higher spending. Sometimes the direction of causation is hard to determine. For example, does a larger police force *detect* more crimes or does a higher crime rate cause a larger police force to be hired? And sometimes a third factor causes both correlated variables. For example, advances in communication technology have caused both a fall in the price of phone calls and an increase in the quantity of calls. So the correlation between the price and quantity of phone calls has a deeper cause.

Sometimes, the direction of cause and effect can be determined by looking at the timing of events. But this method must be handled with care because of a problem known as the *post hoc* fallacy.

**Post Hoc *Fallacy*** Another Latin phrase—*post hoc ergo propter hoc*—means "after this, therefore because of this." The **post hoc fallacy** is the error of reasoning that a first event *causes* a second event because the first occurred before the second. Suppose you are a visitor from a far-off world. You observe lots of people shopping in early December, and then you see them opening gifts and celebrating on Christmas Day. Does the shopping cause Christmas, you wonder? After a deeper study, you discover that Christmas causes the shopping. A later event causes an earlier event.

Just looking at the timing of events often doesn't help to unravel cause and effect in economics. For example, the stock market booms, and some months later

**Correlation**
The tendency for the values of two variables to move in a predictable and related way.

**Post hoc fallacy**
The error of reasoning that a first event *causes* a second event because the first occurred before the second.

the economy expands—jobs and incomes grow. Did the stock market boom cause the economy to expand? Possibly, but perhaps businesses started to plan the expansion of production because a new technology that lowered costs had become available. As knowledge of the plans spread, the stock market reacted to *anticipate* the economic expansion.

To disentangle cause and effect, economists use economic models to interpret correlations. And when they can do so, economists perform experiments.

### Economic Experiments

Economic experiments put real subjects in a decision-making situation and vary the influence of interest to discover how the subjects respond to one factor at a time. Most economic experiments are done using students as the subjects. But some use the actual people whose behavior economists want to understand and predict. An example of an economic experiment on actual subjects is one designed to discover the effects of changing the way welfare benefits are paid in New Jersey. Another experiment was conducted to discover how telecommunications companies would bid in different types of auctions for the airwave frequencies they use to transmit cellular telephone messages. Governments have made billions of dollars using the results of this experiment.

## CHECKPOINT 1.2

Study Guide pp. 5–7

Practice Online 1.2

**2**  **Describe the work of economists as social scientists.**

### Practice Problems 1.2

1. Classify each of the following statements as positive or normative:
   a. There is too much poverty in the United States.
   b. An increase in the gas tax will cut pollution.
   c. Cuts to social security in the United States have been too deep.

2. Provide two examples of the *post hoc* fallacy.

### Exercises 1.2

1. Classify each of the following statements as positive or normative:
   a. More scholarships to students from poor families will reduce U.S. poverty.
   b. Free trade will harm developing countries.
   c. Cuts to public education in the United States have been too high.

2. How might an economist test one of the positive statements in exercise 1?

### Solutions to Practice Problems 1.2

**1a.** A normative statement. It cannot be tested.
**1b.** A positive statement. An experiment will test it.
**1c.** A normative statement. It cannot be tested.

**2.** Examples are: New Year celebrations cause January sales. A booming stock market causes a Republican president to be elected.

## 1.3 THE ECONOMIC WAY OF THINKING

You've seen that to understand what, how, and for whom goods and services are produced, economists build and test models of peoples' choices and the interactions of those choices. Five core ideas summarize the economic way of thinking about people's choices, and these ideas form the basis of all microeconomic models. The ideas are

- People make *rational choices* by comparing *costs* and *benefits*.
- *Cost* is what you *must give up* to get something.
- *Benefit* is what you gain when you get something and is measured by what you *are willing to give up* to get it.
- A rational choice is made on the *margin*.
- People respond to *incentives.*

### ■ Rational Choice

The most basic idea of economics is that in making choices, people act rationally. A **rational choice** is one that uses the available resources to most effectively satisfy the wants of the person making the choice.

Only the wants and preferences of the person making the choice are relevant to determine its rationality. For example, you might like chocolate ice cream more than vanilla ice cream, but your friend prefers vanilla. So it is rational for you to choose chocolate and for your friend to choose vanilla.

A rational choice might turn out to have been not the best choice after the event. A farmer might decide to plant wheat rather than soybeans. Then, when the crop comes to market, the price of soybeans might be much higher than the price of wheat. The farmer's choice was rational when it was made, but subsequent events made it less profitable than a different choice.

The idea of rational choice provides an answer to the first question: What goods and services will get produced and in what quantities? The answer is: Those that people rationally choose to produce!

But how do people choose rationally? Why have we chosen to build an interstate highway system and not an interstate high-speed railroad system? Why have most people chosen to use Microsoft's Windows operating system rather than another? Why do more people today choose to drink bottled water and sports energy drinks than in the past?

We make rational choices by comparing *costs* and *benefits*. But economists think about costs and benefits in a special and revealing way. Let's look at the economic concepts of cost and benefit.

**Rational choice**
A choice that uses the available resources to most effectively satisfy the wants of the person making the choice.

### ■ Cost: What You *Must Give Up*

Whatever you choose to do, you could have done something else instead. You could have done lots of things other than what you actually did. But one of these other things is the *best* alternative given up. This alternative that you *must* give up to get something is the **opportunity cost** of the thing that you get. The thing that you could have chosen—the highest-valued alternative forgone—is the cost of the thing that you did choose.

"There's no such thing as a free lunch" is not a clever but empty saying. It expresses the central idea of economics: that every choice involves a cost.

**Opportunity cost**
The opportunity cost of something is the best thing you *must* give up to get it.

We use the term *opportunity cost* to emphasize that when we make a choice in the face of scarcity, we give up an opportunity to do something else. You can quit school right now, or you can remain in school. Suppose that if you quit school, the best job you can get is at McDonald's, where you can earn $10,000 during the year. The opportunity cost of remaining in school includes the things that you could have bought with this $10,000. The opportunity cost also includes the value of the leisure time that you must forgo to study.

Opportunity cost is *only* the alternative forgone. It does not include all the expenditures that you make. For example, when you contemplate whether to remain in school, your expenditure on tuition is part of the opportunity cost of remaining in school. But the cost of your school meal voucher is *not* part of the opportunity cost of remaining in school. You must buy food whether you remain in school or not.

**Sunk cost**
A previously incurred and irreversible cost.

Also, past expenditures that cannot be reversed are not part of opportunity cost. Suppose you've paid your term's tuition and it is nonrefundable. If you now contemplate quitting school, the paid tuition is irrelevant. It is called a sunk cost. A **sunk cost** is a previously incurred and irreversible cost. Whether you remain in school or quit school, having paid the tuition, the tuition is not part of the opportunity cost of remaining in school.

## ■ Benefit: Gain Measured by What You Are *Willing to Give Up*

**Benefit**
The benefit of something is the gain or pleasure that it brings.

The **benefit** of something is the gain or pleasure that it brings. Benefit is how a person *feels* about something. You might be extremely anxious to get the latest version of a video game. It will bring you a large benefit. And you might have almost no interest in the latest Yo Yo Ma cello concerto CD. It will bring you a small benefit.

Economists measure the benefit of something by what a person is *willing to give up* to get it. You can buy CDs, sodas, or magazines. The sodas or magazines that you are *willing to give up* to get a CD measure the benefit you get from a CD.

*For these students, the opportunity cost of being in school is worth bearing.*

*For the fast-food worker, the opportunity cost of remaining in school is too high.*

## ■ On the Margin

A choice on the **margin** is a choice that is made by comparing *all* the relevant alternatives systematically and incrementally. For example, you must choose how to divide the next hour between studying and e-mailing your friends. To make this choice, you must evaluate the costs and benefits of the alternative possible allocations of your next hour. You choose on the margin by considering whether you will be better off or worse off if you spend an extra few minutes studying or an extra few minutes e-mailing.

The margin might involve a small change, as it does when you're deciding how to divide an hour between studying and e-mailing friends. Or it might involve a large change, as it does, for example, when you're deciding whether to remain in school for another year. Attending school for part of the year is no better (and might be worse) than not attending at all—it is not a *relevant* alternative. So you likely will want to commit the entire year to school or to something else. But you still choose on the margin. It is just that the marginal change is now a change for one year rather than a change for a few minutes.

**Margin**
A choice on the margin is a choice that is made by comparing *all* the relevant alternatives systematically and incrementally.

### Marginal Cost

The opportunity cost of a one-unit increase in an activity is called **marginal cost**. Marginal cost is what you *must* give up to get *one more* unit of something. Think about your marginal cost of going to the movies for a third time in a week. Your marginal cost is what you must give up to see that one additional movie. It is *not* what you give up to see all three movies. The reason is that you've already given up something for two movies, so you don't count this cost as resulting from the decision to see the third movie.

The marginal cost of any activity usually increases as you do more of it. You know that going to the movies decreases your study time and lowers your grade. Suppose that seeing a second movie in a week lowers your grade by five percentage points. Seeing a third movie will lower your grade by more than five additional percentage points. Your marginal cost of moviegoing is increasing.

**Marginal cost**
The opportunity cost that arises from a one-unit increase in an activity. The marginal cost of something is what you *must* give up to get *one more* unit of it.

### Marginal Benefit

The benefit of a one-unit increase in an activity is called marginal benefit. **Marginal benefit** is what you gain when you get *one more* unit of something. Think about your marginal benefit from the movies. You've been to the movies twice this week, and you're contemplating going for a third time. Your marginal benefit is the benefit you will get from the one additional movie. It is *not* the benefit you get from all three movies. The reason is that you already have had the benefit from two movies, so you don't count this benefit as resulting from the third movie.

Marginal benefit is *measured by* the most you *are willing to* give up to get *one more* unit of something. And a fundamental feature of marginal benefit is that it usually diminishes. The benefit from seeing the first movie in the week is greater than the benefit from seeing the second movie in the week. Because the marginal benefit decreases as you see more movies in the week, *you are willing to give up less* to see one more movie. You know that going to the movies decreases your study time and lowers your grade. Suppose that you were willing to give up ten percentage points to see your second movie. You won't be willing to take such a big hit on your grades to see the third movie in a week. Your marginal benefit of moviegoing is decreasing.

**Marginal benefit**
The benefit that arises from a one-unit increase in an activity. The marginal benefit of something is *measured* by what you *are willing to* give up to get *one more* unit of it.

## Making a Rational Choice

So will you go to the movies for that third time in a week? If the marginal cost is less than the marginal benefit, your rational choice will be to see the third movie. If the marginal cost exceeds the marginal benefit, your rational choice will be to spend the evening studying. We make a rational choice and use our scarce resources in the way that makes us as well off as possible when we take those actions for which marginal cost is less than or equal to marginal benefit.

## ■ Responding to Incentives

In making our choices, we respond to incentives—we respond to "carrots" and "sticks." The carrots that we face are marginal benefits. The sticks are marginal costs. A change in marginal benefit or a change in marginal cost brings a change in the incentives that we face and leads us to change our actions.

Most students believe that the payoff from studying just before a test is greater than the payoff from studying a month before a test. In other words, as a test date approaches, the marginal benefit of studying increases and the *incentive* to study becomes stronger. For this reason, we observe an increase in study time and a decrease in leisure pursuits during the last few days before a test. And the more important the test, the greater is this effect.

A change in marginal cost also changes incentives. For example, suppose that last week, you found your course work easy. You scored 100 percent on all your practice quizzes. The marginal cost of taking off an evening to enjoy a movie was low. Your grade on this week's test will not suffer. So you have an incentive to enjoy a movie feast. But this week, suddenly, the going has gotten tough. You are just not getting it. Your practice test scores are low, and you know that if you take off even one evening, your grade on next week's test will suffer. The marginal cost of seeing a movie is higher this week than last week. So you now have an incentive to give the movies a miss and study.

The central idea of economics is that we can measure changes in incentives, and these measurements enable us to predict the choices that people make as their circumstances change.

*Changes in marginal benefit and marginal cost change the incentive to study or to enjoy a movie.*

# CHECKPOINT 1.3

**3** **Explain five core ideas that define the economic way of thinking.**

**Study Guide pp. 7–9**

<u>**Practice Online 1.3**</u>

## Practice Problem 1.3

Kate usually plays tennis for two hours a week, and her grade on each math test is usually 70 percent. Last week, after playing two hours of tennis, Kate thought long and hard about playing for another hour. She decided to play another hour of tennis and cut her study time by one additional hour. But the grade on last week's math test was 60 percent.
a. What was Kate's opportunity cost of the third hour of tennis? →10% on her test
b. Given that Kate made the decision to play the third hour of tennis, what can you conclude about the comparison of her marginal benefit and marginal cost of the second hour of tennis? 10% per hour
c. Was Kate's decision to play the third hour of tennis rational?
d. Did Kate make her decision on the margin?

## Exercises 1.3

1.  Bill Gates gives away a lot of money: $200 million to put computers in libraries that can't afford them and $135 million to universities, cancer research, a children's hospital, and the Seattle Symphony. Doesn't Bill Gates experience scarcity? Are his donations rational? In making these donations, might Bill Gates have responded to any incentive?

2.  Steve Fossett spent a lot of money trying to be the first person to circumnavigate the world in a hot-air balloon. Anheuser-Busch offered a prize of $1 million for the first balloonist to do so in 15 days nonstop. What was the opportunity cost of Steve Fossett's adventure? But Steve Fossett was not the first person to circumnavigate the world in a balloon, so did he get any benefits? Why did Anheuser-Busch offer the prize?

3.  Tony is an engineering student, and he is considering taking an extra course in history. List the things that might be part of his costs and benefits of the history course. Think of an incentive that might encourage him to take the course.

## Solution to Practice Problem 1.3

a.  Kate's opportunity cost of the third hour of tennis was the ten percentage point drop in her grade. If Kate had not played tennis for the third hour, she would have studied and her grade would not have dropped. The best alternative forgone is her opportunity cost of the third hour of tennis.
b.  The marginal benefit from the second hour of tennis must have exceeded the marginal cost of the second hour because Kate chose to play tennis for the third hour. If the marginal benefit did not exceed the marginal cost, she would have chosen to study and not play tennis for the third hour.
c.  If for Kate marginal benefit exceeded marginal cost, her decision was rational.
d.  Kate made her decision on the margin because she considered the benefit and cost of *one additional hour*.

## 1.4 WHY ECONOMICS IS WORTH STUDYING

In 1961, Mick Jagger, then the 19-year-old lead singer with a group that would become the Rolling Stones, enrolled in an economics degree program at the London School of Economics. During the day, he was learning about opportunity cost, and each night, his rock group was earning today's equivalent of $120. Mick soon realized that his opportunity cost of remaining in school was too high, and so he dropped out. (A faculty advisor is reputed to have told Mick that he would not make much money in a rock band. But within a few months, the Rolling Stones, along with the Beatles, shot to international stardom and multimillion-dollar recording contracts!)

Mick Jagger used one of the big ideas of economics to make his own rational decision. And you can do the same. Let's look at the benefits and costs of studying economics and check that the benefits outweigh the costs.

Two main benefits from studying economics are

* Understanding
* Expanded career opportunities

### ■ Understanding

George Bernard Shaw, the great Irish dramatist and thinker, wrote, "Economy is the art of making the most of life." Life is certainly full of economic problems, some global or national in scope and some personal.

Every day, on television, on the Internet, and in newspapers and magazines, we hear and read about global or national economic issues: Should Nike pay higher wages to its workers in Asia? Is there too much economic inequality in the world today? How can we improve health care, welfare, and education? Are taxes too high or too low? Will the Federal Reserve increase interest rates next week?

And every day in your own life, you're confronted with personal economic choices: Will you buy pizza or pasta? Will you skip class today? Will you put your summer earnings in the bank or the stock market?

Studying economics equips you with tools and insights that help you to understand the world's problems, to participate in the political debate that surrounds them, and to understand and solve your personal economic problems.

John Maynard Keynes, a famous British economist of the twentieth century, wrote, "The ideas of economists . . . , both when they are right and when they are wrong, are more powerful than is commonly understood. Indeed the world is ruled by little else. Practical men [and women, he would have written today], who believe themselves to be quite exempt from any intellectual influences, are usually the slaves of some defunct economist."

Keynes was correct. You can't ignore economic ideas. They are all around you. You use them every day in your personal life and in your work. You use them when you vote and when you argue with your friends. But you don't need to be the slave of some defunct economist. By studying economics, you will learn how to develop your own ideas and to test them against the ideas of others. As you progress with your study of economics, you will start to listen to the news and read your newspaper with a deeper understanding of what's going on. You will also find yourself increasingly using the economics that you are learning when you make your own economic choices.

## ■ Expanded Career Opportunities

Robert Reich, a former U.S. Secretary of Labor, predicts that the three big jobs of the twenty-first century will be what he calls *problem identifying*, *problem solving*, and *strategic brokering*. The people who are good at these tasks command soaring incomes. And there is no better way to train yourself in these skills than to study economics. You can think of economics as a workout regimen for your brain. Almost everything that you study in economics is practice at thinking abstractly and rigorously about concrete things. You will constantly be asking, "What if?" Although students of economics learn many useful economic concepts, it is the training and practice in abstract thinking that really pays off.

Most students of economics don't go on to major in the subject. And even those who do major in economics don't usually go on to become economists. Rather, they work in fields such as banking, business, management, finance, insurance, real estate, marketing, law, government, journalism, health care, and the arts. A course in economics is a very good choice for a pre-med, pre-law, or pre-MBA student.

Economics graduates are not the highest-paid professionals. But they are close to the top, as you can see in Figure 1.2. Engineers and computer scientists, for example, earn up to 20 percent more than economics graduates. Economics graduates earn more than most others, and significantly, they earn more than business graduates.

---

**FIGURE 1.2**
Average Incomes

**Practice Online**

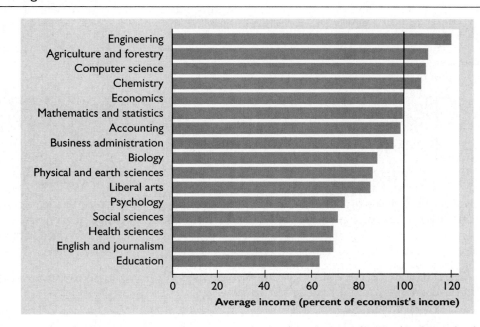

Graduates in disciplines that teach *problem identifying*, *problem solving*, and *strategic brokering* (engineering, computer science, and economics) are at the top of the earnings distribution.

SOURCES: U.S. Department of Commerce, Bureau of the Census, *Educational Background and Economic Status: Spring 1990*, Current Population Reports, Series P-70, No. 32, and *Statistical Abstract of the United States*, 1994, Table 246, and authors' calculations.

### ■ The Costs of Studying Economics

Regardless of what you study, you must buy textbooks and supplies and pay tuition. So these expenses are *not* part of the opportunity cost of studying economics.

One cost of studying economics is forgone knowledge of some other subject. If you work hard at studying economics, you must forgo learning some other subject. You can't study everything.

Another cost, and the main cost of studying economics, is forgone leisure time. Economics is a demanding subject, and it takes time to master. Most students say that they find it difficult. They often complain that they understand the subject when they read the textbook or listen to their instructor but then, when they take an exam, they just can't figure out the correct answers.

The trick is practice, or learning-by-doing. Economics is not a subject that you learn by memorizing things. You must memorize definitions and technical terms. But beyond that, memory is not your main mental tool. Working problems and learning how to analyze and solve problems are the key. And this activity is time consuming.

### ■ Benefits Versus Costs

So which is larger: the benefit or the cost? Economics says that only you can decide. You are the judge of value or benefit to yourself. So you must weigh the benefits and the costs that we've identified (and consider any others that are important to *you*).

If you're clear that the benefits outweigh the costs, you're well on your way to having a good time in your economics course. If the costs outweigh the benefits, don't waste your time. Life is too short.

If you're on the fence, try to get more information. But if you remain on the fence, complete this one course in economics and then decide.

# CHECKPOINT 1.4

**Study Guide pp. 9–10**

**Practice Online 1.4**

**4** **Explain why economics is worth studying.**

## Practice Problem 1.4

A student is choosing between an economics course and a popular music course. List two opportunity costs and two benefits from taking a course in economics.

## Exercise 1.4

Why did Mick Jagger quit his economics course? What are some of the benefits that Mick Jagger might have given up?

## Solution to Practice Problem 1.4

Opportunity costs include the leisure forgone and forgone appreciation of popular music. Benefits include expanded career opportunities, better understanding of the world, and better problem-solving skills.

# CHAPTER CHECKPOINT

## Key Points

**1** **Define economics, distinguish between microeconomics and macro-economics, and explain the questions economics tries to answer.**

- Economics is the social science that studies the choices that we make as we cope with scarcity and the incentives that influence and reconcile our choices.
- Microeconomics explains how choices end up determining *what* goods and services get produced, *how* they get produced, and *for whom* they get produced.
- Macroeconomics explains how choices influence the standard of living, the cost of living, and economic fluctuations.

**2** **Describe the work of economists as social scientists.**

- Positive statements are about what is, and they can be tested. Normative statements are about what ought to be, and they cannot be tested.
- To explain the economic world, economists build and test economic models.
- Economists use the *ceteris paribus* assumption to try to disentangle cause and effect, and they use natural experiments, statistical investigations, and economic experiments.

**3** **Explain five core ideas that define the economic way of thinking.**

- People make rational choices by comparing costs and benefits.
- Cost is what you *must* give up to get something.
- Benefit is what you gain when you get something and is measured by what you *are willing to* give up to get it.
- A rational choice is made on the margin.
- People respond to incentives.

**4** **Explain why economics is worth studying.**

- The benefits of studying economics are understanding of the economic world and expanded career opportunities.
- The costs of studying economics are forgone knowledge of some other subject and leisure time.

## Key Terms

Benefit, 14
Business cycle, 6
*Ceteris paribus*, 10
Correlation, 11
Cost of living, 5
Deflation, 5
Economic model, 9
Economic theory, 9
Economics, 3

Goods and services, 4
Great Depression, 6
Incentive, 2
Inflation, 5
Macroeconomics, 3
Margin, 15
Marginal benefit, 15
Marginal cost, 15
Microeconomics, 3

Opportunity cost, 13
*Post hoc* fallacy, 11
Rational choice, 13
Scarcity, 2
Standard of living, 5
Sunk cost, 14
Unemployment, 5

## Exercises

1. Provide three examples of scarcity that illustrate why even the wealthiest people who live in the most lavish luxury still face scarcity.

2. Provide two examples of incentives, one a carrot and the other a stick, that have influenced major government decisions during the past few years.

3. Think about the following news items and label each as involving a micro-economic or a macroeconomic issue:
   a. An increase in the tax on cigarettes will decrease teenage smoking.
   b. It would be better if the United States spent more on cleaning up the environment and less on space exploration.
   c. A government scheme called "work for welfare" will reduce the number of people unemployed.
   d. An increase in the number of police on inner-city streets will reduce the crime rate.

4. Think about the following news items and label each as involving a What, How, or For Whom question:
   a. Today most stores use computers to keep their inventory records, whereas 20 years ago most stores used paper records.
   b. Health care professionals and drug companies say that Medicaid drug rebates should be available to everyone in need.
   c. A doubling of the gas tax might lead to a better public transit system.

5. Think about the following news items and label each as a positive or a normative statement. In the United States,
   a. The poor pay too much for housing.
   b. The number of farms has decreased over the last 50 years.
   c. The population in rural areas has remained constant over the past decade.

6. Explain how economists try to unscramble cause and effect. Explain why economists use the *ceteris paribus* assumption.

7. What is correlation? What approaches do economists use to try to sort out the cause-and-effect relationship that a correlation might indicate? Describe each of these approaches.

8. What is the *post hoc* fallacy? Provide two examples of the *post hoc* fallacy.

9. Pam, Pru, and Pat are deciding how they will celebrate the New Year. Pam prefers to go on a cruise, is happy to go to Hawaii, but does not want to go skiing. Pru prefers to go skiing, is happy to go to Hawaii, but does not want to go on a cruise. Pat prefers to go to Hawaii or to take a cruise but does not want to go skiing. Their decision is to go to Hawaii. Is this decision rational? What is the opportunity cost of the trip to Hawaii for each of them? What is the benefit each gets?

10. Your school has decided to increase the intake of new students next year. What economic concepts would your school consider in reaching its decision? Would the school make its decision at the margin?

11. In California, most vineyards use machines and a few workers to pick grapes, while some vineyards use no machines and many workers. Which vineyards have made a rational choice? Explain your answer.

## Critical Thinking

12. The largest lottery jackpot prizes in U. S. history were $363 million and $331 million, both won in the Big Game Jackpot.
    a. Do the people who buy lottery tickets face scarcity?
    b. Do the winners of big prizes face scarcity after receiving their winners' checks?
    c. Do you think lotteries have both microeconomic effects and macroeconomic effects or only microeconomic effects? Explain.
    d. How do you think lotteries change what and for whom goods and services are produced?
    e. Think about the statement "Lotteries create more problems than they solve and should be banned." Which part of this statement is positive and how might it be tested? Which part of this statement is normative?
    f. Do people face a marginal cost and a marginal benefit when they decide to buy a lottery ticket?
    g. Does a person who buys a lottery ticket make a rational choice?
    h. Do the people who buy lottery tickets respond to incentives?
    i. How do you think the size of the jackpot affects the number of lottery tickets sold? What role do incentives play in this response?

13. "Spider-Man" was the most successful movie of 2002, with box office receipts of more than $400 million. Creating a successful movie brings pleasure to millions, generates work for thousands, and makes a few people rich.
    a. What contribution does a movie like "Spider-Man" make to coping with scarcity?
    b. Does the decision to make a blockbuster movie mean that some other more desirable activities get fewer resources than they deserve?
    c. Was your answer to part **b** a positive or a normative answer? Explain.
    d. Who decides whether a movie is going to be a blockbuster?
    e. How do you think the creation of a blockbuster movie influences what, how, and for whom goods and services are produced?
    f. What do you think are some of the marginal costs and marginal benefits that the producer of a movie faces?
    g. Suppose that Tobey Maguire had been offered a bigger and better part in another movie and that to hire him for "Spider-Man," the producer had to double Tobey's pay. What incentives were changed? How might the changed incentives have changed the choices that people made?

14. Think about each of the following situations and explain how they affect incentives and might change the choices that people make.
    a. Drought hits the Midwest.
    b. The World Series begins tonight, and there is a thunderstorm warning in effect for the stadium.
    c. The price of a personal computer falls to $50.
    d. Political instability in the Middle East cuts world oil production and sends the price of gasoline to $2 a gallon.
    e. Your school builds a new parking garage that increases the number of parking places available but doubles the price of parking on campus.
    f. A math professor awards grades based on the percentage of questions answered correctly and an economics professor awards grades based on rank in class—the top 10 percent get As, the bottom 10 percent get Cs, and the rest of the class get Bs regardless of the percentage of questions answered correctly.

Practice Online # Web Exercises

If you haven't already done so, take a few minutes to visit your Foundations Web site, sign in, and obtain your username and password. Browse the site and become familiar with its structure and content. You'll soon appreciate that this Web site is a very useful and powerful learning tool. For each chapter, you will find quizzes, e-text, e-study guide, interactive tutorials and graphics, and animations of your textbook figures. You will also find the links you need to work the Web exercises.

**Use the links on your Foundations Web site to work the following exercises.**

15. Visit some news Web sites and review today's economic news. Summarize a news article that deals with an economic issue that interests you. Say whether the story deals with a microeconomic or a macroeconomic issue.

16. Visit the Campaign for Tobacco-Free Kids. Obtain data on changes in state tobacco taxes and changes in state tobacco consumption.
    a. Calculate the percentage change in tobacco taxes in each of the states for which you have data.
    b. Make a graph that plots the percentage change in the tobacco tax on the $x$-axis and the percentage change in state tobacco consumption on the $y$-axis.
    c. Describe the relationship between these two variables. (Look at pages 25, 26, and 27 if you need help with making and interpreting your graph.)
    d. How would you expect a rise in the tobacco tax to influence the incentive for a young person to smoke cigarettes?
    e. Do the data that you've obtained confirm what you expected or were you surprised by the data? Explain your answer.
    f. What can you infer about cause and effect in the data on tobacco taxes and tobacco consumption?
    g. What is the main obstacle to drawing a strong conclusion about the effect of tobacco taxes on tobacco consumption?

17. Visit the *Statistical Abstract of the United States* and obtain data on the levels of average annual pay and the percentage of persons with a bachelor's degree in each of the states.
    a. Which state has the highest average pay and which has the lowest?
    b. Where in the ranking of average pay does your state stand?
    c. Which state has the highest percentage of people with a bachelor's degree and which has the lowest?
    d. Where in the ranking of people with a bachelor's degree does your state stand?
    e. What do you think these numbers tell us about what, how, or for whom goods and services are produced?
    f. What is the difficulty in using these numbers to determine whether education levels influence pay levels?

18. Visit the Inflation Calculator. Then make this choice: You can have $11 and pay the prices of 1800, or you can have $100 and pay the prices of 2000. Which do you prefer and why?

19. Visit the Federal Reserve and view the latest edition of the Beige Book. What are the recent changes in the standard of living and the cost of living in the United States and of your region?

**When you have completed your study of this appendix, you will be able to**

**1** Interpret a scatter diagram, a time-series graph, and a cross-section graph.

**2** Interpret the graphs used in economic models.

**3** Define and calculate slope.

**4** Graph relationships among more than two variables.

### ■ Basic Idea

A graph represents a quantity as a distance and enables us to visualize the relationship between two variables. To make a graph, we set two lines called *axes* perpendicular to each other, like those in Figure A1.1. The vertical line is called the *y*-axis, and the horizontal line is called the *x*-axis. The common zero point is called the *origin*. In Figure A1.1, the *x*-axis measures temperature in degrees Fahrenheit. A movement to the right shows an increase in temperature, and a movement to the left shows a decrease in temperature. The *y*-axis represents ice cream consumption, measured in gallons per day. To make a graph, we need a value of the variable on the *x*-axis and a corresponding value of the variable on the *y*-axis. For example, if the temperature is 40°F, ice cream consumption is 5 gallons a day at point *A* in the graph. If the temperature is 80°F, ice cream consumption is 20 gallons a day at point *B* in the graph. Graphs like that in Figure A1.1 can be used to show any type of quantitative data on two variables.

---

### ■ FIGURE A1.1

Making a Graph

### Practice Online

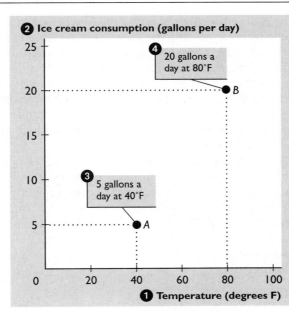

All graphs have axes that measure quantities as distances.

**1** The horizontal axis (*x*-axis) measures temperature in degrees Fahrenheit. A movement to the right shows an increase in temperature.

**2** The vertical axis (*y*-axis) measures ice cream consumption in gallons per day. A movement upward shows an increase in ice cream consumption.

**3** Point *A* shows that 5 gallons of ice cream are consumed on a day when the temperature is 40°F.

**4** Point *B* shows that 20 gallons of ice cream are consumed on a day when the temperature is 80°F.

## ■ Interpreting Data Graphs

A **scatter diagram** is a graph of the value of one variable against the value of another variable. It is used to reveal whether a relationship exists between two variables and to describe the relationship. Figure A1.2 shows two examples.

Figure A1.2(a) shows the relationship between expenditure and income. Each point shows expenditure per person and income per person in the United States in a given year from 1992 to 2002. The points are "scattered" within the graph. The label on each point shows its year. The point marked 96 shows that in 1996, income per person was $21,100 and expenditure per person was $20,100. This scatter diagram reveals that as income increases, expenditure also increases.

Figure A1.2(b) shows the relationship between the number of minutes of international phone calls made from the United States and the average price per minute. This scatter diagram reveals that as the price per minute falls, the number of minutes called increases.

A **time-series graph** measures time (for example, months or years) on the $x$-axis and the variable or variables in which we are interested on the $y$-axis. Figure A1.2(c) shows an example. In this graph, time (on the $x$-axis) is measured in years, which run from 1972 to 2002. The variable that we are interested in is the price of coffee, and it is measured on the $y$-axis.

A time-series graph conveys an enormous amount of information quickly and easily, as this example illustrates. It shows when the value is

1. High or low. When the line is a long way from the $x$-axis, the price is high, as it was in 1977. When the line is close to the $x$-axis, the price is low, as it was in 2002.
2. Rising or falling. When the line slopes upward, as in 1976, the price is rising. When the line slopes downward, as in 1978, the price is falling.
3. Rising or falling quickly and slowly. If the line is steep, then the price is rising or falling quickly. If the line is not steep, the price is rising or falling slowly. For example, the price rose quickly in 1976 and slowly in 1993. The price fell quickly in 1978 and slowly in 1982.

A time-series graph also reveals whether the variable has a trend. A **trend** is a general tendency for the value of a variable to rise or fall. You can see that the price of coffee had a general tendency to fall from the mid-1970s to the early 1990s. That is, although the price rose and fell, it had a general tendency to fall.

With a time-series graph, we can compare different periods quickly. Figure A1.2(c) shows that the 1990s were different from the 1970s. The price of coffee fluctuated more violently in the 1970s than it did in the 1990s. This graph conveys a wealth of information, and it does so in much less space than we have used to describe only some of its features.

A **cross-section graph** shows the values of an economic variable for different groups in a population at a point in time. Figure A1.2(d) is an example of a cross-section graph. It shows the percentage of people who participate in selected sports activities in the United States in 2000. This graph uses bars rather than dots and lines, and the length of each bar indicates the participation rate. Figure A1.2(d) enables you to compare the participation rates in these ten sporting activities. And you can do so much more quickly and clearly than by looking at a list of numbers.

## ■ FIGURE A1.2
Data Graphs

Practice Online

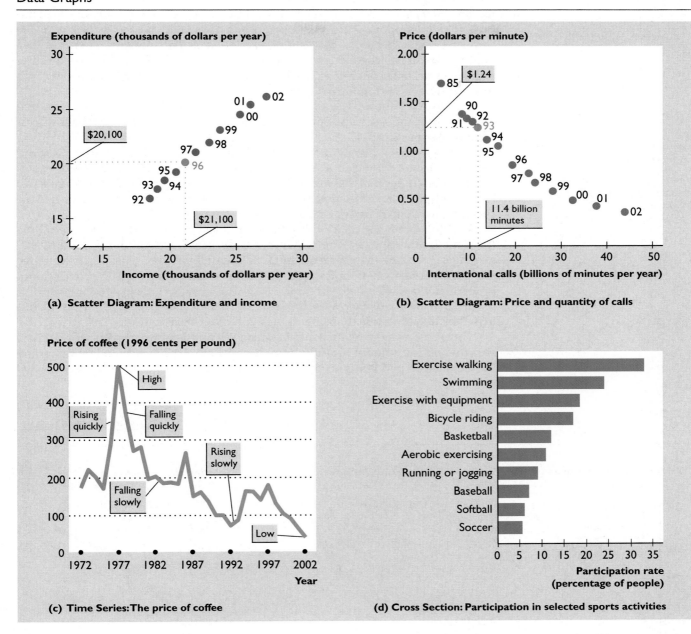

**(a) Scatter Diagram: Expenditure and income**

**(b) Scatter Diagram: Price and quantity of calls**

**(c) Time Series: The price of coffee**

**(d) Cross Section: Participation in selected sports activities**

A scatter diagram reveals the relationship between two variables. In part (a), as income increases, expenditure increases. In part (b), as the price per minute falls, the number of minutes called increases.

A time-series graph plots the value of a variable on the *y*-axis against time on the *x*-axis. Part (c) plots the price of coffee each year from 1972 to 2002. The graph shows when the price of coffee was high and low, when it increased and decreased, and when it changed quickly and slowly.

A cross-section graph shows the value of a variable across the members of a population. Part (d) shows the participation rate in the United States in each of ten sporting activites in 2000.

## ■ Interpreting Graphs Used in Economic Models

We use graphs to show the relationships among the variables in an economic model. An *economic model* is a simplified description of the economy or of a component of the economy such as a business or a household. It consists of statements about economic behavior that can be expressed as equations or as curves in a graph. Economists use models to explore the effects of different policies or other influences on the economy in ways similar to those used to test model airplanes in wind tunnels and models of the climate.

Figure A1.3 shows graphs of the relationships between two variables that move in the same direction. Such a relationship is called a **positive relationship** or **direct relationship**.

Part (a) shows a straight-line relationship, which is called a **linear relationship**. The distance traveled in 5 hours increases as the speed increases. For example, point *A* shows that 200 miles are traveled in 5 hours at a speed of 40 miles an hour. And point *B* shows that the distance traveled increases to 300 miles if the speed increases to 60 miles an hour.

Part (b) shows the relationship between distance sprinted and recovery time (the time it takes the heart rate to return to its normal resting rate). An upward-sloping curved line that starts out quite flat but then becomes steeper as we move along the curve away from the origin describes this relationship. The curve slopes upward and becomes steeper because the extra recovery time needed from sprinting another 100 yards increases. It takes less than 5 minutes to recover from sprinting 100 yards but more than 10 minutes to recover from sprinting 200 yards.

Part (c) shows the relationship between the number of problems worked by a student and the amount of study time. An upward-sloping curved line that starts out quite steep and becomes flatter as we move away from the origin shows this

**Positive relationship or direct relationship**
A relationship between two variables that move in the same direction.

**Linear relationship**
A relationship that graphs as a straight line.

---

### ■ FIGURE A1.3
Positive (Direct) Relationships

**Practice Online**

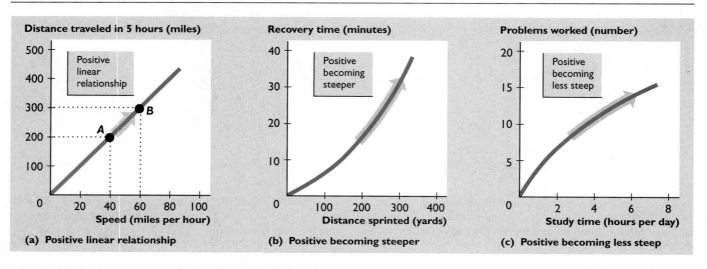

**(a) Positive linear relationship**

**(b) Positive becoming steeper**

**(c) Positive becoming less steep**

Part (a) shows that as speed increases, the distance traveled increases along a straight line.

Part (b) shows that as the distance sprinted increases, recovery time increases along a curve that becomes steeper.

Part (c) shows that as study time increases, the number of problems worked increases along a curve that becomes less steep.

relationship. Study time becomes less effective as you increase the hours worked and become more tired.

Figure A1.4 shows relationships between two variables that move in opposite directions. Such a relationship is called a **negative relationship** or **inverse relationship**.

Part (a) shows the relationship between the number of hours for playing squash and the number of hours for playing tennis when the total number of hours available is five. One extra hour spent playing tennis means one hour less playing squash and vice versa. This relationship is negative and linear.

Part (b) shows the relationship between the cost per mile traveled and the length of a journey. The longer the journey, the lower is the cost per mile. But as the journey length increases, the cost per mile decreases, and the fall in the cost gets smaller. This feature of the relationship is shown by the fact that the curve slopes downward, starting out steep at a short journey length and then becoming flatter as the journey length increases. This relationship arises because some of the costs are fixed, such as auto insurance, and the fixed costs are spread over a longer journey.

Part (c) shows the relationship between the amount of leisure time and the number of problems worked by a student. Increasing leisure time produces an increasingly large reduction in the number of problems worked. This relationship is a negative one that starts out with a gentle slope at a small number of leisure hours and becomes steeper as the number of leisure hours increases. This relationship is a different view of the idea shown in Figure A1.3(c).

Many relationships in economic models have a maximum or a minimum. For example, firms try to make the largest possible profit and to produce at the lowest possible cost. Figure A1.5 shows relationships that have a maximum or a minimum.

**Negative relationship or inverse relationship**
A relationship between two variables that move in opposite directions.

---

■ **FIGURE A1.4**
Negative (Inverse) Relationships

**Practice Online**

---

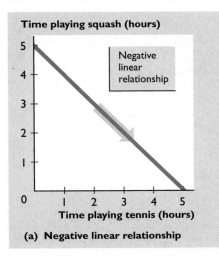

**(a)  Negative linear relationship**

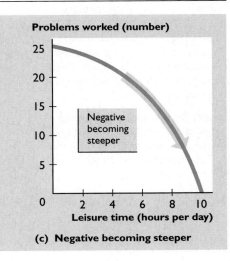

**(b)  Negative becoming less steep**

**(c)  Negative becoming steeper**

Part (a) shows that as the time playing tennis increases, the time playing squash decreases along a straight line.

Part (b) shows that as the journey length increases, the cost of the trip falls along a curve that becomes less steep.

Part (c) shows that as leisure time increases, the number of problems worked decreases along a curve that becomes steeper.

### FIGURE A1.5
Maximum and Minimum Points

Practice Online

In part (a), as the rainfall increases, the curve ❶ slopes upward as the yield per acre rises, ❷ is flat at point A, the maximum yield, and then ❸ slopes downward as the yield per acre falls.

In part (b), as the speed increases, the curve ❶ slopes downward as the cost per mile falls, ❷ is flat at the minimum point B, and then ❸ slopes upward as the cost per mile rises.

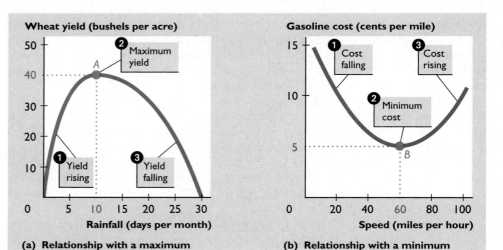

(a)  Relationship with a maximum

(b)  Relationship with a minimum

Part (a) shows the relationship that starts out sloping upward, reaches a maximum, and then slopes downward. Part (b) shows a relationship that begins sloping downward, falls to a minimum, and then slopes upward.

Finally, there are many situations in which, no matter what happens to the value of one variable, the other variable remains constant. Sometimes we want to show two variables that are unrelated in a graph. Figure A1.6 shows two graphs in which the variables are independent.

### FIGURE A1.6
Variables That Are Unrelated

Practice Online

In part (a), as the price of bananas increases, the student's grade in economics remains at 75 percent. These variables are unrelated, and the curve is horizontal.

In part (b), the vineyards of France produce 3 billion gallons of wine no matter what the rainfall in California is. These variables are unrelated, and the curve is vertical.

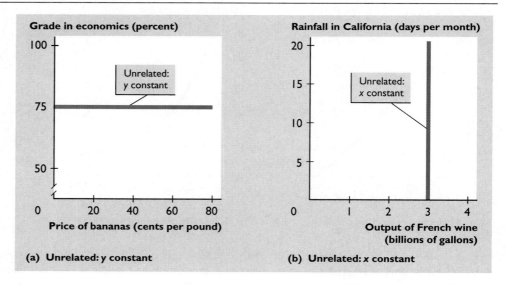

(a)  Unrelated: y constant

(b)  Unrelated: x constant

## ■ The Slope of a Relationship

We can measure the influence of one variable on another by the slope of the relationship. The **slope** of a relationship is the change in the value of the variable measured on the $y$-axis divided by the change in the value of the variable measured on the $x$-axis. We use the Greek letter $\Delta$ (delta) to represent "change in." So $\Delta y$ means the change in the value of $y$, and $\Delta x$ means the change in the value of $x$, and the slope of the relationship is

$$\Delta y \div \Delta x.$$

If a large change in $y$ is associated with a small change in $x$, the slope is large and the curve is steep. If a small change in $y$ is associated with a large change in $x$, the slope is small and the curve is flat.

Figure A1.7 shows you how to calculate slope. The slope of a straight line is the same regardless of where on the line you calculate it—the slope is constant. In part (a), when $x$ increases from 2 to 6, $y$ increases from 3 to 6. The change in $x$ is +4—that is, $\Delta x$ is 4. The change in $y$ is +3—that is, $\Delta y$ is 3. The slope of that line is 3/4. In part (b), when $x$ increases from 2 to 6, $y$ *decreases* from 6 to 3. The change in $y$ is *minus* 3—that is, $\Delta y$ is –3. The change in $x$ is plus 4—that is, $\Delta x$ is 4. The slope of the curve is –3/4. In part (c), we calculate the slope at a point on a curve. To do so, place a ruler on the graph so that it touches point $A$ and no other point on the curve, then draw a straight line along the edge of the ruler. The slope of this straight line is the slope of the curve at point $A$. This slope is 3/4.

**Slope**
The change in the value of the variable measured on the $y$-axis divided by the change in the value of the variable measured on the $x$-axis.

---

**FIGURE A1.7**

Calculating Slope

**Practice Online**

---

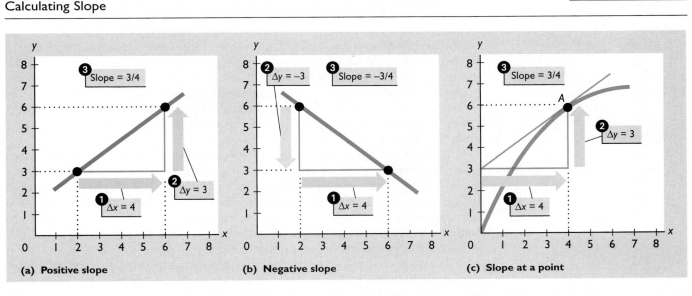

**(a) Positive slope**    **(b) Negative slope**    **(c) Slope at a point**

In part (a), ❶ when $\Delta x$ is 4, ❷ $\Delta y$ is 3, so ❸ the slope ($\Delta y/\Delta x$) is 3/4.

In part (b), ❶ when $\Delta x$ is 4, ❷ $\Delta y$ is –3, so ❸ the slope ($\Delta y/\Delta x$) is –3/4.

In part (c), the slope of the curve at point $A$ equals the slope of the red line. ❶ When $\Delta x$ is 4, ❷ $\Delta y$ is 3, so ❸ the slope ($\Delta y/\Delta x$) is 3/4.

## ■ Relationships Among More Than Two Variables

We have seen that we can graph the relationship between two variables as a point formed by the *x* and *y* values. But most of the relationships in economics involve relationships among many variables, not just two. For example, the amount of ice cream consumed depends on the price of ice cream and the temperature. If ice cream is expensive and the temperature is low, people eat much less ice cream than when ice cream is inexpensive and the temperature is high. For any given price of ice cream, the quantity consumed varies with the temperature; and for any given temperature, the quantity of ice cream consumed varies with its price.

Figure A1.8 shows a relationship among three variables. The table shows the number of gallons of ice cream consumed per day at various temperatures and ice cream prices. How can we graph these numbers?

To graph a relationship that involves more than two variables, we use the *ceteris paribus* assumption.

### Ceteris Paribus

The Latin phrase *ceteris paribus* means "other things remaining the same." Every laboratory experiment is an attempt to create *ceteris paribus* and isolate the relationship of interest. We use the same method to make a graph.

Figure A1.8(a) shows an example. This graph shows what happens to the quantity of ice cream consumed when the price of ice cream varies while the temperature remains the same. The curve labeled 70°F shows the relationship between ice cream consumption and the price of ice cream if the temperature is 70°F. The numbers used to plot that curve are those in the first and fourth columns of the table in Figure A1.8. For example, if the temperature is 70°F, 10 gallons are consumed when the price is 60¢ a scoop and 18 gallons are consumed when the price is 30¢ a scoop. The curve labeled 90°F shows consumption as the price varies if the temperature is 90°F.

We can also show the relationship between ice cream consumption and temperature while the price of ice cream remains constant, as shown in Figure A1.8(b). The curve labeled 60¢ shows how the consumption of ice cream varies with the temperature when the price of ice cream is 60¢ a scoop, and a second curve shows the relationship when the price of ice cream is 15¢ a scoop. For example, at 60¢ a scoop, 10 gallons are consumed when the temperature is 70°F and 20 gallons when the temperature is 90°F.

Figure A1.8(c) shows the combinations of temperature and price that result in a constant consumption of ice cream. One curve shows the combination that results in 10 gallons a day being consumed, and the other shows the combination that results in 7 gallons a day being consumed. A high price and a high temperature lead to the same consumption as a lower price and a lower temperature. For example, 10 gallons of ice cream are consumed at 90°F and 90¢ a scoop, at 70°F and 60¢ a scoop, and at 50°F and 45¢ a scoop.

With what you've learned about graphs in this Appendix, you can move forward with your study of economics. There are no graphs in this textbook that are more complicated than the ones you've studied here.

### FIGURE A1.8

Graphing a Relationship Among Three Variables

**Practice Online**

| Price (cents per scoop) | Ice cream consumption (gallons per day) | | | |
|---|---|---|---|---|
| | **30°F** | **50°F** | **70°F** | **90°F** |
| 15 | 12 | 18 | 25 | 50 |
| 30 | 10 | 12 | 18 | 37 |
| 45 | 7 | 10 | 13 | 27 |
| 60 | 5 | 7 | 10 | 20 |
| 75 | 3 | 5 | 7 | 14 |
| 90 | 2 | 3 | 5 | 10 |
| 105 | 1 | 2 | 3 | 6 |

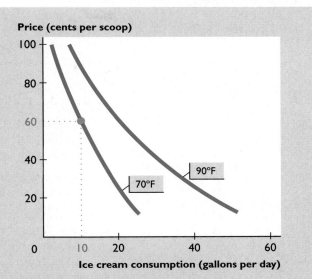

(a) Price and consumption at a given temperature

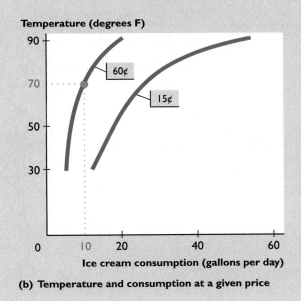

(b) Temperature and consumption at a given price

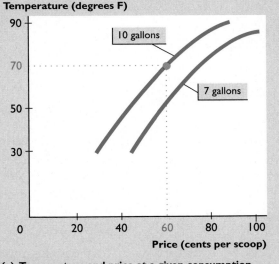

(c) Temperature and price at a given consumption

The table tells us how many gallons of ice cream are consumed each day at different prices and different temperatures. For example, if the price is 60¢ a scoop and the temperature is 70°F, 10 gallons of ice cream are consumed. This set of values is highlighted in the table and each part of the figure.

Part (a) shows the relationship between price and consumption when temperature is held constant. One curve holds temperature at 90°F, and the other at 70°F.

Part (b) shows the relationship between temperature and consumption when price is held constant. One curve holds the price at 60¢ a scoop, and the other at 15¢ a scoop.

Part (c) shows the relationship between temperature and price when consumption is held constant. One curve holds consumption at 10 gallons, and the other at 7 gallons.

Study Guide pp. 14–19

Practice Online A1.1

## Exercises

The spreadsheet provides data on the U.S. economy: Column A is the year; the other columns are actual and projected expenditures per person in dollars per year on recorded music (column B), Internet services (column C), and movies in theaters (column D). Use this spreadsheet to answer exercises 1, 2, 3, 4, and 5.

*Music  Internet  Theaters*

| | A | B | C | D |
|---|---|---|---|---|
| 1 | 1992 | 43 | 4 | 23 |
| 2 | 1993 | 47 | 5 | 24 |
| 3 | 1994 | 56 | 6 | 25 |
| 4 | 1995 | 57 | 11 | 25 |
| 5 | 1996 | 57 | 17 | 27 |
| 6 | 1997 | 55 | 26 | 29 |
| 7 | 1998 | 56 | 32 | 30 |
| 8 | 1999 | 58 | 37 | 31 |
| 9 | 2000 | 62 | 43 | 32 |
| 10 | 2001 | 66 | 48 | 33 |
| 11 | 2002 | 69 | 53 | 34 |

1. Draw a scatter diagram to show the relationship between expenditure on recorded music and expenditure on Internet services. Describe the relationship.

2. Draw a scatter diagram to show the relationship between expenditure on Internet services and expenditure on movies in theaters. Describe the relationship.

3. Draw a scatter diagram to show the relationship between expenditure on recorded music and expenditure on movies in theaters. Describe the relationship.

4. Draw a time-series graph of expenditure on Internet services. Say in which year or years (a) expenditure was highest, (b) expenditure was lowest, (c) expenditure increased the most, and (d) expenditure increased the least. Also, say whether the data show a trend and describe its direction.

5. Draw a time-series graph of expenditure on recorded music. Say in which year or years (a) expenditure was highest, (b) expenditure was lowest, (c) expenditure increased the most, and (d) expenditure increased the least. Also, say whether the data show a trend and describe its direction.

6. Draw a graph to show the relationship between the two variables $x$ and $y$:

| $x$ | 0 | 1 | 2 | 3 | 4 | 5 | 6 | 7 | 8 |
|---|---|---|---|---|---|---|---|---|---|
| $y$ | 0 | 1 | 4 | 9 | 16 | 25 | 36 | 49 | 64 |

   a. Is the relationship positive or negative?
   b. Calculate the slope of the relationship between $x$ and $y$ when $x$ equals 2 and when $x$ equals 4.
   c. How does the slope of the relationship change as the value of $x$ increases?
   d. Think of some economic relationships that might be similar to this one.

7. Draw a graph to show the relationship between the two variables $x$ and $y$:

| $x$ | 0 | 1 | 2 | 3 | 4 | 5 | 6 | 7 | 8 |
|---|---|---|---|---|---|---|---|---|---|
| $y$ | 60 | 49 | 39 | 30 | 22 | 15 | 9 | 4 | 0 |

   a. Is the relationship positive or negative?
   b. Calculate the slope of the relationship between $x$ and $y$ when $x$ equals 2 and when $x$ equals 4.
   c. How does the slope of the relationship change as the value of $x$ increases?
   d. Think of some economic relationships that might be similar to this one.

| Price (dollars per ride) | Balloon rides (number per day) | | |
|---|---|---|---|
| | 50°F | 70°F | 90°F |
| 5 | 32 | 50 | 40 |
| 10 | 27 | 40 | 32 |
| 15 | 18 | 32 | 27 |
| 20 | 10 | 27 | 18 |

8. The table provides data on the price of a balloon ride, the temperature, and the number of rides a day. Draw graphs to show the relationship between:
   a. The price and the number of rides, holding the temperature constant.
   b. The number of rides and the temperature, holding the price constant.
   c. The temperature and the price, holding the number of rides constant.

# The U.S. and Global Economies

# CHAPTER 2

## CHAPTER CHECKLIST

**When you have completed your study of this chapter,
you will be able to**

1 Describe what, how, and for whom goods and services are produced in
the United States.

2 Use the circular flow model to provide a picture of how households,
firms, and governments interact.

3 Describe the macroeconomic performance—standard of living, cost of
living, and economic fluctuations—of the United States and other
economies.

You've learned that economics is the social science that studies the choices that people, businesses, and governments make to cope with *scarcity* and the *incentives* that influence and reconcile our choices. These choices and the interactions among them determine *what*, *how*, and *for whom* goods and services are produced. These choices also determine the standard of living and the cost of living and bring economic fluctuations—recessions and expansions.

Most of your economics course explains the principles and theories that *explain* and in some cases enable economists to *predict* choices and their consequences. But before we turn to this task, we are going to *describe* the main features of the U.S. and global economies. In this chapter, you will learn *what*, *how*, and *for whom* goods and services are produced; about the resources available and how they are used; and about the standard of living, the cost of living, and economic fluctuations around the world.

## 2.1 WHAT, HOW, AND FOR WHOM?

Walk around a shopping mall and pay close attention to the range of goods and services that are being offered for sale. Go inside some of the shops and look at the labels to see where various items are manufactured. The next time you travel on an interstate highway, look at the large trucks and pay attention to the names and products printed on their sides and the places in which the trucks are registered. Open the Yellow Pages and flip through a few sections. Notice the huge range of goods and services that businesses are offering.

You've just done a sampling of *what* goods and services are produced and consumed in the United States today.

### ■ What Do We Produce?

We divide the vast array of goods and services produced into four large groups:

- Consumption goods and services
- Investment goods
- Government goods and services
- Export goods and services

**Consumption goods** and **services**
Goods and services that are bought by individuals and used to provide personal enjoyment and contribute to a person's standard of living.

**Consumption goods and services** are items that are bought by individuals and used to provide personal enjoyment and contribute to a person's standard of living. They include items such as housing, SUVs, popcorn and soda, movies and chocolate bars, microwave ovens and inline skates, and dental and dry cleaning services.

**Investment goods**
Goods that are bought by businesses to increase their productive resources.

**Investment goods** are goods that are bought by businesses to increase their productive resources. They include items such as auto assembly lines and shopping malls, airplanes, and oil tankers.

**Government goods and services**
Goods and services that are bought by governments.

**Government goods and services** are items that are bought by governments. Governments purchase missiles and weapons systems, travel services, Internet services, police protection, roads, and paper and paper clips.

**Export goods and services**
Goods and services produced in one country and sold in other countries.

**Export goods and services** are items produced in one country and sold in other countries. U.S. export goods and services include the airplanes produced by Boeing that Singapore Airlines buys, the computers produced by Dell that Europeans buy, and licenses sold by U.S. film companies to show U.S. movies in European movie theaters.

Figure 2.1(a) provides a snapshot of the division of total production in the United States in 2002 into these four groups. You can see that consumption goods and services have the largest share at 61 percent of the total. Investment goods accounts for 13 percent of total production. Goods and services bought by governments take 17 percent of the total, and 9 percent is exported.

Figure 2.1(b) shows the production of the largest five services and goods. Real estate services are the largest item and represent 11 percent of the value of total production. The main component of this item is the services of rental and owner-occupied housing. Retail and wholesale trades are the next two largest categories. Health services and education complete the largest five services.

The largest categories of goods—construction, electronic equipment such as computers, food, industrial equipment, and chemicals—each account for less than 4 percent of the value of total production.

<u>**Practice Online**</u>

■ **FIGURE 2.1**
What We Produce

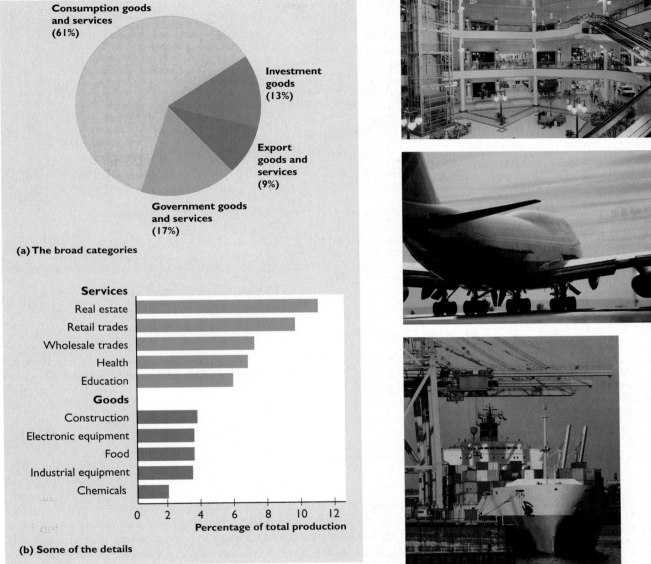

(a) The broad categories

(b) Some of the details

Source: Bureau of Economic Analysis.

In 2002, consumption goods and services accounted for 61 percent of total production. Investment goods accounted for 13 percent, government goods and services accounted for 17 percent, and export goods and services accounted for 9 percent of total production.

Real estate services, retail and wholesale trades, health, and education are the largest five services produced. Construction, electronic equipment, food, industrial equipment, and chemicals are the largest five goods produced. Services production exceeds goods production and is growing faster.

# Eye on the Past

## Changes in What We Produce

Sixty years ago, one American in four worked on a farm. That number has shrunk to one in thirty-five. The number of people who produce goods—in mining, construction, and manufacturing—has also shrunk from one person in three to one in five. In contrast, the number of people who produce services has expanded from one in two to almost four out of five. These changes in employment reflect changes in what we produce—services.

**Employment (percentage of total)**

Services

Mining, construction, and manufacturing

Agriculture

1940  1950  1960  1970  1980  1990  2000

**Year**

SOURCE: U.S. Census Bureau, *Statistical Abstract of the United States*, 2000.

## ■ How Do We Produce?

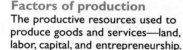

**Factors of production**
The productive resources used to produce goods and services—land, labor, capital, and entrepreneurship.

Goods and services are produced by using productive resources. Economists call the productive resources **factors of production**. Factors of production are grouped into four categories:

- Land
- Labor
- Capital
- Entrepreneurship

### Land

**Land**
The "gifts of nature," or *natural resources*, that we use to produce goods and services.

In economics, **land** includes all the "gifts of nature" that we use to produce goods and services. Land is what, in everyday language, we call *natural resources*. It includes land in the everyday sense, minerals, energy, water, and air, and wild plants, animals, birds, and fish. Some of these resources are renewable, and some are nonrenewable. The U.S. Geological Survey maintains a national inventory of the quantity and quality of natural resources and monitors changes to that inventory.

The United States covers almost 2 billion acres. About 45 percent of the land is forest, lakes, and national parks. In 2000, almost 50 percent of the land was used for agriculture and 5 percent was urban, but urban land use is growing and agricultural land use is shrinking.

Our land surface and water resources are renewable, and some of our mineral resources can be recycled. But many mineral resources, and all those that we use to create energy, can be used only once. They are nonrenewable resources. Of these, the United States has vast known coal reserves but much smaller known reserves of oil and natural gas.

## Labor

**Labor** is the work time and work effort that people devote to producing goods and services. It includes the physical and mental efforts of all the people who work on farms and construction sites and in factories, shops, and offices. The Census Bureau and Bureau of Labor Statistics measure the nation's labor force every month.

In the United States in 2002, 144 million people had jobs or were available for work. Some worked full time, some part time, and some were unemployed but looking for an acceptable job. The total amount of time worked during 2002 was about 234 billion hours.

The quantity of labor increases as the adult population increases. The quantity of labor also increases if a larger percentage of the population takes jobs. During the past 50 years, a larger proportion of women have taken paid work and this trend has increased the quantity of labor.

The quality of labor depends on how skilled people are. Economists use a special name for human skill: human capital. **Human capital** is the knowledge and skill that people obtain from education, on-the-job training, and work experience. You are building your own human capital right now as you work on your economics course and other subjects. And your human capital will continue to grow when you get a full-time job and become better at it. Human capital improves the *quality* of labor. Figure 2.2 shows that today more than 80 percent of the U.S. population has completed high school and 25 percent has a college or university degree.

**Labor**
The work time and work effort that people devote to producing goods and services.

**Human capital**
The knowledge and skill that people obtain from education, on-the-job training, and work experience.

---

**■ FIGURE 2.2**
Measures of Human Capital

**Practice Online**

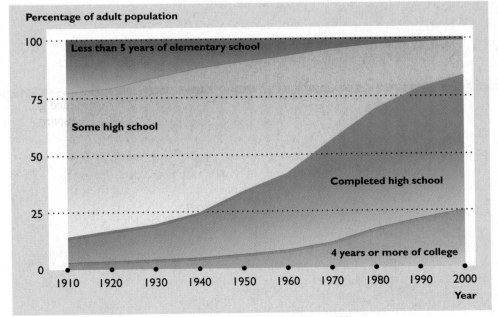

In 2000, 25 percent of the population had 4 years or more of college, up from 3 percent in 1910. An additional 58 percent had completed high school, up from 11 percent in 1910.

SOURCE: U.S. Census Bureau, *Statistical Abstract of the United States*, 2002.

## How We Produce in the New Economy

The new economy consists of the jobs and businesses that produce Internet services, e-commerce, database and other information services, and other computer-driven services. The new economy also consists of the biotechnology industries.

These new economy sectors are indeed growing rapidly. But they are not really the heart of tomorrow's economy.

Tomorrow's economy, like today's economy, will be an increasingly service-oriented economy.

In 1996, some 15 million people worked in general clerical and sales jobs. By 2006, their number will be swelled by another 2 million workers, an increase of 14 percent since 1996. Clerical work and retail selling are the core of tomorrow's economy.

Health care and personal care make up a second large and fast-growing area. The 6 million workers in these jobs will grow to almost 8 million by 2006.

Food preparation and serving will grow by 1 million workers to more than 7 million by 2006. This increase continues the trend toward people buying an ever-increasing proportion of their meals away from home.

The education sector will also expand quickly with close to a million more teachers by 2006, an increase of 33 percent since 1996.

The computer-driven economy will expand rapidly too. In fact, it will grow more quickly than any of the areas we've just reviewed. In 1996, about 1 million people worked in this sector. By 2006, this number will have more than doubled.

These projections through 2006 reinforce the strong sense that our economy is increasingly a service economy.

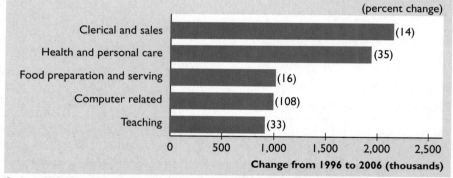

SOURCE: U.S. Census Bureau, *Statistical Abstract of the United States*, 2000.

## Capital

In everyday language, we talk about money, stocks, and bonds as being capital. These items are *financial capital*, and they are not productive resources. They enable people to provide businesses with financial resources, but they are *not* used to produce goods and services. They are not capital.

**Capital** consists of the tools, instruments, machines, buildings, and other constructions that have been produced in the past and that businesses now use to produce goods and services. Capital includes hammers and screwdrivers, computers, auto assembly lines, office towers and warehouses, dams and power plants, airports and airplanes, shirt factories, and cookie shops. The Bureau of Economic Analysis in the U.S. Department of Commerce keeps track of the total value of capital, which grows over time. In the United States today, it is around $20 trillion. The global value of capital exceeds $130 trillion.

**Capital**
Tools, instruments, machines, buildings, and other constructions that have been produced in the past and that businesses now use to produce goods and services.

## Entrepreneurship

**Entrepreneurship** is the human resource that organizes labor, land, and capital. Entrepreneurs come up with new ideas about what and how to produce, make business decisions, and bear the risks that arise from these decisions.

The quantity of entrepreneurship is hard to describe or measure. At some periods, there appears to be a great deal of imaginative entrepreneurship around. People such as Sam Walton, who created Wal-Mart, one of the world's largest retailers; Bill Gates, who founded the Microsoft empire; and Michael Dell, who established Dell Computers, are examples of extraordinary entrepreneurial talent. But these highly visible entrepreneurs are just the tip of an iceberg that consists of hundreds of thousands of people who run businesses, large and small.

**Entrepreneurship**
The human resource that organizes labor, land, and capital.

## ■ For Whom Do We Produce?

Who gets the goods and services that are produced depends on the incomes that people earn and the goods and services that they choose to buy. A large income enables a person to buy large quantities of goods and services. A small income leaves a person with few options and small quantities of goods and services.

People earn their incomes by selling the services of the factors of production they own. **Rent** is paid for the use of land, **wages** are paid for the services of labor, **interest** is paid for the use of capital, and entrepreneurs receive a **profit** (or incur a **loss**) for running their businesses.

Which factor of production in the United States earns more income: labor or capital? Figure 2.3(a) provides the answer.

**Rent**
Income paid for the use of land.

**Wages**
Income paid for the services of labor.

**Interest**
Income paid for the use of capital.

**Profit (or loss)**
Income earned by an entrepreneur for running a business.

---

### ■ FIGURE 2.3
### For Whom?

**Practice Online**

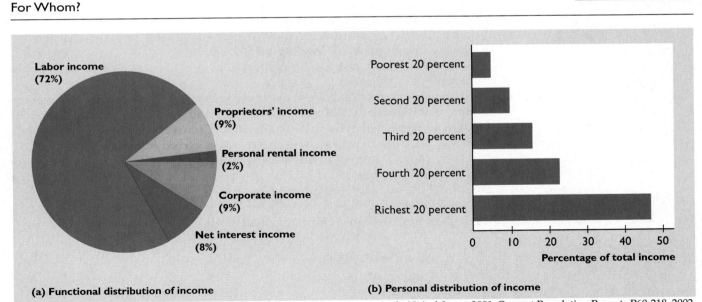

**(a) Functional distribution of income**

Labor income (72%)
Proprietors' income (9%)
Personal rental income (2%)
Corporate income (9%)
Net interest income (8%)

**(b) Personal distribution of income**

Poorest 20 percent
Second 20 percent
Third 20 percent
Fourth 20 percent
Richest 20 percent

Percentage of total income

SOURCES: Bureau of Economic Analysis and U.S. Census Bureau, *Money Income in the United States: 2001*, Current Population Reports P60-218, 2002.

Incomes determine who consumes the goods and services produced. In 2002, labor income was 72 percent of total income, capital income (corporate income and net interest income) was 17 percent, and proprietors' income, which includes both wages and rent, was almost 9 percent. Personal rental income was 2 percent of the total. More than 70 percent of total income is from labor. The richest 20 percent of the population receives almost 50 percent of total income. The poorest 20 percent receives only 5 percent of total income.

**Functional distribution of income**

The distribution of income among the factors of production.

**Personal distribution of income**

The distribution of income among households.

The figure shows the **functional distribution of income**, which is the distribution of income among the factors of production. Labor earns most of the income: 72 percent of total income in 2002. Capital income—corporate income and net interest income—was 17 percent in 2002. The proprietors of businesses, whose earnings are a mixture of labor and capital income, earned 9 percent of total income in 2002. Personal rental income was 2 percent in 2002. These percentages remain remarkably constant over time.

The data in Figure 2.3(a) tell us how income is distributed among the factors of production. But the data don't tell us how income is distributed among individuals.

You know of lots of people who earn very large incomes. Tiger Woods wins several million dollars a year in prize money and earns substantially more than this amount in endorsements. The average salary of major league baseball players in 2002 was $2.4 million, and some stars, such as Barry Bonds, Sammy Sosa, Manny Ramirez, Kevin Brown, Carlos Delgado, and Alex Rodriguez received between $15 million and $22 million a year.

You know of even more people who earn very small incomes. Servers at McDonald's average around $6.50 an hour; checkout clerks, gas station attendants, and textile and leather workers earn less than $10 an hour.

Figure 2.3(b) shows the **personal distribution of income** after households have paid their income taxes and received benefits from governments. Households are divided into five groups, each of which represents 20 percent of all households. If incomes were equal, each 20 percent group would earn 20 percent of total income. You know that incomes are unequal, and the figure provides a measure of just how unequal they are.

The poorest 20 percent of households receives only 5 percent of total income. The average income of this group in 2001 was about $10,000.

The second poorest 20 percent receives 10 percent of total income. The average income of this group in 2001 was about $25,000.

The middle 20 percent receives 16 percent of total income. The average income of this group in 2001 was about $43,000.

All three of these groups—the poorest 60 percent of households—receive only 31 percent of total income.

The second richest 20 percent receives 23 percent of total income. The average income in this group in 2001 was about $67,000 and the highest income was about $85,000. So 80 percent of the households in the United States have incomes of less than $85,000. Only 20 percent have incomes that exceed this amount.

The richest 20 percent of households receives 47 percent of total income. We don't know the highest income in this group, but some of the famous names that we started out with are examples of high earners.

Based on these numbers, you can see that the 20 percent of households with the highest incomes can afford to buy half of the goods and services produced.

# CHECKPOINT 2.1

**1** **Describe what, how, and for whom goods and services are produced in the United States.**

Study Guide pp. 24–26

Practice Online 2.1

## Practice Problems 2.1

1. Name the four broad categories of goods and services that we use in economics, provide an example of each (different from those in the chapter), and say what percentage of total production each accounted for in 2002.
2. Name the four factors of production and the incomes they earn.
3. Distinguish between the functional distribution of income and the personal distribution of income.
4. In the United States, which factor of production earns the largest share of income and what percentage does it earn?

## Exercises 2.1

1. What is the distinction between consumption goods and services and investment goods? Which one of them brings an increase in productive resources?
2. Describe the changes that have occurred in the education levels of the U.S. labor force during the last few decades.
3. If everyone were to consume an equal quantity of goods and services, what percentage of total income would the poorest 20 percent of individuals have to receive from higher-income groups? What percentage would the second poorest 20 percent have to receive?
4. Compare the percentage of total U. S. income that labor earns with the percentage earned by all the other factors of production combined.

## Solutions to Practice Problems 2.1

1. The four categories are consumption goods and services, investment goods, government goods and services, and export goods and services. An example of a consumption service is a haircut, of an investment good is an oil rig, of a government service is police protection, and of an export good is a computer chip sold to Ireland. Of total production, consumption goods and services are 61 percent; investment goods are 13 percent; government goods and services are 17 percent; and export goods and services are 9 percent.
2. The factors of production are land, labor, capital, and entrepreneurship. Land earns rent; labor earns wages; capital earns interest; and entrepreneurship earns profit or incurs a loss.
3. The functional distribution of income shows the percentage of total income received by each factor of production. The personal distribution of income shows the percentage of total income received by households.
4. Labor is the factor of production that earns the largest share of income in the United States. In 2002, labor earned 72 percent of total income.

## 2.2 CIRCULAR FLOWS

**Circular flow model**
A model of the economy that shows the circular flow of expenditures and incomes that result from decision makers' choices, and the way those choices interact to determine what, how, and for whom goods and services are produced.

**Households**
Individuals or groups of people living together.

**Firms**
The institutions that organize the production of goods and services.

**Market**
Any arrangement that brings buyers and sellers together and enables them to get information and do business with each other.

**Goods markets**
Markets in which goods and services are bought and sold.

**Factor markets**
Markets in which factors of production are bought and sold.

We can organize the data you've just studied using the **circular flow model**—a model of the economy that shows the circular flow of expenditures and incomes that result from decision makers' choices and the way those choices interact to determine what, how, and for whom goods and services are produced. Figure 2.4 shows the circular flow model.

### ■ Households and Firms

**Households** are individuals or groups of people living together. The 109 million households in the United States own the factors of production—land, labor, capital, and entrepreneurship—and choose the quantities of these resources to provide to firms. Households also choose the quantities of goods and services to buy.

**Firms** are the institutions that organize the production of goods and services. The 20 million firms in the United States choose the quantities of the factors of production to hire and the quantities of goods and services to produce.

### ■ Markets

Households choose the quantities of the factors of production to provide to firms, and firms choose the quantities of the services of the factors of production to hire. Households choose the quantities of goods and services to buy, and firms choose the quantities of goods and services to produce. How are these choices coordinated and made compatible? The answer is: by markets.

A **market** is any arrangement that brings buyers and sellers together and enables them to get information and do business with each other. An example is the market in which oil is bought and sold—the world oil market. The world oil market is not a place. It is the network of oil producers, oil users, wholesalers, and brokers who buy and sell oil. In the world oil market, decision makers do not meet physically. They make deals by telephone, fax, and the Internet.

Figure 2.4 identifies two types of markets: goods markets and factor markets. **Goods markets** are markets in which goods and services are bought and sold. **Factor markets** are markets in which factors of production are bought and sold.

### ■ Real Flows and Money Flows

When households choose the quantities of land, labor, capital, and entrepreneurship to offer in factor markets, they respond to the incomes they receive—rent for land, wages for labor, interest for capital, and profit for entrepreneurship. When firms choose the quantities of factors to hire, they respond to the rent, wages, interest, and profits they must pay to households.

Similarly, when firms choose the quantities of goods and services to produce and offer for sale in goods markets, they respond to the amounts that they receive from the expenditures that households make. And when households choose the quantities of goods and services to buy, they respond to the amounts they must pay to firms.

Figure 2.4 shows the flows that result from these choices made by households and firms. The real flows are shown in orange. These are the flows of the factors of production that go from households through factor markets to firms and the goods and services that go from firms through goods markets to households. The money flows go in the opposite direction. These flows are the payments made in exchange for factors of production (blue flow) and expenditures on goods and services (red flow).

Lying behind these real flows and money flows are millions of individual choices about what to consume, what to produce, and how to produce. These choices result in buying plans by households and selling plans by firms in goods markets. And the choices result in selling plans by households and buying plans by firms in factor markets. When these buying plans and selling plans are carried out, they determine the prices that people pay and the incomes they earn and so determine for whom goods and services are produced. You'll learn in Chapter 4 how markets coordinate the buying plans and selling plans of households and firms and make them compatible.

Firms produce most of the goods and services that we consume. But governments provide some of the services that we enjoy. And governments play a big role in modifying for whom goods and services are produced by changing the distribution of income. So we're now going to look at the role of governments in the U.S. economy and add them to the circular flow model.

## ■ FIGURE 2.4
The Circular Flow Model

**Practice Online**

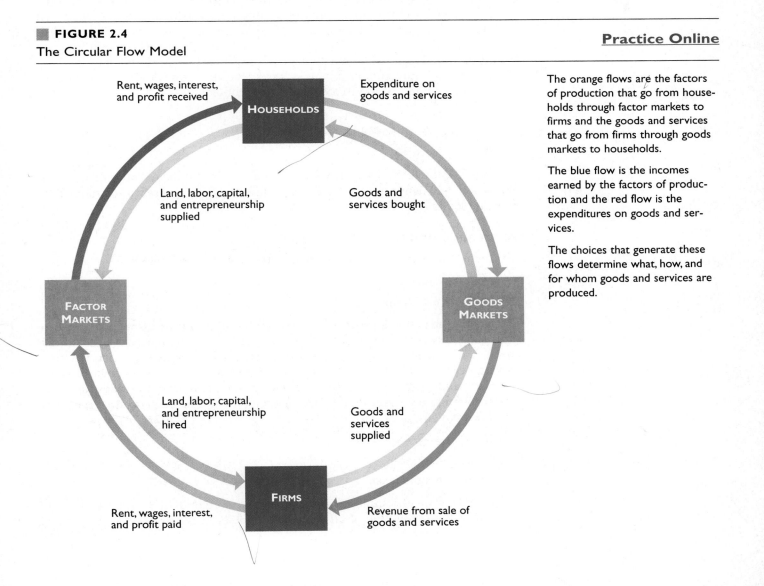

The orange flows are the factors of production that go from households through factor markets to firms and the goods and services that go from firms through goods markets to households.

The blue flow is the incomes earned by the factors of production and the red flow is the expenditures on goods and services.

The choices that generate these flows determine what, how, and for whom goods and services are produced.

# ■ Governments

More than 86,000 organizations operate as governments in the United States. Some are tiny like the Yuma, Arizona, school district and some are enormous like the U.S. federal government. We divide governments into two levels:

- Federal government
- State and local government

## Federal Government

The federal government's major expenditures are to provide

1. Goods and services
2. Social security and welfare payments
3. Transfers to state and local governments

The goods and services provided by the federal government include the legal system, which defines property rights and enforces contracts, and national defense. Social security and welfare benefits, which include income for retired seniors and programs such as Medicare and Medicaid, are transfers from the federal government to households. Transfers to state and local governments are payments designed to provide more equality across the states and regions.

The federal government finances its expenditures by collecting a variety of taxes. The main taxes paid to the federal government are

1. Personal income taxes
2. Corporate (business) income taxes
3. Social security taxes

In 2002, the federal government spent and raised in taxes more than $2 trillion—about 20 percent of the total value of all the goods and services produced in the United States in that year.

## State and Local Government

The state and local governments' major expenditures are to provide

1. Goods and services
2. Welfare benefits

The goods and services provided by state and local governments include the state courts and law enforcement authorities, schools, roads, garbage collection and disposal, water supplies, and sewage management. Welfare benefits provided by state governments include unemployment benefits and other aid to low-income families.

State and local governments finance these expenditures by collecting taxes and receiving transfers from the federal government. The main taxes paid to state and local governments are

1. Sales taxes
2. Property taxes
3. State income taxes

In 2002, state and local governments spent more than $1.3 trillion—about 13 percent of the total value of all the goods and services produced in the United States in that year.

## ■ Governments in the Circular Flow

Figure 2.5 adds governments to the circular flow model. As you study this figure, first notice that the outer circle is the same as Figure 2.4. In addition to these flows, governments buy goods and services from firms. The red arrows that run from governments through the goods markets to firms show this expenditure.

Households and firms pay taxes to governments. The green arrows running directly from households and firms to governments show these flows. Also, the governments make money payments to households and firms. The green arrows running directly from governments to households and firms show these flows. Taxes and transfers are direct transactions with governments and do not go through the goods markets and factor markets.

Not part of the circular flow and not visible in Figure 2.5, governments provide the legal framework within which all transactions occur. For example, they operate the courts and legal system that enable contracts to be written and enforced.

■ **FIGURE 2.5**

**Practice Online**

Governments in the Circular Flow

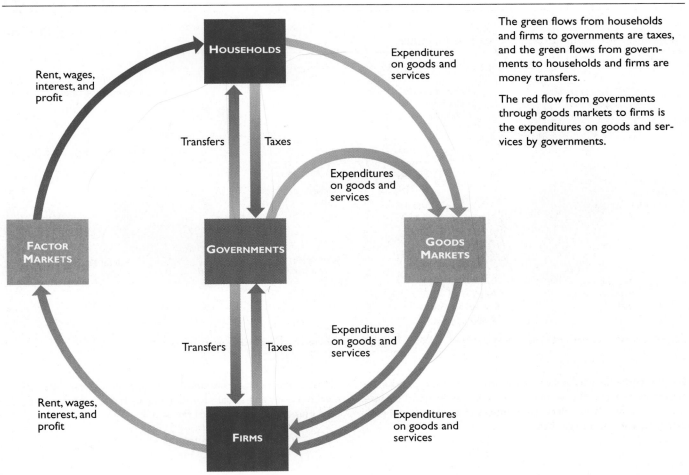

The green flows from households and firms to governments are taxes, and the green flows from governments to households and firms are money transfers.

The red flow from governments through goods markets to firms is the expenditures on goods and services by governments.

## ■ Federal Government Expenditures and Revenue

What are the main items of expenditures by the federal government on goods and services and transfers? And what are its main sources of tax revenue? Figure 2.6 answers these questions.

You can see that by far the largest part of what the federal government spends is on social security benefits and other transfers to persons. National defense also takes a big slice of the federal government's expenditures. The interest payment on the national debt is another large item. The **national debt** is the total amount that the federal government has borrowed to make expenditures that exceed tax revenue—to run a government budget deficit. The national debt is a bit like a large credit card balance. And paying the interest on the national debt is like paying the minimum required monthly payment.

Transfers to other levels of government also use up a large part of the federal government's expenditures. Purchases of goods and services (other than national defense) are relatively small, and subsidies and aid to other countries take a tiny slice of expenditures.

Most of the tax revenue of the federal government—almost a half of it—comes from personal income taxes. And two thirds of the rest comes from social security taxes. Corporate income taxes are a small part of the federal government's revenue.

**National debt**
The total amount that the federal government has borrowed to make expenditures that exceed tax revenue—to run a government budget deficit.

---

**FIGURE 2.6**

Federal Government Expenditures and Revenue

**Practice Online**

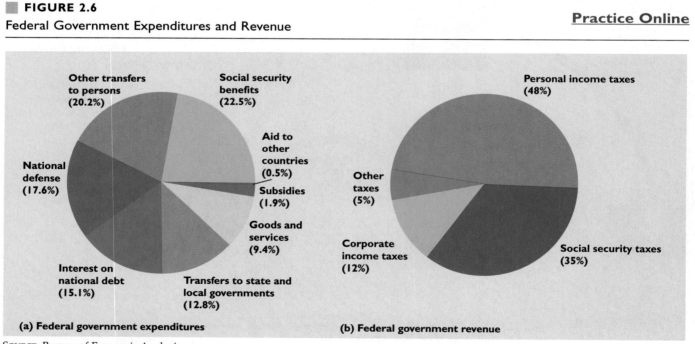

**(a) Federal government expenditures**

**(b) Federal government revenue**

SOURCE: Bureau of Economic Analysis.

Social security benefits and other transfers to persons are the largest slice of federal government expenditures. National defense, interest on the national debt, and transfers to state and local governments also are a large share.

Most of the federal government's revenue comes from personal income taxes and social security taxes. Corporate income taxes are only a small part of total revenue.

## ■ State and Local Government Expenditures and Revenue

What are the main items of expenditures by the state and local governments on goods and services and transfers? And what are their main sources of revenue? Figure 2.7 answers these questions.

You can see that education is by far the largest part of the expenditures of state and local governments. This item covers the cost of public schools, colleges, and universities. It absorbs 40 percent of total expenditures—approximately $520 billion, or $1,870 per person.

Welfare benefits are the second largest item, and it takes 20 percent of total expenditures. Highways are the next largest item, and they account for 8 percent of total expenditures. The remaining 32 percent is spent on other local public goods and services such as police services, garbage collection and disposal, sewage management, and water supplies.

Sales taxes and transfers from the federal government bring in similar amounts—about 25 percent of total revenue. Property taxes account for 21 percent of total revenue. Individual income taxes account for 15 percent, and corporate income taxes account for 3 percent. The remaining 13 percent comes from other taxes such as estate taxes.

---

■ **FIGURE 2.7**                                                                __Practice Online__

State and Local Government Expenditures and Revenue

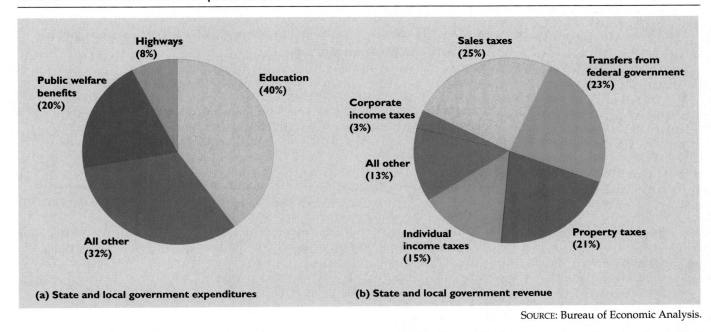

(a) State and local government expenditures

(b) State and local government revenue

SOURCE: Bureau of Economic Analysis.

Education, highways, and public welfare benefits are the largest slice of state and local government expenditures.

Most of the state and local government revenue comes from sales taxes, property taxes, and transfers from the federal government.

# Eye on the Global Economy

## Production and People in the World Today

In the United States, 5 percent of the world's people produce 22 percent of the value of the world's output. The figure shows the percentages of population and production for other nations and regions.

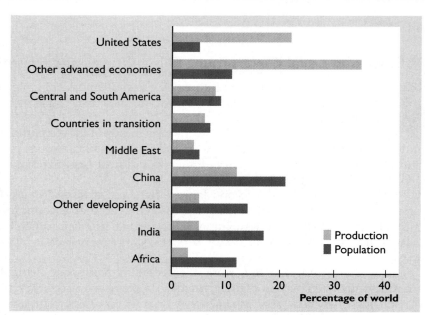

SOURCE: International Monetary Fund, *World Economic Outlook* database.

---

# CHECKPOINT 2.2

Study Guide pp. 27–29

Practice Online 2.2

**2** Use the circular flow model to provide a picture of how households, firms, and governments interact.

## Practice Problem 2.2

What are the real flows and money flows that run between households, firms, and governments in the circular flow model?

## Exercises 2.2

1. What are the choices made by households and firms that determine what, how, and for whom goods and services are produced? Where, in the circular flow model, do those choices appear?
2. How do the actions of governments modify what, how, and for whom goods and services are produced? Where, in the circular flow model, do those choices appear?

## Solution to Practice Problem 2.2

The real flows are the services of factors of production from households to firms and the goods and services from firms to households and from firms to governments. The money flows are factor incomes, household and government expenditures on goods and services, taxes, and transfers.

## 2.3 MACROECONOMIC PERFORMANCE

Macroeconomic performance has three dimensions:

- Standard of living
- Cost of living
- Economic fluctuations

### ■ Standard of Living

The standard of living depends on the quantities of goods and services produced and the number of people among whom those goods and services are shared. The greater the value of production per person, the higher is the standard of living, other things remaining the same. For the world as a whole, the average value of goods and services produced is $21 per person per day. But there is an enormous range around that average. Let's begin our exploration of global living standards by looking at the size and distribution of the population.

### World Population

Visit the Web site of the U.S. Census Bureau and find the population clocks. On September 8, 2002, the U.S. clock recorded a population of 287,991,639. The world clock recorded a global population of 6,248,847,500. The U.S. clock ticks along showing a population increase of one person every 14 seconds. The world clock spins much faster, adding 34 people in the same 14 seconds.

### Classification of Countries

The world's 6.25 billion (and rising) population lives in 184 economies classified by the International Monetary Fund into three broad groups:

- Advanced economies
- Developing economies
- Transition economies

***Advanced Economies***  Advanced economies are the 28 countries (or areas) that have the highest standards of living. The United States, Japan, Italy, Germany, France, the United Kingdom, and Canada belong to this group. So do four new industrial Asian economies: Hong Kong, South Korea, Singapore, and Taiwan. The other advanced economies include Australia, New Zealand, and most of the rest of Western Europe. Almost 1 billion people live in the advanced economies.

***Developing Economies***  Developing economies are the 128 countries in Africa, Asia, the Middle East, Europe, and Central and South America that have not yet achieved a high standard of living for their people. The standard of living in these economies varies a great deal, but in all cases, it is much lower than that in the advanced economies, and in some cases, it is extremely low. Almost 5 billion people live in the developing economies.

***Transition Economies***  Transition economies are the 28 countries in Europe and Asia that were, until the early 1990s, part of the Soviet Union or its satellites. These countries include Russia, Hungary, Poland, and the Czech Republic.

The economies in this group are small—only 200 million people in total—but are important because they are in transition (hence the name) from a system of state-owned production, central economic planning, and heavily regulated markets to a system of free enterprise and unregulated markets.

### Living Standards Around the World

Figure 2.8 shows the distribution of living standards around the world in 2002, measured in dollars per day. You can see that in the United States, the average income is $100 a day. This number tells you that an average person in the United States can buy goods and services that cost $100, which is close to five times the world average. Canada has an average income close to 90 percent of that in the United States. Japan, Germany, France, Italy, the United Kingdom, and the other advanced economies have average incomes around two thirds that of the United States. Living standards fall off quickly as we move farther down the table, with India and the African continent achieving average incomes of only $5 a day.

Most people live in the countries that have incomes below the world average. You can see this fact by looking at the population numbers shown in the figure. The poorest five countries or regions—China, Central Asia, Other Asia, India, and Africa—have a total population of 4 billion.

---

### ■ FIGURE 2.8

**The Standard of Living Around the World**

**Practice Online**

---

Average income per person ranges from $5 a day in Africa to $100 a day in the United States. The world average is $21 a day. Russia and Central and South America have incomes that are close to the world average.

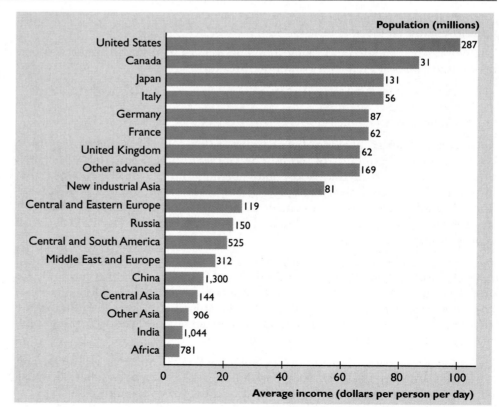

SOURCE: International Monetary Fund, *World Economic Outlook*, April 2002, Washington, D.C.

## Unemployment and Living Standards

Unemployment is another factor that influences the standard of living. If jobs are easy to find, then when people lose their jobs they will find new ones after only a short period of unemployment. But if jobs are hard to find, then when people lose their jobs they will find new ones only after a long period of unemployment.

Unemployment rates vary enormously around the world. In the United States, the average unemployment rate during the past 20 years has been 6 percent. That is, for every 100 people in the labor force, 94 have jobs and 6 are looking for jobs but can't find them. At this average unemployment rate, it takes an unemployed person an average of about 15 weeks to find an acceptable job.

Figure 2.9 shows the distribution of unemployment rates among developed countries, on the average for the 1980s and 1990s. (Note that the European Union average includes some of the other countries shown separately.)

The United States has one of the world's lowest unemployment rates. Only Japan and the new industrial economies of Asia (Hong Kong, Korea, Singapore, and Taiwan) have lower rates. Canada, the European Union, and other advanced economies have higher rates. And two members of the European Union—Spain and Ireland—have extremely high unemployment rates.

Figure 2.9 does *not* show the unemployment rates of the developing and transition economies. Why not? No one knows what they are. Data on unemployment is expensive to collect, and only the rich advanced economies devote resources to its measurement. Even though developing and transition economies do not measure unemployment rates, they are likely to be substantially higher than those in the advanced economies and might even exceed the high rate of Spain.

Why unemployment rates differ across economies is a difficult question to answer and is one of the challenges of macroeconomics.

---

### ▣ FIGURE 2.9
Unemployment Rates Around the World

**Practice Online**

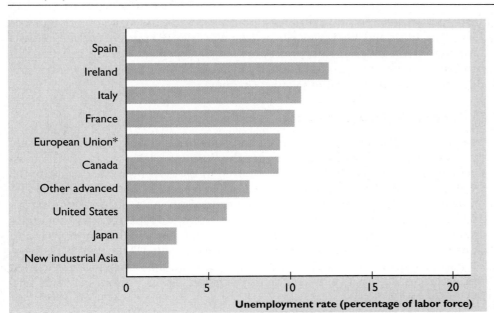

Unemployment rate (percentage of labor force)

SOURCE: International Monetary Fund, *World Economic Outlook*, April 2002, Washington, D.C.

During the 1980s and 1990s, the average unemployment rate in Spain was much higher than in most advanced economies. The unemployment rate in the United States is among the lowest, but it is not as low as in Japan and in the new industrial Asian economies.

---

\* The European Union average is the average for all 15 member countries, including Spain, Ireland, Italy, and France.

## ■ Cost of Living

The cost of living is the amount of money it takes to buy the goods and services that achieve a given standard of living. In the United States, we measure money in dollars. So the cost of living in the United States is the number of dollars it takes to buy the goods and services that achieve a given standard of living. In the United Kingdom, it is the number of pounds; in Japan, the number of yen; in Russia, the number of rubles; and in Indonesia, the number of rupiahs.

### Prices in Different Currencies

To make this idea concrete, think about the price of a Big Mac. Table 2.1 shows some prices in 10 currencies. The average price of a Big Mac in the United States is $2.50. In the United Kingdom, it is £2.00, and in Japan, it is ¥294. So in the United Kingdom, it costs a smaller number of money units to buy a Big Mac than it does in United States, and in Japan, it costs a larger number of money units. But the price of a Big Mac is actually *more* in the United Kingdom than in either the United States or Japan. The reason is that a pound is worth $1.55, so £2.00 is equivalent to $3.10. And a pound is worth 182 yen, so £2.00 is equivalent to ¥364.

### Inflation

The number of money units that something costs is not very important, but the rate at which the number of money units is changing is important. A rising cost of living, called inflation (see p. 5), is measured by the percentage change in the cost of living. Most countries experience inflation, but its rate varies enormously. In the United States, the inflation rate during the 1980s and 1990s was 3 percent a year. To put this number in perspective, a Big Mac that cost $2.50 in 2002 cost $1.80 in 1992 and $1.30 in 1982. Inflation at this rate is not generally regarded as a big problem. But it is a problem that we need to understand.

Most of the advanced economies have low inflation rates, as you can see in Figure 2.10. But the developing economies have higher inflation rates, some of them spectacularly so. In Central and South America, the average inflation rate during the 1980s and 1990s was 107 percent a year. A 100 percent change means a doubling. At this inflation rate, prices are rising by 6 percent a *month*. Inflation this rapid poses huge problems as people try to avoid holding onto money and struggle to cope with an ever-falling value of money.

## ■ Economic Fluctuations

Economies expand at an uneven pace and sometimes shrink for a while. These ebbs and flows of economic activity are the business cycle (see p. 6). The most recent recessions in the United States occurred in 1991 when production fell by 1.3 percent and in 2001 when production fell by 0.6 percent.

The most serious recent recessions occurred in Asia. Japan's production shrank by 1 percent and production in the new industrial Asian economies shrank by 2.4 percent in 1998 amidst a crisis of confidence in their currencies and financial systems. Many firms failed during this so-called Asia crisis. The deepest and lengthiest recession of the 1990s was in the transition economies. Production in Russia and its neighbors decreased by 33 percent between 1990 and 1994.

Figure 2.11 shows the recessions and expansions that we've just described.

**TABLE 2.1 THE PRICE OF A BIG MAC IN TEN CURRENCIES**

| Country or Region | Name of currency | Price of a Big Mac |
|---|---|---|
| United Kingdom | Pound | 2.00 |
| United States | Dollar | 2.50 |
| Euro area | Euro | 2.67 |
| Brazil | Real | 3.60 |
| South Africa | Rand | 9.70 |
| Israel | Shekel | 13.90 |
| Russia | Ruble | 35.00 |
| Japan | Yen | 294 |
| South Korea | Won | 3,000 |
| Indonesia | Rupiah | 14,700 |

**FIGURE 2.10**
Inflation Rates Around the World

Practice Online

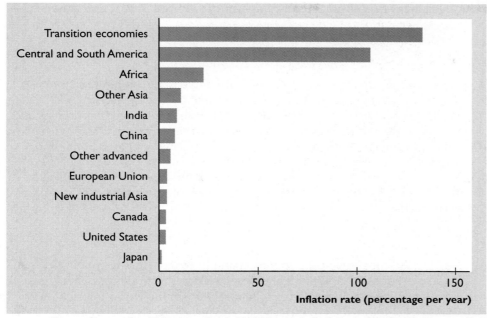

The most severe inflation has occurred in the transition economies (Russia and its neighbors) and Central and South America. In the United States and the other advanced economies, inflation rates were very low during the 1990s.

SOURCE: International Monetary Fund, *World Economic Outlook*, April 2002, Washington, D.C.

**FIGURE 2.11**
Business Cycles in the Global Economy

Practice Online

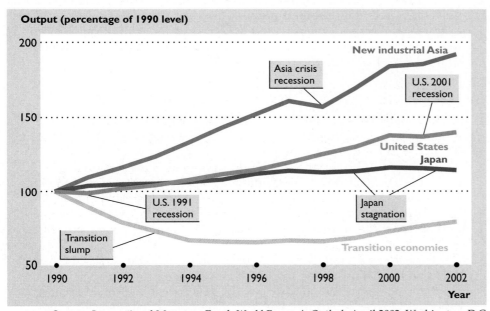

The United States had recessions in 1991 and 2001. Japan and the new industrial countries of Asia had a sharp recession in 1998. The transition economies had a long and deep recession for most of the 1990s.

SOURCE: International Monetary Fund, *World Economic Outlook*, April 2002, Washington, D.C.

Study Guide pp. 29–31

Practice Online 2.3

**3** Describe the macroeconomic performance—standard of living, cost of living, and economic fluctuations—of the United States and other economies.

## Practice Problems 2.3

1. What percentage of the world's population live in developing economies and what was the range of incomes that these people earned in 2002?
2. What percentage of the world's population live in advanced economies and what was the range of incomes that these people earned in 2002?
3. What percentage of the world's population live in the United States and what was the average income that Americans earned in 2002?
4. Which countries or regions experienced high inflation during the 1990s?
5. Which countries or regions experienced recession during the 1990s and the early 2000s?

## Exercises 2.3

1. What is the current world population and how rapidly is it growing? What is the current U.S. population and how rapidly is it growing? Is the U.S. population becoming larger or smaller relative to the world population?
2. Classify the following countries as (a) advanced, (b) developing, or (c) transition: Canada, Bolivia, Brazil, China, Colombia, Germany, Ghana, India, Japan, Korea, New Zealand, Russia, Singapore, the United States, Vietnam.
3. What was the average income in the world as a whole in 2002? Which regions or nations were closest to that world average, which were the farthest above it, and which were the farthest below it?
4. What was the average U.S. inflation rate during the 1990s? Is inflation at this rate considered to be a serious problem? Why or why not?
5. Compare and contrast the most recent U.S. recession with the most recent recessions in Asia and the transition economies. Which was the deepest? Which lasted the longest?

## Solutions to Practice Problems 2.3

1. Approximately 80 percent of the world's population lives in developing economies. In 2002, their average daily incomes ranged from $5 in Africa to $21 in Central and South America.
2. Approximately 16 percent of the world's population lives in advanced economies. In 2002, their average daily incomes ranged from about $55 in the new industrial economies of Asia to $100 in the United States.
3. In 2002, the population of the United States was 287 million—about 5 percent of the world's 6.25 billion population. The average income in the United States was $100 a day.
4. The transition economies and parts of Central and South America experienced high inflation during the 1990s.
5. The transition economies, Japan, and the new industrial economies of Asia experienced recession during the 1990s. The United States was in recession in 1991 and 2001, but for the rest of the 1990s it experienced expansion.

# CHAPTER CHECKPOINT

## Key Points

**1** **Describe what, how, and for whom goods and services are produced in the United States.**

- Consumption goods and services represent 61 percent of total production; investment goods represent 13 percent.
- Goods and services are produced by using the four factors of production: land, labor, capital, and entrepreneurship.
- The incomes people earn—rent for land, wages for labor, interest for capital, and profit for entrepreneurship—and the taxes they pay and benefits they receive from government determine who gets what is produced.

**2** **Use the circular flow model to provide a picture of how households, firms, and governments interact.**

- The circular flow model shows the real flows of factors and goods and the corresponding money flows of incomes and expenditures.
- Governments in the circular flow receive taxes, make transfers, and buy goods and services.
- Social security, other transfers to persons, national defense, interest on the national debt, and transfers to other levels of government make up most of the federal government's expenditures, and personal income taxes pay the largest share of these expenditures.
- Education, welfare benefits, and highways account for most of the expenditures of the state and local governments, and sales taxes, transfers from the federal government, and property taxes pay for these expenditures.

**3** **Describe the macroeconomic performance—standard of living, cost of living, and economic fluctuations—of the United States and other economies.**

- The standard of living, measured by income per person per day, ranges from an average of $5 in Africa to $100 in the United States.
- Inflation is low in most of the world but has been rapid in the transition economies (Russia and others) and in Central and South America.
- The United States had recessions in 1991 and 2001. Japan, the new industrial economies of Asia, and the transition economies had recessions during the 1990s.

## Key Terms

Capital, 40
Circular flow model, 44
Consumption goods and services, 36
Entrepreneurship, 41
Export goods and services, 36
Factor markets, 44
Factors of production, 38
Firms, 44

Functional distribution of income, 42
Goods markets, 44
Government goods and services, 36
Households, 44
Human capital, 39
Interest, 41
Investment goods, 36
Labor, 39

Land, 38
Market, 44
National debt, 48
Personal distribution of income, 42
Profit (or loss), 41
Rent, 41
Wages, 41

## Exercises

1.  Which of the following items are not consumption goods and services and why?
    a.  A chocolate bar
    b.  A ski lift
    c.  A gold ball
    d.  An interstate highway
    e.  An airplane
    f.  A stealth bomber

2.  Which of the following items are not investment goods and why?
    a.  An auto assembly line
    b.  A shopping mall
    c.  A golf ball
    d.  An interstate highway
    e.  An oil tanker
    f.  A construction worker

3.  Which of the following items are not factors of production and why?
    a.  Vans used by a baker to deliver bread
    b.  1,000 shares of Amazon.com stock
    c.  Undiscovered oil
    d.  A garbage truck
    e.  A pack of bubble gum
    f.  The President of the United States
    g.  Disneyland

4.  Think about the trends in what and how goods and services are produced:
    a.  Which jobs will grow fastest during the next decade? Explain your answer.
    b.  What types of jobs will most people most likely be doing 50 years from now? Explain your answer.
    c.  What do you think will happen to the quantity of human capital over the next decade? Explain your answer.
    d.  Do you think that at some future time, there will be no jobs? Why or why not?

5.  You've seen that the distribution of income is unequal. Why do you think it is unequal?

6.  The government grew larger through the mid-1980s and shrank slightly after that time. Why do you think the government grew until the mid-1980s and then began to shrink slightly?

7.  Review the sources of government revenue and determine who pays most of the taxes: workers, businesses, or consumers. Do the same groups that pay most of the federal taxes also pay most of the state and local taxes?

8.  On a graph of the circular flow model, label the flows in which the following items occur:
    a.  Capital owned by households and used by firms
    b.  Computers sold by firms to governments and households
    c.  Labor hired by firms
    d.  Land rented to businesses
    e.  Taxes paid by households and firms
    f.  Unemployment benefits
    g.  Wages paid by firms
    h.  Dividends paid by businesses
    i.  Profit paid to entrepreneurs

# Critical Thinking

9. You've seen in this chapter that the United States is increasingly becoming a service-producing economy. The production of food and manufactured goods is a shrinking proportion of total production. We continue to consume large quantities of food and manufactures, but these items increasingly are produced in other parts of the world and imported into the United States.

    Reflecting on these facts do you think that we should be concerned that much of our food and most of our clothing, electronic goods, and other manufactured goods come from abroad? Organize your answer around the following five points:

   a. In what ways should we be concerned?
   b. Who in the United States do you think benefits from the availability of cheap foreign-produced food, clothing, electronic goods, and other manufactured goods?
   c. Who in the United States do you think bears the cost of cheap foreign-produced food, clothing, electronic goods, and other manufactured goods?
   d. Who in the rest of the world do you think benefits from the United States buying foreign-produced food, clothing, electronic goods, and other manufactured goods?
   e. Who in the rest of the world do you think bears the cost of the United States buying cheap foreign-produced food, clothing, electronic goods, and other manufactured goods?

10. Although our urban areas use only a bit more than 100 million acres of our 1,944 million acres of land, urban use has increased by 35 million acres in just 20 years. In light of this change, do you think that we should be concerned that too much of our land is becoming urban? Organize your answer around the following five points:
   a. What type of land gets transferred to urban use?
   b. Who benefits from the transfer of an acre of farmland to an acre of suburban housing?
   c. Who bears the cost of the transfer of an acre of farmland to an acre of suburban housing?
   d. What steps could be taken to slow the transfer of farmland to urban use?
   e. Is there a case for not just slowing the transfer of farmland to urban use but either stopping it completely or even trying to reverse the trend?

11. "If the trends in schooling continue, at some point in the future, everyone will have a college degree and no one will be available to work as a janitor or garbage collector." Critically evaluate this statement.

12. "Income is unequally distributed, but because wages account for more than 70 percent of total income, so any redistribution from the rich to the poor means taking from wage earners to give to others." What is wrong with the reasoning in this statement?

13. You've seen that the government grew larger through the mid-1980s and shrank slightly after that time. Do you think the government is too big or too small? Provide your reasons.

14. You've seen that all levels of government get only a small part of their revenues from taxing businesses. Why do you think businesses pay a small share of taxes? Wouldn't it be better if businesses paid more taxes and individuals paid less? Explain your answer.

<u>**Practice Online**</u>   ## Web Exercises

**Use the links on your Foundations Web site to work the following exercises.**

15. Review the special "20th Century Statistics" section of the 1999 *Statistical Abstract of the United States* and find the table that describes the trends in food consumption.
    a. Describe the trends in the consumption of the eight categories of food and drink shown in the table since 1970. Which item has increased most? Which item has increased least?
    b. Can you think of reasons for the trends that you've found?

16. Review the special "20th Century Statistics" section of the 1999 *Statistical Abstract of the United States* and find the table that describes trends in the characteristics of housing and the items that people own.
    a. Describe the trend in the ownership of homes. Do more people own or rent their homes today than the proportions in 1940?
    b. Describe the trend in the ownership of mobile homes and trailers.
    c. Describe the trend in plumbing facilities.
    d. Describe the trend in vehicle ownership.
    e. Describe the trend in telephone ownership.
    f. Can you explain the trends that you've found?

17. Review the special "20th Century Statistics" section of the 1999 *Statistical Abstract of the United States* and find the table that describes trends in transportation.
    a. Describe the trend in air travel.
    b. Describe the trend in the price of air travel.
    c. Can you explain the trends that you've found?
    d. How might these trends be influenced by the events of September 11, 2001?

18. Review the special "20th Century Statistics" section of the 1999 *Statistical Abstract of the United States* and find the table that describes trends in transportation.
    a. Describe the trend in road travel.
    b. Can you explain the trend that you've found?
    c. How might this trend be influenced by the events of September 11, 2001?

19. Visit the regional income pages of the Bureau of Economic Analysis at the U.S. Department of Commerce.
    a. Obtain data on per capita personal income for the states as a percentage of U.S. per capita personal income.
    b. Which state has the highest per capita income and which has the lowest?
    c. Where in the ranking does your state stand?
    d. Can you think of reasons for the ranking that you've found?
    e. Does the ranking change much from year to year? Why or why not?

20. Visit the University of Michigan's Statistical Resources on the Web.
    a. Find data that interest you and that provide information about what, how, and for whom goods and services are produced.
    b. Find data that tell you about the size and the growth of government.
    c. Find data that tell you about the scale and trends in international trade.

# CHAPTER 3

# The Economic Problem

When you have completed your study of this chapter,
you will be able to

1. Use the production possibilities frontier to illustrate the economic problem.

2. Calculate opportunity cost.

3. Define efficiency and describe an efficient use of resources.

4. Explain how people gain from specialization and trade.

5. Explain how technological change and increases in capital and human capital expand production possiblities.

You learned in Chapter 1 that all economic problems arise from scarcity, that scarcity forces us to make choices, and that in making choices, we try to get the most value out of our scarce resources by comparing marginal costs and marginal benefits. You learned in Chapter 2 what, how, and for whom goods and services are produced in the U.S. economy. And you used your first economic model, the circular flow model, to illustrate the choices and interactions that determine what, how, and for whom goods and services are produced.

In this chapter, you will study another economic model: one that illustrates scarcity, choice, and cost and that helps us to understand the choices that people and societies actually make. You will also learn about the central idea of economics—*efficiency*. And you will discover how we gain by specializing and trading with each other and how economic growth expands our production possibilities.

## 3.1 PRODUCTION POSSIBILITIES

Every working day in the mines, factories, shops, and offices and on the farms and construction sites across the United States, we produce a vast array of goods and services. In the United States in 2002, 234 billion hours of labor equipped with $20 trillion worth of capital produced $10 trillion worth of goods and services. Globally, 6 trillion hours of labor and $100 trillion of capital produced $47 trillion worth of goods and services.

Although our production capability is enormous, it is limited by our available resources and by technology. At any given time, we have fixed quantities of the factors of production and a fixed state of technology. Because our wants exceed our resources, we must make choices. We must rank our wants and decide which wants to satisfy and which to leave unsatisfied. In using our scarce resources, we make rational choices.

To make a rational choice, we must determine the costs and benefits of the alternatives. In the rest of this chapter, we're going to study an economic model that makes the ideas of scarcity, costs and benefits, and rational choice more concrete. We're also going to learn about the economic concept of efficiency.

To illustrate the limits to production, we focus our attention on two goods only and hold the quantities produced of all the other goods and services constant. That is, we use the *ceteris paribus* assumption. We look at a *model* of the economy in which everything remains the same except for the production of the two goods we are currently considering.

### ■ Production Possibilities Frontier

**Production possibilities frontier**
The boundary between the combinations of goods and services that can be produced and the combinations that cannot be produced, given the available factors of production and the state of technology.

The **production possibilities frontier** is the boundary between the combinations of goods and services that can be produced and the combinations that cannot be produced, given the available factors of production—land, labor, capital, and entrepreneurship—and the state of technology. Let's look at the production possibilities frontier for bottled water and CDs.

Land can be used for either water-bottling plants or CD factories. Labor can be trained to work as water bottlers or as CD makers. Capital can be devoted to tapping springs and making water filtration plants or to the computers and lasers that make CDs. And entrepreneurs can devote their creative talents to managing water resources and bottling factories or to running electronics businesses that make CDs. In every case, the more resources that get used to produce bottled water, the fewer are left for producing CDs.

We can illustrate the production possibilities frontier by using either a table or a graph. The table in Figure 3.1 describes six production possibilities for bottled water and CDs—alternative combinations of quantities of these two goods that we can produce.

One possibility, in column *A*, is to devote no factors of production to making bottled water, so bottled water production is zero. In this case, we can devote all the factors of production to making CDs and produce 15 million a year. Another possibility, in column *B*, is to devote resources to bottled water production that are sufficient to produce 1 million bottles a year. But the resources that are being used in water-bottling plants must be taken from CD factories. So we can now produce only 14 million CDs a year. Columns *C*, *D*, *E*, and *F* show other possible combinations of the quantities of these two goods that we can produce. In column *F*, we use all our resources to produce 5 million bottles of water a year and have no resources to devote to producing CDs.

The graph in Figure 3.1 illustrates the production possibilities frontier, *PPF*, for bottled water and CDs. It is a graph of the production possibilities in the table. The *x*-axis shows the production of bottled water, and the *y*-axis shows the production of CDs. Each point on the graph labeled *A* through *F* represents the corresponding column in the table. For example, point *B* represents the production of 1 million bottles of water and 14 million CDs. These quantities also appear in column *B* of the table.

The *PPF* is a valuable tool for illustrating the effects of scarcity and its consequences. It puts three features of production possibilities in sharp focus. They are the distinctions between

- Attainable and unattainable combinations
- Full employment and unemployment
- Tradeoffs and free lunches

---

■ **FIGURE 3.1**

The Production Possibilities Frontier

**Practice Online**

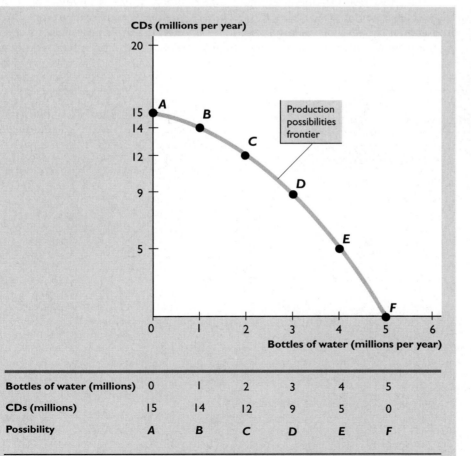

The table and the graph show the production possibilities frontier for bottled water and CDs. Point *A* tells us that if we produce no bottled water, the maximum quantity of CDs we can produce is 15 million a year. Points *A, B, C, D, E,* and *F* in the figure represent the columns of the table. The line passing through these points is the production possibilities frontier.

| Bottles of water (millions) | 0 | 1 | 2 | 3 | 4 | 5 |
|---|---|---|---|---|---|---|
| CDs (millions) | 15 | 14 | 12 | 9 | 5 | 0 |
| Possibility | *A* | *B* | *C* | *D* | *E* | *F* |

## Attainable and Unattainable Combinations

Because the *PPF* shows the *limits* to production, it separates attainable combinations from unattainable ones. We can produce combinations of bottled water and CDs that are smaller than those on the *PPF*, and we can produce any of the combinations *on* the *PPF*. These combinations of bottled water and CDs are attainable. But we cannot produce combinations that are larger than those on the *PPF*. These combinations are unattainable.

Figure 3.2 emphasizes the attainable and unattainable combinations. Only the points on the *PPF* and inside it (in the orange area) are attainable. The combinations of bottled water and CDs beyond the *PPF* (in the white area), such as the combination at point *G*, are unattainable. These points illustrate combinations that cannot be produced with our current resources and technology. The *PPF* tells us that we can produce 4 million bottles of water and 5 million CDs at point *E* or 2 million bottles of water and 12 million CDs at point *C*. But we cannot produce 4 million bottles of water and 12 million CDs at point *G*.

## Full Employment and Unemployment

Full employment occurs when all the available factors of production are being used. Unemployment occurs when some factors of production are not used.

The most noticed unemployment affects labor. There is always some unemployed labor, and in a recession, the amount of unemployment can be large. But land and capital can also be unemployed. Land is often unemployed while its owner is trying to work out the land's most valuable use. Look around where you live and

---

■ **FIGURE 3.2**
Attainable and Unattainable Combinations

**Practice Online**

The production possibilities frontier, *PPF*, separates attainable combinations from unattainable ones. We can produce at any point inside the *PPF* (the orange area) or *on* the frontier. Points outside the production possibilities frontier such as point *G* are unattainable.

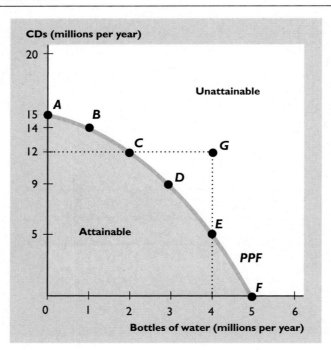

you'll probably be able to find at least one or two city blocks that are currently unemployed. Capital often lies idle. For example, thousands of automobiles are unemployed in parking lots; and restaurant tables and kitchens are often unemployed.

Figure 3.3 illustrates the effects of unemployment. With unemployed resources, the economy might produce at point *H*. Here, with some resources *employed*, it is possible to produce 3 million bottles of water and 5 million CDs. But with full employment, it is possible to move to points such as *D* or *E*. At point *D*, there are more CDs and the same quantity of bottled water as at point *H*. And at point *E*, there are more bottles of water and the same quantity of CDs as at point *H*.

## Tradeoffs and Free Lunches

A **tradeoff** is a constraint or limit to what is possible that forces an exchange or a substitution of one thing for something else. If the federal government devotes more resources to finding a cure for AIDS and cuts its transfers to state and local governments, a move that forces state and local governments to increase class sizes and cut back on school libraries and computer facilities, we face a tradeoff between health care and education. If the federal government devotes more resources to national defense and fewer resources to NASA's space exploration program, we face a tradeoff between defense and the space program.

If lumber producers cut down fewer trees to conserve spotted owls, we face a tradeoff between paper products and wildlife. If Ford Motor Company decreases the production of trucks to produce more SUVs, we face a tradeoff between two types of vehicle. If a student decides to take an extra course and cut back on her weekend job, she faces a tradeoff between course credits and income.

**Tradeoff**
A constraint or limit to what is possible that forces an exchange or a substitution of one thing for something else.

---

**■ FIGURE 3.3**
Full Employment and Unemployment

**Practice Online**

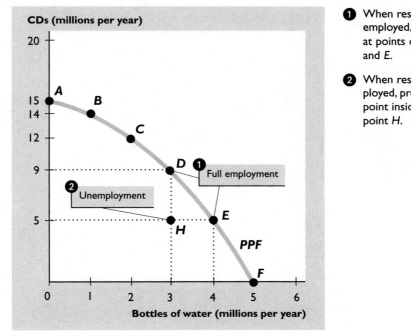

❶ When resources are fully employed, production occurs at points on the *PPF* such as *D* and *E*.

❷ When resources are unemployed, production occurs at a point inside the frontier such as point *H*.

The *PPF* in Figure 3.4 illustrates the idea of a tradeoff. If we produce at point *E* and would like to produce more CDs, we must forgo some bottled water. For example, we might move from point *E* to point *D*. We exchange some bottles of water for some CDs.

Economists often express the central idea of economics—that every choice involves an opportunity cost—with the saying "There is no such thing as a free lunch." (See Chapter 1, p. 13.) But suppose some resources are not being used or are not being used in their most productive way. Isn't it then possible to avoid opportunity cost and get a free lunch?

The answer is yes. You can see this answer in Figure 3.4. If production is taking place *inside* the *PPF* at point *H*, then it is possible to move to point *D* and increase the production of CDs by using currently unused resources or by using resources in their most productive way. There is a free lunch.

So when production takes place at a point on the *PPF*, we face a tradeoff. But we don't face a tradeoff if we produce inside the *PPF*. More of some goods and services can be produced without producing less of some others.

Because of scarcity and the attempt to get the most out of our scarce resources, we do not leave factors of production idle or use them unproductively if we can avoid it. And if such a situation arises, people seek ways of putting their resources to productive employment. It is for these reasons that economists emphasize the tradeoff idea and deny the existence of free lunches. We might *occasionally* get a free lunch, but we *persistently* face tradeoffs.

**FIGURE 3.4**
Tradeoffs and Free Lunches

**Practice Online**

① When production is *on* the *PPF*, we face a tradeoff. If we are producing 5 million CDs a year at point *E*, to produce 9 million CDs at point *D*, we must trade some bottled water for CDs and move along the *PPF*.

② When production is *inside* the *PPF*, there is a free lunch. If we are producing 5 million CDs a year at point *H*, to produce 9 million CDs at point *D*, we move to the *PPF* and get a free lunch.

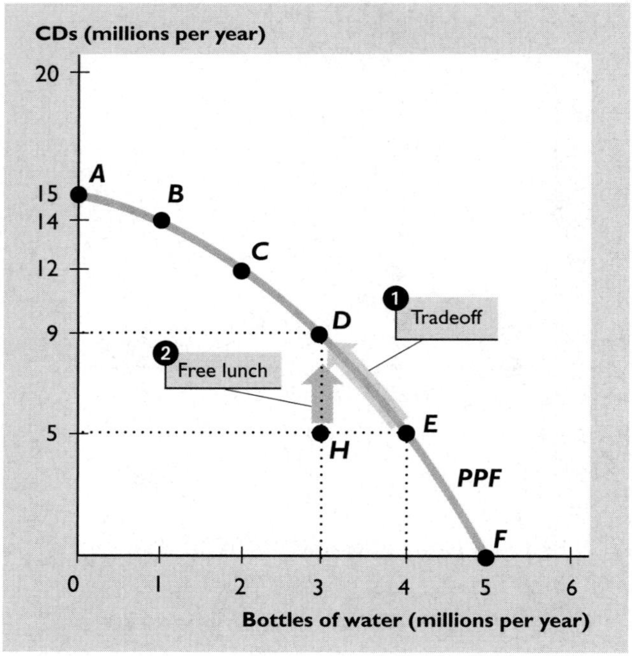

**b.** If the college puts a rent ceiling on rooms of $650 a month, what is the rent and how many rooms are rented?

**c.** If the college puts a rent ceiling of $550 a month, what is the rent and how many rooms are rented?

**d.** If the college strictly enforced the rent ceiling of $550 a month, is the on-campus housing market efficient? Explain why or why not.

**e.** If a black market develops, how high could the black market rent be? Explain.

**f.** If a black market develops, is the housing market fair? Explain.

**TABLE 3**

| Rent (dollars per month) | Quantity demanded | Quantity supplied |
|---|---|---|
| | (rooms) | |
| 500 | 2,500 | 2,000 |
| 550 | 2,250 | 2,000 |
| 600 | 2,000 | 2,000 |
| 650 | 1,750 | 2,000 |
| 700 | 1,500 | 2,000 |
| 750 | 1,250 | 2,000 |

8. During the 1996 Olympic Games, many residents of Atlanta left the city and rented out their homes. Despite the increase in the quantity of housing available, rents soared. If at the same time, the city of Atlanta had imposed a rent ceiling, describe how the housing market would have functioned.

9. Concerned about the political fallout from rising gas prices, the government decides to impose a price ceiling on gasoline of $1.00 a gallon.
   **a.** Explain how the market for gasoline would react to this price ceiling if
      (i) The oil-producing nations increased production and drove the equilibrium price of gasoline to 90 cents a gallon.
      (ii) A global shortage of oil sent the equilibrium price of gasoline to $2.00 a gallon.
   **b.** Which of the situations in part **a** would result in an efficient use of resources? Explain why.

10. Suppose the government introduced a ceiling on the fees that lawyers are permitted to charge.
   **a.** Explain the effects of such a ceiling on
      (i) The amount of work done by lawyers.
      (ii) The consumer surplus of people who hire lawyers.
      (iii) The producer surplus of law firms.
   **b.** Would this fee ceiling result in an efficient use of resources? Why or why not?

11. Table 4 shows the demand and supply schedules for student workers at on-campus venues.
   **a.** What is the equilibrium wage rate of student workers, and what is the equilibrium number of students employed?
   **b.** Is the market for student workers at on-campus venues efficient?
   **c.** If the college introduces a minimum wage of $5.50 an hour, how many student workers are employed and how many are unemployed?
   **d.** If the college introduces a minimum wage of $6.50 an hour, how many student workers are employed and how many are unemployed?
   **e.** Is the minimum wage of $6.50 an hour efficient? Is it fair?
   **f.** Who gains and who loses from the minimum wage of $6.50 an hour?

**TABLE 4**

| Wage rate (dollars per hour) | Quantity demanded | Quantity supplied |
|---|---|---|
| | (student workers) | |
| 5.00 | 600 | 300 |
| 5.50 | 500 | 350 |
| 6.00 | 400 | 400 |
| 6.50 | 300 | 450 |
| 7.00 | 200 | 500 |
| 7.50 | 100 | 550 |

12. Bakers earn $15 an hour, gas pump attendants earn $6 an hour, and copy shop workers earn $7 an hour. If the government introduces a minimum wage of $7 an hour, explain how the markets for bakers, gas pump attendants, and copy shop workers will respond initially to the minimum wage.

## Critical Thinking

13. The government of the U.S. Virgin Islands seeks your help to evaluate two sales tax schemes. In scheme A, food is not taxed, luxury goods are taxed at 10 percent, and all other goods are taxed at 5 percent. In scheme B, there is a flat 3 percent tax on all goods and services. The government asks you to explain what research must be undertaken and what features of the markets for food, luxury goods, and other goods will influence.

    a. How the prices and the quantities of food, luxury goods, and all other goods will differ under the two schemes.
    b. The excess burden of the taxes under the two schemes. Which tax would be more efficient if both schemes generated the same amount of tax revenue?

14. The New York City Rent Guidelines Board is mandated to establish rent adjustments for the nearly one million apartments and houses that are subject to the city's Rent Stabilization Law. The board holds public hearings to consider testimony from owners, tenants, advocacy groups, and housing industry experts. Write a brief report to the New York City Rent Guidelines Board that explains why it is not possible to improve on permitting the market forces of supply and demand to determine rents at the levels that make the quantity demanded and quantity supplied equal.

15. "Market prices might be fine in a rich country, but in a poor developing African nation where there are shortages of most items, without government control of prices everything would be too expensive." Do you agree or disagree with this statement? Use the concepts of efficiency and fairness to explain why.

## Web Exercises

**Use the links on your Foundations Web site to work the following exercises.**

<u>Practice Online</u>   16. Obtain data on the sales tax rates in each state.
    a. Which state has the highest sales tax rate and which states have the lowest?
    b. Which states have the most exemptions?
    c. Compare California and its neighbors, Nevada and Washington. In which state do you think consumer surplus and producer surplus (per person) is greatest? Why?

17. Visit the Web site of the Harvard Living Wage Campaign.
    a. What is the campaign for a living wage?
    b. How would you distinguish the minimum wage from a living wage?
    c. If the Living Wage Campaign succeeds in getting wages increased above their equilibrium levels, what do you predict its effect would be?
    d. Would a living wage above the equilibrium wage be efficient?
    e. Who would gain and who would lose from a living wage above the equilibrium wage?
    f. Would a living wage above the equilibrium wage be fair?

# CHAPTER 8

# Externalities

When you have completed your study of this chapter,
you will be able to

**1** Explain why negative externalities lead to inefficient overproduction
and how property rights, pollution charges, and taxes can achieve a
more efficient outcome.

**2** Explain why positive externalities lead to inefficient underproduction
and how public provision, subsidies, vouchers, and patents can achieve a
more efficient outcome.

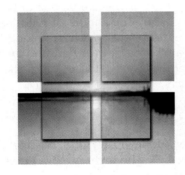

You learned in Chapter 6 that markets are not
always efficient. And you saw in Chapter 7 some
government actions that create inefficiency. In
this chapter, we study markets in which governments can help to achieve a more efficient outcome. In these markets, the actions of buyers and
sellers affect other people, for ill or good, in ways
that are ignored by the market participants.

We burn huge quantities of coal and oil that bring acid
rain and global warming, and we dump toxic waste into
rivers, lakes, and oceans. These environmental issues are
simultaneously everybody's problem and nobody's problem.
How can we create incentives that make us consider the
damage that we inflict on others every time we turn on our
heating or air conditioning?

Almost every day, we hear about a new discovery in medicine, engineering, chemistry, physics, and even economics.
Advances in knowledge bring benefits to all, not just to the scientists who make the advances. How much should we spend on
the education and research that make these advances possible?

# EXTERNALITIES IN OUR DAILY LIVES

**Externality**
A cost or a benefit that arises from production that falls on someone other than the producer; or a cost or benefit that arises from consumption that falls on someone other than the consumer.

**Negative externality**
A production or consumption activity that creates an external cost.

**Positive externality**
A production or consumption activity that creates an external benefit.

An **externality** is a cost or a benefit that arises from production that falls on someone other than the producer; or a cost or a benefit that arises from consumption that falls on someone other than the consumer. Before we embark on the two main tasks of this chapter, we're going to review the range of externalities, classify them, and give some everyday examples.

First, an externality can arise from either a production activity or a consumption activity. Second, it can be either a **negative externality**, which imposes an external cost, or a **positive externality**, which provides an external benefit. So there are four types of externalities:

- Negative production externalities
- Positive production externalities
- Negative consumption externalities
- Positive consumption externalities

## ■ Negative Production Externalities

When the U.S. Open tennis tournament is being played at Flushing Meadows, players, spectators, and television viewers around the world share a negative production externality that many New Yorkers experience every day—the noise of airplanes taking off from Kennedy Airport. Aircraft noise imposes a large cost on millions of people who live under the flight paths to airports in every major city.

Logging and the clearing of forests is the source of another negative production externality. These activities destroy the habitat of wildlife and influence the amount of carbon dioxide in the atmosphere, which has a long-term effect on temperature. So these external costs are borne by everyone and by future generations.

Pollution, which we examine in more detail in the next section, is a major example of this type of externality.

## ■ Positive Production Externalities

To produce orange blossom honey, Honey Run Honey of Chico, California, locates beehives next to an orange orchard. The honeybees collect pollen and nectar from the orange blossoms to make the honey. At the same time, they transfer pollen between the blossoms, which helps to fertilize them. Two positive production

*Negative production externality.*

*Positive production externality.*

externalities are present in this example. Honey Run Honey gets a positive production externality from the owner of the orange orchard. And the orange grower gets a positive production externality from Honey Run.

## ■ Negative Consumption Externalities

Negative consumption externalities are a source of irritation for most of us. Smoking tobacco in a confined space creates fumes that many people find unpleasant and that pose a health risk. So smoking in restaurants and on airplanes generates a negative externality. To avoid this negative externality, many restaurants and all airlines ban smoking. But while a smoking ban avoids a negative consumption externality for most people, it imposes a negative consumption externality on smokers. The majority, for whom the ban is in place, impose a cost on the minority—the smokers who would prefer to enjoy the consumption of tobacco while dining or taking a plane trip.

Noisy parties and outdoor rock concerts are other examples of negative consumption externalities. And they are also examples of the fact that a simple ban on an activity is not a solution. Banning noisy parties avoids the external cost on sleep-seeking neighbors, but it results in the sleepers imposing an external cost on the fun-seeking partygoers.

Permitting dandelions to grow in lawns, not picking up leaves in the fall, allowing a dog to bark loudly or to foul a neighbor's lawn, and letting your cell phone ring in class are other examples of negative consumption externalities.

## ■ Positive Consumption Externalities

When you get a flu vaccination, you lower your risk of being infected during the winter. But if you avoid the flu, your neighbor, who didn't get vaccinated, has a better chance of remaining healthy. Flu vaccinations generate positive consumption externalities.

When its owner restores a historic building, everyone who sees the building gets pleasure from it. Similarly, when someone erects a spectacular home—such as those built by Frank Lloyd Wright during the 1920s and 1930s—or other exciting building—such as the Chrysler and Empire State Buildings in New York or the Wrigley Building in Chicago—an external consumption benefit flows to everyone who has an opportunity to view it.

Education, which we examine in more detail in this chapter, is another and a major example of this type of externality.

*Negative consumption externality.*          *Positive consumption externality.*

# 8.1 NEGATIVE EXTERNALITIES: POLLUTION

You've just seen that pollution is an example of a negative externality. Both production and consumption activities create pollution. But here, we'll focus on pollution as a negative production externality. When a chemical factory dumps waste into a river, the people who live by the river and use it for fishing and boating bear the cost of the pollution. The chemical factory does not consider the cost of pollution when it decides the quantity of chemicals to produce. Its supply curve is based on its own costs, not on the costs that it inflicts on others. You're going to discover that when external costs are present, we produce more output than the efficient quantity and we get more pollution than the efficient quantity.

Pollution and other environmental problems are not new. Preindustrial towns and cities in Europe had severe sewage disposal problems that created cholera epidemics and plagues that killed millions. Nor is the desire to find solutions to environmental problems new. The development in the fourteenth century of a pure water supply and the hygienic disposal of garbage and sewage are examples of early contributions to improving the quality of the environment.

Popular discussions about pollution and the environment often pay little attention to economics. They focus on physical aspects of the environment, not on costs and benefits. A common assumption is that activities that damage the environment are morally wrong and must cease. In contrast, an economic study of the environment emphasizes costs and benefits. Economists talk about the efficient amount of pollution or environmental damage. This emphasis on costs and benefits does not mean that economists, as citizens, don't share the same goals as others and value a healthy environment. Nor does it mean that economists have the right answers and everyone else has the wrong ones. Rather, economics provides a set of tools and principles that help to clarify the issues.

The starting point for an economic analysis of the environment is the distinction between private costs and social costs.

## ■ Private Costs and Social Costs

**Marginal private cost**
The cost of producing an additional unit of a good or service that is borne by the producer of that good or service.

**Marginal external cost**
The cost of producing an additional unit of a good or service that falls on people other than the producer.

**Marginal social cost**
The marginal cost incurred by the entire society—by the producer and by everyone else on whom the cost falls. It is the sum of marginal private cost and marginal external cost.

A *private cost* of production is a cost that is borne by the producer of a good or service. *Marginal cost* is the cost of producing an *additional unit* of a good or service. So **marginal private cost** (*MC*) is the cost of producing an additional unit of a good or service that is borne by the producer of that good or service.

You've seen that an *external cost* is a cost of producing a good or service that is *not* borne by the producer but borne by other people. A **marginal external cost** is the cost of producing an additional unit of a good or service that falls on people other than the producer.

**Marginal social cost** (*MSC*) is the marginal cost incurred by the entire society—by the producer and by everyone else on whom the cost falls—and is the sum of marginal private cost and marginal external cost. That is,

$$MSC = MC + \text{Marginal external cost.}$$

We express costs in dollars. But we must always remember that a cost is an opportunity cost—the best thing we give up to get something. A marginal external cost is what someone other than the producer of a good or service must give up when the producer makes one more unit of the item. Something real that people value, such as a clean river or clean air, is given up.

## Valuing an External Cost

Economists use market prices to put a dollar value on the cost of pollution. For example, suppose that there are two similar rivers, one polluted and the other clean. Five hundred identical homes are built along the side of each river. The homes on the clean river rent for $2,500 a month, and those on the polluted river rent for $1,500 a month. If the pollution is the only detectable difference between the two rivers and the two locations, the rent decrease of $1,000 per month is the cost of the pollution. For the 500 homes, the external cost is $500,000 a month.

## External Cost and Output

Figure 8.1 shows an example of the relationship between output and cost in a chemical industry that pollutes. The marginal cost curve, MC, describes the private marginal cost borne by the firms that produce the chemical. Marginal cost increases as the quantity of the chemical produced increases. If the firms dump waste into a river, they impose an external cost that increases with the amount of the chemical produced. The marginal social cost curve, MSC, is the sum of marginal private cost and marginal external cost. For example, when output is 4,000 tons a month, marginal private cost is $100 a ton, marginal external cost is $125 a ton, and marginal social cost is $225 a ton.

   In Figure 8.1, as the quantity of the chemical produced increases, the amount of pollution increases and the external cost of pollution increases. The quantity of the chemical produced and the pollution created depend on how the market for the chemical operates. First, we'll see what happens when the industry is free to pollute.

### FIGURE 8.1
An External Cost

**Practice Online**

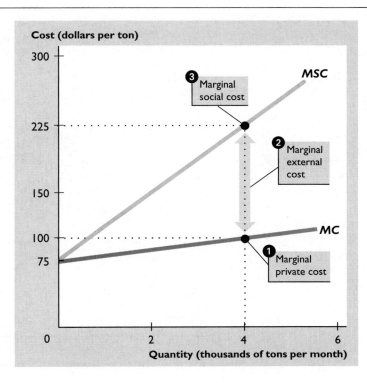

The MC curve shows the private marginal cost borne by the factories that produce a chemical. The MSC curve shows the sum of marginal private cost and marginal external cost. When output is 4,000 tons of chemicals a month, ❶ marginal private cost is $100 a ton, ❷ marginal external cost is $125 a ton, and ❸ marginal social cost is $225 a ton.

## ■ Production and Pollution: How Much?

When an industry is unregulated, the amount of pollution it creates depends on the market equilibrium price and quantity of the good produced. Figure 8.2 illustrates the outcome in the market for a pollution-creating chemical.

The demand curve for the chemical is *D*. This curve also measures the marginal benefit, *MB*, to the buyers of the chemical (see Chapter 6, p. 144). The supply curve is *S*. This curve also measures the marginal private cost, *MC*, of the producers (see Chapter 6, p. 147). The supply curve is the marginal private cost curve because when firms make their production and supply decisions, they consider only the costs that they will bear. Market equilibrium occurs at a price of $100 a ton and a quantity of 4,000 tons a month.

This equilibrium is inefficient. You learned in Chapter 6 that the allocation of resources is efficient when marginal benefit equals marginal cost. But we must count all the costs—private and external—when we compare marginal benefit and marginal cost. So with an external cost, the allocation is efficient when marginal benefit equals marginal *social* cost. This outcome occurs when the quantity of the chemical produced is 2,000 tons a month. The market equilibrium overproduces by 2,000 tons a month and creates a deadweight loss, the gray triangle.

How can the people who live by the polluted river get the chemical factories to decrease their output of the chemical and create less pollution? If some method can be found to achieve this outcome, everyone—the owners of the factories and the residents of the riverside homes—can gain. Let's explore some solutions.

---

### ▨ FIGURE 8.2
#### Inefficiency with an External Cost

Practice Online

The market supply curve is the marginal private cost curve, *S = MC*. The demand curve is the marginal benefit curve, *D = MB*.

❶ Market equilibrium at a price of $100 a ton and 4,000 tons a month is inefficient because

　❷ marginal social cost exceeds
　❸ marginal benefit.

❹ The efficient quantity is 2,000 tons a month.

❺ The gray triangle shows the deadweight loss created by the pollution externality.

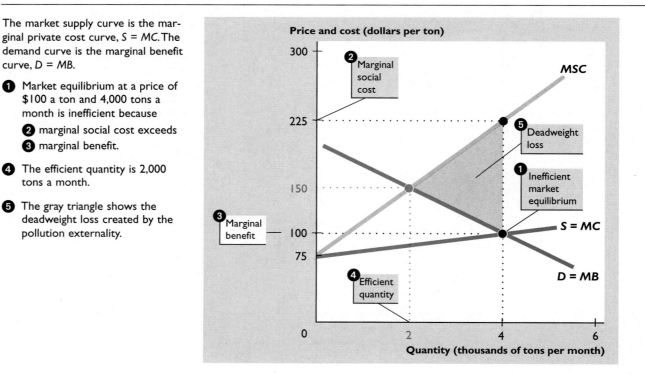

## ■ Property Rights

Sometimes it is possible to reduce the inefficiency arising from an externality by establishing a property right where one does not currently exist. **Property rights** are legally established titles to the ownership, use, and disposal of factors of production and goods and services that are enforceable in the courts.

Suppose that the chemical factories own the river and the 500 homes alongside it. The rent that people are willing to pay depends on the amount of pollution. Using the earlier example, people are willing to pay $2,500 a month to live alongside a pollution-free river but only $1,500 a month to live with the pollution created by 4,000 tons of chemical a month. If the factories produce this quantity, they lose $1,000 a month for each home and a total of $500,000 a month.

The chemical factories are now confronted with the cost of their pollution decision. They might still decide to pollute, but if they do, they face the opportunity cost of their actions—forgone rent from the people who live by the river.

Figure 8.3 illustrates the outcome by using the same example as in Figure 8.2. With property rights in place, the original marginal cost curve no longer measures all the costs that the factories face in producing the chemical. It excludes the pollution cost that they must now bear. The former *MSC* curve now becomes the marginal private cost curve *MC*. All the costs fall on the factories, so the market supply curve is based on all the marginal costs and is the curve labeled $S = MC$.

Market equilibrium now occurs at a price of $150 a ton and a quantity of 2,000 tons a month. This outcome is efficient. The factories still produce some pollution, but it is the efficient quantity.

**Property rights**
Legally established titles to the ownership, use, and disposal of factors of production and goods and services that are enforceable in the courts.

---

### ■ FIGURE 8.3
Property Rights Achieve an Efficient Outcome

**Practice Online**

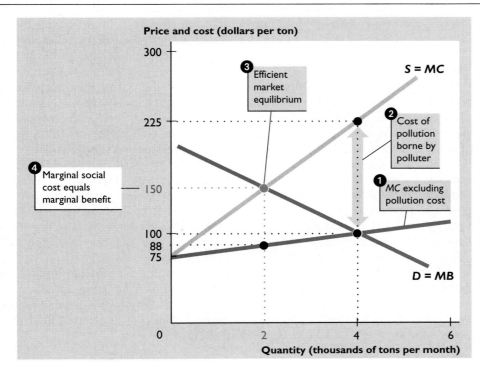

❶ With property rights, the marginal cost curve that excludes the cost of pollution shows only part of the producers' marginal cost.

The marginal private cost curve includes ❷ the cost of pollution, so the supply curve is $S = MC$.

❸ Market equilibrium is at a price of $150 a ton and a quantity of 2,000 tons a month and is efficient because ❹ marginal social cost equals marginal benefit.

## ■ The Coase Theorem

Does it matter how property rights are assigned? Does it matter whether the polluter or the victim of the pollution owns the resource that might be polluted? Until 1960, everyone—including economists who had thought long and hard about the problem—thought that it did matter. But in 1960, Ronald Coase had a remarkable insight, now called the Coase theorem.

The **Coase theorem** is the proposition that if property rights exist, only a small number of parties are involved, and transactions costs are low, then private transactions are efficient. There are no externalities because the transacting parties take all the costs and benefits into account. Furthermore, it doesn't matter who has the property rights.

**Coase theorem**
The proposition that if property rights exist, only a small number of parties are involved, and transactions costs are low, then private transactions are efficient and the outcome is not affected by who is assigned the property right.

### Application of the Coase Theorem

Let's apply the Coase theorem to the polluted river. In the example that we've just studied, the factories own both the river and the homes. Suppose that instead, the residents own both their homes and the river. Now the factories must pay a fee to the homeowners for the right to dump their waste. The greater the quantity of waste dumped into the river, the more the factories must pay. So again, the factories face the opportunity cost of the pollution they create. The quantity of chemicals produced and the amount of waste dumped are the same whoever owns the homes and the river. If the factories own them, they bear the cost of pollution because they receive a lower income from home rents. And if the residents own the homes and the river, the factories bear the cost of pollution because they must pay a fee to the homeowners. In both cases, the factories bear the cost of their pollution and dump the efficient amount of waste into the river.

The Coase solution works only when transactions costs are low. **Transactions costs** are the opportunity costs of conducting a transaction. For example, when you buy a house, you incur a series of transactions costs. You might pay a realtor to help you find the best place and a financial planner to help you get the best loan, and you pay a lawyer to run checks that assure you that the seller owns the property and that after you've paid for it, the ownership has been properly transferred to you.

**Transactions costs**
The opportunity costs of conducting a transaction.

In the example of the homes alongside a river, the transactions costs that are incurred by a small number of chemical factories and a few homeowners might be low enough to enable them to negotiate the deals that produce an efficient outcome. But in many situations, transactions costs are so high that it would be inefficient to incur them. In these situations, the Coase solution is not available.

Suppose, for example, that everyone owns the airspace above their homes up to, say, 10 miles. If someone pollutes your airspace, you can charge a fee. But to collect the fee, you must identify who is polluting your airspace and persuade them to pay you. Imagine the cost to you and the 50 million people who live in your part of the United States (and perhaps in Canada or Mexico) of negotiating and enforcing agreements with the several thousand factories that emit sulfur dioxide and create acid rain that falls on your property!

In this situation, we use public choices through governments to cope with externalities. But the transactions costs that prevent us from using the Coase solution are opportunity costs, and governments can't wave a magician's wand to eliminate them. So attempts by the government to deal with externalities offer no easy solution. Let's look at some of these attempts.

## ■ Government Actions in the Face of External Costs

The three main methods that governments use to cope with externalities are

- Emission charges
- Marketable permits
- Taxes

### Emission Charges

Emission charges confront a polluter with the external cost of pollution and provide an incentive to seek new technologies that are less polluting. In the United States, the Environmental Protection Agency (EPA) sets emission charges, which are, in effect, a price per unit of pollution. The more pollution a firm creates, the more it pays in emission charges. This method of dealing with environmental externalities has been used only modestly in the United States, but it is common in Europe. For example, in France, Germany, and the Netherlands, water polluters pay a waste disposal charge.

To work out the emission charge that achieves efficiency, the regulator must determine the marginal external cost of pollution at different levels of output and levy a charge on polluters that equals that cost. The polluter then incurs a marginal cost that includes both private and external costs. But to achieve the efficient outcome, the regulator needs a lot of information about the polluting industry that, in practice, is not available.

Another way of overcoming excess pollution is to issue firms with pollution quotas that they can buy and sell—with marketable permits. Let's look at this alternative.

### Marketable Permits

An alternative to an emission charge is to assign each polluter an emission limit. Provided that the marginal benefit and marginal cost are assessed correctly, the same efficient outcome can be achieved with emission limits as with emission charges. But in the case of emission limits, a cap must be set for each polluter.

Marketable permits are a clever way of overcoming the need for the regulator to know every firm's marginal cost schedule. The government issues each firm an emissions permit, and firms can buy and sell these permits. Firms with a low marginal cost of reducing pollution sell permits and firms with a high marginal cost of reducing pollution buy permits. The market in permits determines the price at which firms trade permits. And firms buy or sell permits until their marginal cost of pollution equals the market price.

The 1990 Clear Air Act and the 1994 Regional Clean Air Incentives Market (RECLAIM) in the Los Angeles basin successfully use this method of dealing with pollution. The method provides an even stronger incentive than do emission charges to find technologies that pollute less because the price of a permit to pollute rises as the demand for permits increases.

### Taxes

The government can use taxes as an incentive for producers to cut back on an activity that creates an external cost. By setting the tax rate equal to the marginal external cost, firms can be made to behave in the same way as they would if they bore the cost of the externality directly.

## Pollution Trends

Air quality in the United States is getting better. Lead has been almost eliminated, and sulfur dioxide, carbon monoxide, and suspended particulates have been reduced substantially. But nitrogen dioxide and ozone have persisted at close to their 1975 levels.

The earth's average temperature has increased over the past 100 years, and most of the increase occurred before 1940. No one knows why this temperature increase has occurred, but some scientists believe the cause to be carbon dioxide emissions from road transportation and electric utilities, methane created by cows and other livestock, nitrous oxide emissions of electric

utilities and from fertilizers, and chlorofluorocarbons (CFCs) from refrigeration equipment and (in the past) aerosols.

The ozone layer in the earth's atmosphere protects us from cancer-

causing ultraviolet rays from the sun. A hole in the ozone layer over Antarctica is getting bigger. How our industrial activity influences the ozone layer is not well understood, but some scien-

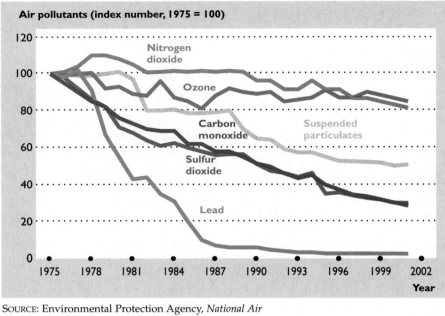

SOURCE: Environmental Protection Agency, *National Air Quality: 2001 Status and Trends*, 1999.

## Effects of Government Actions

To see how government actions can change market outcomes in the face of externalities, let's return to the example of the chemical factories and the river.

Assume that the government has assessed the marginal external cost accurately and imposes a tax on the factories that exactly equals this cost.

Figure 8.4 illustrates the effects of this tax. The demand curve and marginal benefit curve $D = MB$ and the firms' marginal cost curve $MC$ are the same as in Figure 8.2. The pollution tax equals the marginal external cost of the pollution. We add this tax to marginal cost to find the market supply curve. This curve is the one labeled $S = MC + tax = MSC$. This curve is the market supply curve because it tells us the quantities supplied at each price given the firms' marginal cost and the tax they must pay. This curve is also the marginal social cost curve because the pollution tax has been set equal to the marginal external cost.

Demand and supply now determine the market equilibrium price at $150 a ton and the equilibrium quantity at 2,000 tons a month. At this scale of chemical production, the marginal social cost is $150 and the marginal benefit is $150, so the outcome is efficient. The firms incur a marginal cost of $88 a ton and pay a tax of $62 a ton. The government collects tax revenue of $124,000 a month.

tists think that CFCs are one source of ozone layer depletion.

The largest sources of water pollution are the dumping of industrial waste and treated sewage in lakes and rivers and the runoff from fertilizers. A more dramatic source is the accidental spilling of crude oil into the oceans such as the *Exxon Valdez* spill in Alaska in 1989 and an even larger spill from the *Prestige* off Spain in 2002. The most frightening is the dumping of nuclear waste into the ocean by the former Soviet Union.

Land pollution arises from dumping toxic waste products. Ordinary household garbage does not pose a pollution problem unless dumped garbage seeps into the water supply. This possibility increases as less suitable landfill sites are used. It is estimated that 80 percent of existing landfills in the United States will be full by 2010.

Some densely populated regions (such as New York and New Jersey) and densely populated countries (such as Japan and the Netherlands), where

land costs are high, are seeking less costly alternatives to landfill, such as recycling and incineration. Recycling is an apparently attractive alternative, but it requires an investment in new technologies to be effective. Incineration is a high-cost alternative to landfill, and it produces air pollution. These alternatives become efficient only when the cost of using landfills is high, as it is in densely populated regions and countries.

## FIGURE 8.4
A Pollution Tax

Practice Online

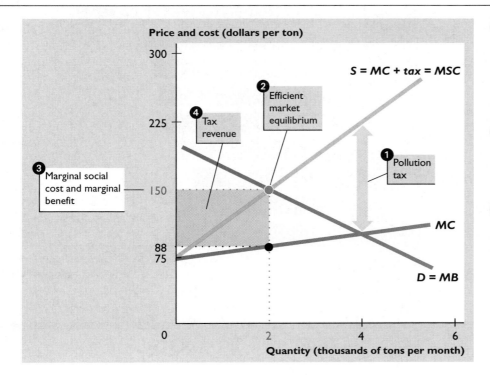

❶ A pollution tax is imposed that is equal to the marginal external cost of pollution. The supply curve becomes the marginal private cost curve, *MC*, plus the tax—the curve labeled *S = MC + tax*.

❷ Market equilibrium is at a price of $150 a ton and a quantity of 2,000 tons a month and is efficient because ❸ marginal social cost equals marginal benefit.

❹ The government collects tax revenue shown by the purple rectangle.

## A Carbon Fuel Tax?

Most countries tax gasoline at a much higher rate than does the United States. Why don't we have a higher gas tax to encourage a large reduction in emissions?

The question becomes even more pressing when we consider not only the current levels of greenhouse gases but also their projected future levels. In 1990, annual carbon emissions worldwide were a staggering 6 billion tons. By 2050, with current policies, that annual total is predicted to be 24 billion tons.

Part of the reason we do not have a higher gas tax is that many people do not accept the scientific evidence that emissions produce global warming. Climatologists are uncertain about how carbon emissions translate into atmospheric concentrations—about how the flow of emissions translates into a stock of pollution. The main uncertainty arises because carbon drains from the atmosphere into the oceans and vegetation at a rate that is not well understood. Climatologists are also uncertain about the connection between carbon concentration and temperature. And economists are uncertain about how a temperature increase translates into economic costs and benefits. Some economists believe that the costs and benefits are almost zero, while others believe that a temperature increase of 5.4 degrees Fahrenheit by 2090 will reduce the total output of goods and services by 20 percent.

Another factor weighing against a large change in fuel use is that the costs would be borne now, while the benefits, if any, would come many years in the future. To compare future benefits with current costs, we must use an interest rate. If the interest rate is 1 percent a year, a dollar today becomes $2.70 in 100 years. If the interest rate is 5 percent a year, a dollar today becomes more than $131.50 in 100 years. So at an interest rate of 1 percent a year, it is worth spending $1 million in 2000 on pollution control to avoid $2.7 million in environmental damage in 2100. At an interest rate of 5 percent a year, it is worth spending $1 million today only if this expenditure avoids $131.5 million in environmental damage 100 years from now.

Because large uncertain future benefits are needed to justify small current costs, a general tax on carbon fuels is not a high priority on the political agenda.

A final factor working against a large change in fuel use is the international pattern of the use of carbon fuels. Right now, carbon pollution comes in even doses from the industrial countries and the developing countries. But by 2050, three quarters of the carbon pollution will come from the developing countries (if the trends persist).

One reason for the high pollution rate in some developing countries (notably China, Russia, and other Eastern European countries) is that their governments subsidize the use of coal or oil. These subsidies lower producers' marginal costs and encourage the greater use of these fuels. The result is that the quantity of carbon fuels used exceeds the efficient quantity—and by a large amount. It is estimated that by 2050, these subsidies will induce annual global carbon emissions of some 10 billion tons—about two fifths of total emissions. If the subsidies were removed, global emissions in 2050 would be 10 billion tons a year less.

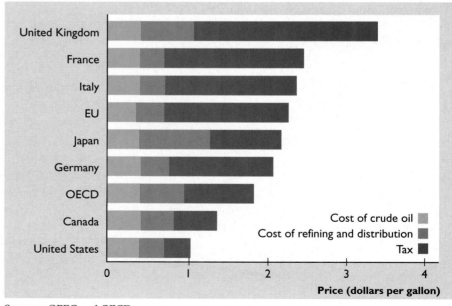

SOURCES: OPEC and OECD.

# CHECKPOINT 8.1

**I** Explain why negative externalities lead to inefficient overproduction and how property rights, pollution charges, and taxes can achieve a more efficient outcome.

**Study Guide pp. 118–122**

**Practice Online 8.1**

## Practice Problem 8.1

Figure 1 illustrates the unregulated market for pesticide. When the factories produce pesticide, they also create waste, which they dump into a lake on the outskirts of the town. If the marginal external cost of the dumped waste is equal to the marginal private cost of producing the pesticide, then the marginal social cost of producing the pesticide is double the marginal private cost.
a. What is the quantity of pesticide produced if no one owns the lake?
b. What is the efficient quantity of pesticide?
c. If the residents of the town own the lake, what is the quantity of pesticide produced and how much do the pesticide factories pay to residents of the town?
d. If the pesticide factories own the lake, how much pesticide is produced?
e. Suppose that no one owns the lake but that the government levies a pollution tax. What is the tax per ton of pesticide that will achieve the efficient outcome?

**FIGURE 1**

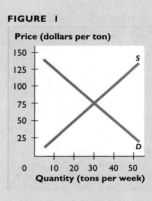

## Exercise 8.1

Suppose that, in Practice Problem 8.1, the marginal external cost increases to twice the marginal private cost, so the marginal social cost of producing the pesticide is 3 times the marginal private cost. With no property rights, the government issues enough marketable permits to the town's residents to enable the factory to produce the efficient output of pesticide.
a. How much pesticide gets produced?
b. What is the price of a permit?
c. How, if at all, would the outcome change if the government allocated the permits to the factories instead of to the town's residents?

## Solution to Practice Problem 8.1

a. The quantity of pesticide produced is 30 tons a week (Figure 2).
b. The efficient quantity of pesticide is 20 tons a week. At the efficient quantity, the marginal benefit to the factories equals the marginal social cost, which is the sum of the marginal private cost and the marginal external cost. When the factories produce 20 tons a week, the marginal social cost is $100 a ton and the marginal benefit is $100 a ton.
c. The quantity of pesticide produced is the efficient quantity, 20 tons a week, and the factories pay the townspeople the marginal external cost of $50 a ton.
d. The factories produce the efficient quantity—20 tons a week.
e. A tax of $50 a ton will achieve the efficient quantity of pesticide produced.

**FIGURE 2**

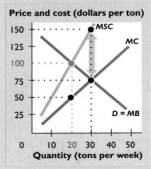

## 8.2 POSITIVE EXTERNALITIES: KNOWLEDGE

Knowledge comes from education and research. To study the economics of knowledge, we must distinguish between private benefits and social benefits.

### ■ Private Benefits and Social Benefits

A *private benefit* is a benefit that the consumer of a good or service receives. *Marginal benefit* is the benefit from an *additional unit* of a good or service. So **marginal private benefit** (*MB*) is the benefit from an additional unit of a good or service that the consumer of that good or service receives.

**Marginal private benefit**
The benefit from an additional unit of a good or service that the consumer of that good or service receives.

**Marginal external benefit**
The benefit from an additional unit of a good or service that people other than the consumer of the good or service enjoy.

**Marginal social benefit**
The marginal benefit enjoyed by society—by the consumers of a good or service and by everyone else who benefits from it. It is the sum of marginal private benefit and marginal external benefit.

You've seen that an *external benefit* is a benefit from a good or service that someone other than the consumer receives. A **marginal external benefit** is the benefit from an additional unit of a good or service that people other than the consumer enjoy.

**Marginal social benefit** (*MSB*) is the marginal benefit enjoyed by society—by the consumers of a good or service (marginal private benefit) plus the marginal benefit enjoyed by others (the marginal external benefit). That is,

$$MSB = MB + \text{Marginal external benefit.}$$

Figure 8.5 shows an example of the relationship between marginal private benefit, marginal external benefit, and marginal social benefit. The marginal benefit curve, *MB*, describes the marginal private benefit—such as expanded job opportunities and higher incomes—enjoyed by college graduates. Marginal private benefit decreases as the quantity of education increases.

---

**■ FIGURE 8.5**
An External Benefit

**Practice Online**

The *MB* curve shows the private marginal benefit enjoyed by the people who receive a college education. The *MSB* curve shows the sum of marginal private benefit and marginal external benefit. When 15 million students attend college, ❶ marginal private benefit is $10,000 per student, ❷ marginal external benefit is $15,000 per student, and ❸ marginal social benefit is $25,000 per student.

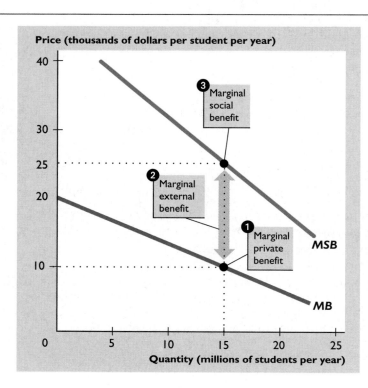

But college graduates generate external benefits. On the average, college graduates communicate more effectively with others and tend to be better citizens. Their crime rates are lower, and they are more tolerant of the views of others. And a society with a large number of college graduates can support activities such as high-quality newspapers and television channels, music, theater, and other organized social activities.

In the example in Figure 8.5, the marginal external benefit is $15,000 per student per year when 15 million students enroll in college. The marginal social benefit curve, *MSB*, is the sum of marginal private benefit and marginal external benefit. For example, when 15 million students a year enroll in college, the marginal private benefit is $10,000 per student and the marginal external benefit is $15,000 per student, so the marginal social benefit is $25,000 per student.

When people make decisions about how much schooling to undertake, they ignore its external benefits and consider only its private benefits. The result is that if education were provided by private schools that charged full-cost tuition, we would produce too few college graduates.

Figure 8.6 illustrates the underproduction if the government left education to the private market. The supply curve is the marginal cost curve of the private schools, *S = MC*. The demand curve is the marginal private benefit curve, *D = MB*. Market equilibrium is at a tuition of $15,000 per student per year and 7.5 million students per year. At this equilibrium, marginal social benefit is $38,000 per student, which exceeds marginal cost by $23,000. There are too few students in college. The efficient number is 15 million, where marginal social benefit equals marginal cost. The gray triangle shows the deadweight loss created by the underproduction.

---

■ **FIGURE 8.6**

Inefficiency with an External Benefit

**Practice Online**

---

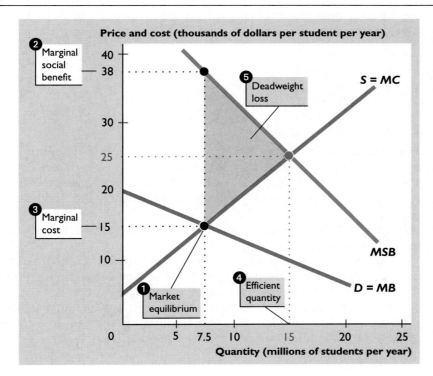

The market demand curve is the marginal private benefit curve, *D = MB*. The supply curve is the marginal cost curve, *S = MC*.

❶ Market equilibrium is at a tuition of $15,000 a year and 7.5 million students and is inefficient because ❷ marginal social benefit exceeds ❸ marginal cost.

❹ The efficient quantity is 15 million students.

❺ The gray triangle shows the deadweight loss created because too few students enroll in college.

Underproduction similar to that in Figure 8.6 would occur at other levels of education—grade school and high school—if an unregulated market produced it. When children learn basic reading, writing, and number skills, they receive the private benefit of increased earning power. But even these basic skills bring the external benefit of developing better citizens.

External benefits also arise from research that leads to the discovery of new knowledge. When Isaac Newton worked out the formulas for calculating the rate of response of one variable to another—calculus—everyone was free to use his method. When a spreadsheet program called VisiCalc was invented, Lotus Corporation and Microsoft were free to copy the basic idea and create 1-2-3 and Excel. When the first shopping mall was built and found to be a successful way of arranging retailing, everyone was free to copy the idea, and malls spread like mushrooms.

Once someone has discovered how to do something, others can copy the basic idea. They do have to work to copy an idea, so they face an opportunity cost. But they do not usually have to pay the person who made the discovery to use it. When people make decisions about how much research to undertake, they ignore its external benefits and consider only its private benefits.

When people make decisions about the quantity of education or the amount of research to undertake, they balance the marginal private cost against the marginal private benefit. They ignore the external benefit. As a result, if we left education and research to unregulated market forces, we would get too little of these activities.

To get closer to producing the efficient quantity of a good or service that generates an external benefit, we make public choices, through governments, to modify the market outcome.

## ■ Government Actions in the Face of External Benefits

Four devices that governments can use to achieve a more efficient allocation of resources in the presence of external benefits, such as those that arise from education and research, are

- Public provision
- Private subsidies
- Vouchers
- Patents and copyrights

### Public Provision

**Public provision** The production of a good or service by a public authority that receives most of its revenue from the government.

**Public provision** is the production of a good or service by a public authority that receives most of its revenue from government. The education services produced by the public universities, colleges, and schools are examples of public provision.

Figure 8.7(a) shows how public provision might overcome the underproduction that arises in Figure 8.6. Public provision cannot lower the cost of production, so marginal cost is the same as before. Marginal private benefit and marginal external benefit are also the same as before.

The efficient quantity occurs where marginal social benefit equals marginal cost. In Figure 8.7(a), this quantity is 15 million students. Tuition is set to ensure that the efficient number of students enrolls. That is, tuition is set at the level that equals the marginal private benefit at the efficient quantity. In Figure 8.7(a), tuition is $10,000 a year. The rest of the cost of the public university is borne by the taxpayers and, in this example, is $15,000 per student per year.

## Private Subsidies

A **subsidy** is a payment that the government makes to private producers. By making the subsidy depend on the level of output, the government can induce private decision makers to consider external benefits when they make their choices.

Figure 8.7(b) shows how a subsidy to private colleges works. In the absence of a subsidy, the marginal cost curve is the market supply curve of private college education, $S = MC$. The marginal benefit is the demand curve, $D = MB$. In this example, the government provides a subsidy to colleges of $15,000 per student per year. We must subtract the subsidy from the marginal cost of education to find the colleges' supply curve. That curve is $S = MC - subsidy$ in the figure. The equilibrium tuition (market price) is $10,000 a year, and the equilibrium quantity is 15 million students. To educate 15 million students, colleges incur a marginal cost of $25,000 a year. The marginal social benefit is also $25,000 a year. So with marginal cost equal to marginal social benefit, the subsidy has achieved an efficient outcome. The tuition and the subsidy just cover the colleges' marginal cost.

Whether a public school operating on government-provided funds or a private school receiving a subsidy does a better job is a difficult question to resolve.

**Subsidy**
A payment that the government makes to private producers that depends on the level of output.

---

**FIGURE 8.7**

Public Provision or Private Subsidy to Achieve an Efficient Outcome

**Practice Online**

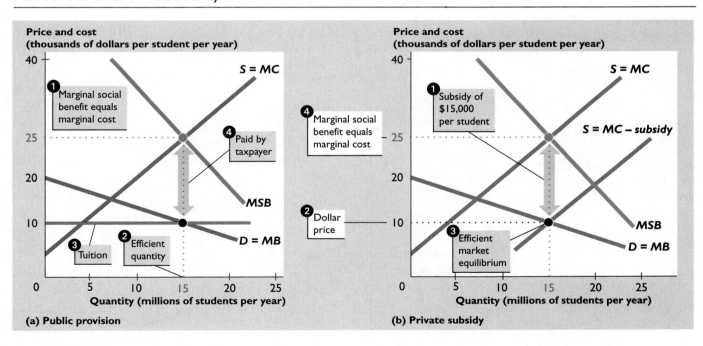

**(a) Public provision**

**(b) Private subsidy**

❶ Marginal social benefit equals marginal cost with 15 million students enrolled in college, the ❷ efficient quantity.

❸ Tuition is set at $10,000 per year, and ❹ the taxpayers cover the remaining $15,000 of marginal cost per student.

With a ❶ subsidy of $15,000 per student, the supply curve is $S = MC - subsidy$. ❷ The equilibrium price is $10,000, and ❸ the market equilibrium is efficient with 15 million students enrolled in college. ❹ Marginal social benefit equals marginal cost.

It turns on the efficiency of alternative mechanisms for monitoring school performance and on the strength of the incentives that school boards and private school operators have to deliver a high-quality service.

### Vouchers

**Voucher**
A token that the government provides to households that can be used to buy specified goods or services.

A **voucher** is a token that the government provides to households, which they can use to buy specified goods or services. Food stamps that the U.S. Department of Agriculture provides under a federal Food Stamp Program are examples of vouchers. The vouchers (stamps) can be spent only on food and are designed to improve the diet and health of extremely poor families.

School vouchers have been advocated as a means of improving the quality of education and have been used in Cleveland and Milwaukee, though a proposition to introduce school vouchers in Michigan was defeated in the 2000 election.

A school voucher allows parents to choose the school their children will attend and to use the voucher to pay part of the cost. The school cashes the vouchers to pay its bills. A voucher could be provided to a college student in a similar way, and although technically not a voucher, a federal Pell Grant has a similar effect.

Because vouchers can be spent only on a specified item, they increase the willingness to pay for that item and so increase the demand for it. Figure 8.8 shows how a voucher system works. The government provides vouchers worth $15,000 per student per year. Parents (or students) use these vouchers to supplement the dollars they pay for college education. The market equilibrium occurs at a price of

---

### ■ FIGURE 8.8
Vouchers Achieve an Efficient Outcome

**Practice Online**

With vouchers, buyers are willing to pay *MB* plus the value of the voucher. ❶ With a voucher worth $15,000, I market equilibrium is efficient. With 15 million students enrolled in college, ❷ marginal social benefit equals marginal cost. The tuition, ❸ the dollar price, is $10,000 and the school collects $15,000 from the government.

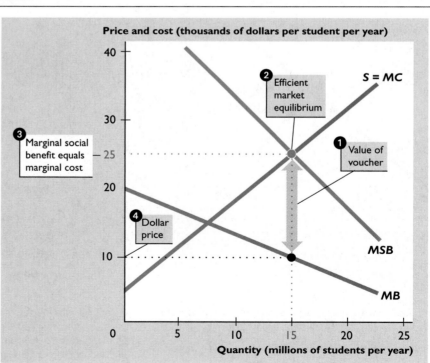

$25,000 per student per year and 15 million students attend college. Each student pays $10,000 tuition, and schools collect an additional $15,000 per student from the voucher.

If the government estimates the value of the external benefit correctly and makes the value of the voucher equal the marginal external benefit, the outcome from the voucher scheme is efficient. Marginal cost equals marginal social benefit, and the deadweight loss is eliminated.

Vouchers are similar to subsidies, but they provide the consumer rather than the producer with the financial resources. Advocates of vouchers say that they offer a more efficient outcome than subsidies do because the consumer can monitor school performance more effectively than the government can.

## Patents and Copyrights

Every inventor benefits from previous inventions. Some inventions are so fundamental that they benefit many subsequent inventors. Some examples are calculus, invented by Newton and Leibniz, and the structure of DNA discovered by Crick and Watson. *Basic research* is the activity that leads to the development of these fundamental tools.

*Research and development* efforts build on the fruits of basic research to refine and improve on earlier advances. For example, each advance in knowledge about how to design and manufacture a processor chip for a PC has brought ever-larger increments in performance and productivity. Similarly, each advance in knowledge about how to design and build an airplane has brought ever larger increments in performance: Orville and Wilbur Wright's "Flyer 1" was a one-seat plane that could hop a farmer's field. The Lockheed Constellation could fly 120 passengers from New York to London, with two refueling stops, not much space, and a lot of noise and vibration. The latest Boeing 747 can carry 450 people nonstop from Los Angeles to Sydney or New York to Tokyo (flights of 7,500 miles that take 14 hours). Examples of the cumulative fruits of research and development efforts such as these can be found in fields as diverse as agriculture, biogenetics, communications, entertainment, medicine, and publishing.

Because discoveries build on previous discoveries, research generates external benefits. So it is necessary to use public policies to ensure that those who develop new ideas have incentives to encourage an efficient level of effort. The main way of providing the right incentives uses the central idea of the Coase theorem and assigns property rights—called **intellectual property rights**—to creators. The legal device for establishing intellectual property rights is the patent or copyright. A **patent** or **copyright** is a government-sanctioned exclusive right granted to the inventor of a good, service, or productive process to produce, use, and sell the invention for a given number of years. A patent enables the developer of a new idea to prevent others from benefiting freely from an invention for a limited number of years. But to obtain the protection of the law, an inventor must make knowledge of the invention public.

Although patents encourage invention and innovation, they do so at an economic cost. While a patent is in place, its holder has a monopoly. And monopoly is another source of inefficiency (which is explained in Chapter 11). But without a patent, the effort to develop new goods, services, or processes is diminished and the flow of new inventions is slowed. So the efficient outcome is a compromise that balances the benefits of more inventions against the cost of temporary monopoly in newly invented activities.

**Intellectual property rights**
The property rights of the creators of knowledge and other discoveries.

**Patent or copyright**
A government-sanctioned exclusive right granted to the inventor of a good, service, or productive process to produce, use, and sell the invention for a given number of years.

Study Guide pp. 122–126

Practice Online 8.2

**2** **Explain why positive externalities lead to inefficient underproduction and how public provision, subsidies, vouchers, and patents can achieve a more efficient outcome.**

## Practice Problem 8.2

Figure 1 shows the marginal private benefit from college education. The marginal cost of a college education is a constant $6,000 a year. The marginal external benefit from a college education is $4,000 per student per year.

**a.** If colleges are private and government has no involvement in college education, how many people will undertake a college education and what will be the tuition?

**b.** What is the efficient number of students?

**c.** If the government decides to provide public colleges, what tuition will these colleges charge to achieve the efficient number of students? How much will taxpayers have to pay?

**d.** If the government decides to subsidize private colleges, what subsidy will achieve the efficient number of college students?

**e.** If the government offers vouchers to those who enroll at a college and no subsidy, what is the value of the voucher that will achieve the efficient number of students?

FIGURE 1

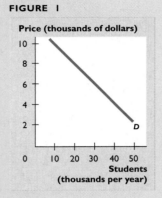

## Exercise 8.2

Figure 2 shows the marginal private benefit from a law degree and the marginal cost of obtaining a law degree. The marginal external benefit is $8,000 per law graduate per year.

**a.** If colleges are private and there is no government involvement in educating lawyers, how many people enroll in law school and what is the tuition?

**b.** What is the efficient number of law students?

**c.** If the government decides to provide public law schools, what tuition will the public schools charge to achieve the efficient number of students?

**d.** If the government decides to subsidize private law schools, what subsidy will achieve the efficient number of students?

**e.** If the government offers vouchers to law students, what is the value of the voucher that will achieve the efficient number of students?

FIGURE 2

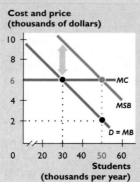

## Solution to Practice Problem 8.2

**a.** The tuition will be $6,000 a year, and 30,000 students will enroll—the intersection of the *MB* and *MC* curves (Figure 3).

**b.** The efficient number of students is 50,000 a year—the intersection of the *MSB* and *MC* curves (Figure 3).

**c.** To enroll 50,000 students, public colleges would charge $2,000 per student and taxpayers would pay $4,000 per student (Figure 3).

**d.** The subsidy would be $4,000 per student, which is equal to the marginal external benefit.

**e.** The value of the voucher will be $4,000 per student. The enrollment will be 50,000 if the tuition is $2,000. But the private college tuition is $6,000, so to get 50,000 students to enroll, the value of the voucher will have to be $4,000.

FIGURE 3

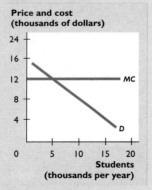

# CHAPTER CHECKPOINT

## Key Points

**1** **Explain why negative externalities lead to inefficient overproduction and how property rights, pollution charges, and taxes can achieve a more efficient outcome.**

- External costs are costs of production that fall on people other than the producer of a good or service. Marginal social cost equals marginal private cost plus marginal external cost.
- Producers take account only of marginal private cost and produce more than the efficient quantity when there is a marginal external cost.
- Sometimes it is possible to overcome a negative externality by assigning a property right.
- When property rights cannot be assigned, governments might overcome a negative externality by using emission charges, marketable permits, or taxes.

**2** **Explain why positive externalities lead to inefficient underproduction and how public provision, subsidies, vouchers, and patents can achieve a more efficient outcome.**

- External benefits are benefits that are received by people other than the consumer of a good or service. Marginal social benefit equals marginal private benefit plus marginal external benefit.
- External benefits from education arise because better-educated people are better citizens, commit fewer crimes, and support social activities.
- External benefits from research arise because once someone has worked out a basic idea, others can copy.
- Vouchers or subsidies to private schools or the provision of public education below cost can achieve a more efficient provision of education.
- Patents and copyrights create intellectual property rights and an incentive to innovate. But they do so by creating a temporary monopoly, the cost of which must be balanced against the benefit of more inventive activity.

## Key Terms

Coase theorem, 200
Copyright, 211
Externality, 194
Intellectual property rights, 211
Marginal external benefit, 206
Marginal external cost, 196

Marginal private benefit, 206
Marginal private cost, 196
Marginal social benefit, 206
Marginal social cost, 196
Negative externality, 194
Patent, 211

Positive externality, 194
Property rights, 199
Public provision, 208
Subsidy, 209
Transactions costs, 200
Voucher, 210

## Exercises

**TABLE 1**

| Pollution cut (percentage) | Property taxes willingly paid (dollars per day) | Total cost of pollution cut (dollars per day) |
|---|---|---|
| 0 | 0 | 0 |
| 10 | 150 | 10 |
| 20 | 285 | 25 |
| 30 | 405 | 45 |
| 40 | 510 | 70 |
| 50 | 600 | 100 |
| 60 | 675 | 135 |
| 70 | 735 | 175 |
| 80 | 780 | 220 |
| 90 | 810 | 270 |

1. A city borders on a polluting steel mill. Table 1 shows the cost of cutting the pollution and the property taxes that people are willing to pay at different levels of pollution. Assume that the property taxes willingly paid measure the total benefit from cleaner air that results from the percentage cut in pollution.
   a. With no pollution control, how much pollution will there be?
   b. What is the efficient percentage decrease in pollution?
   c. If the city owns the steel mill, how much pollution will there be?
   d. If the city is a company town owned by the steel mill, how much pollution will there be?

2. Tom and Larry are working on a project that makes it necessary for them to spend a day together. Tom likes to smoke, and his marginal benefit from one cigar a day is $20. The price of a cigar is $2. Larry dislikes cigar smoke, and his marginal benefit from a smoke-free environment is $25 a day. What is the outcome if they
   a. Meet at Tom's home?
   b. Meet at Larry's home?

3. If in exercise 2, Tom's marginal benefit from one cigar a day is $25 and Larry's marginal benefit from a smoke-free environment is $20 a day, what is the outcome if they:
   a. Meet at Tom's home?
   b. Meet at Larry's home?

**TABLE 2**

| Students (millions per year) | Marginal private benefit (dollars per student per year) |
|---|---|
| 1 | 5,000 |
| 2 | 3,000 |
| 3 | 2,000 |
| 4 | 1,500 |
| 5 | 1,200 |
| 6 | 1,000 |
| 7 | 800 |
| 8 | 500 |

4. The marginal cost of educating a college student is $5,000 a year. Table 2 shows the marginal private benefit schedule from a college education. The marginal external benefit for college education is $2,000 per student per year.
   a. With no public colleges and no government involvement in college education, how many students will enroll and what is the tuition?
   b. If the government subsidizes private colleges and sets the subsidy so that the efficient number of students will enroll in college, what is the subsidy per student? How many students will enroll?
   c. If the government offers vouchers to students (but no subsidy to private colleges) and values the vouchers so that the efficient number of students will enroll in college, what is the value of the voucher? How many students will enroll?

5. For many people, distance education has cut the cost of a college education. If in exercise 4, an Internet course cuts the cost to $3,500 a year and increases the marginal external benefit to $3,000 per student per year, what now are your answers to exercise 4?

6. Suppose that researchers could not obtain patents for their discoveries.
   a. What do you think would happen to the pace of technological change?
   b. Would consumers' or producers' interests be damaged by a lack of patent protection?
   c. Would anyone gain?

7. Suppose that popular singers could not obtain copyrights for their recordings.
   a. What do you think would happen to the quantity and quality of recorded music?
   b. Would consumers be better off because they could buy cheaper CDs? Explain why or why not.

# Critical Thinking

8. The Kyoto Protocol on greenhouse gas emissions was adopted at the United Nations Framework Convention on Climate Change in 1997. The major provision of the protocol is a set of national targets, with dates, for the reduction of greenhouse gas emissions. Countries with large amounts of emissions (of which the United States is one) have the most severe targets. The United States has steadfastly refused to ratify the Kyoto Protocol, but the European Union has ratified it.
   a. Why do you think the United States might be reluctant to ratify the Kyoto Protocol?
   b. Why do you think the European Union was willing to ratify it?
   c. In light of the principles you've learned in this chapter, what types of data would you need to collect if you were to determine whether the emission target for the United States laid out in the Kyoto Protocol is efficient?
   d. What is your own view on whether the United States should ratify the Kyoto Protocol and why?

9. The price of gasoline in Europe is much higher than that in the United States, and the reason is that the gas tax is much higher there than here.
   a. What is the range of externalities that arise from automobiles?
   b. In light of the principles you've learned in this chapter, what is the case *for* increasing the gas tax in the United States to the European level?
   c. In light of the principles you've learned in this chapter, what is the case *against* increasing the gas tax in the United States to the European level?
   d. What is your view on whether the United States should raise the gas tax to the European level and why?

10. The debate over school vouchers often creates more heat than light.
    a. Why do you think that school vouchers are controversial?
    b. In light of the principles you've learned in this chapter, what is the case *for* replacing the existing school funding arrangements with vouchers?
    c. In light of the principles you've learned in this chapter, what is the case *against* replacing the existing school funding arrangements with vouchers?

11. It has been estimated that developing new technologies and figuring out how to use them accounts for more than half of economic growth—the expansion of production possibilities. In light of this fact:
    a. Do you think that the government should subsidize research and development?
    b. Do you think that the government should subsidize basic research?
    c. Do you think it would be a good idea to award prizes to firms for the successful development of a new technology?
    d. Do you think that firms should be given tax breaks for the successful development of a new technology?
    e. Do you think the patent laws should be strengthened so that the inventor of a new technology can be protected from competition for longer than is currently the case?
    f. Provide your own ranking of the alternatives in parts **a** through **e** along with the further alternative of leaving research and development to unregulated market forces. Explain your ranking, being explicit about your assumptions about the efficiency of each approach.

<u>Practice Online</u>    **Web Exercises**

**Use the links on your Foundations Web site to work the following exercises.**

12. Visit the EPA "Search Your Community" page. Enter your zip code in the box provided and press the "Submit" button.
    a. Obtain information about a negative production externality in your neighborhood.
    b. Explain which, if any, of the tools reviewed in this chapter the government is using to address the externality.
    c. Explain how the government's action will work or why you think it will not work. Use the concepts of marginal private cost, marginal external cost, marginal social cost, and efficiency in your explanation.
    d. If you think the current measures for dealing with this externality are not working or are not working well enough, what do you think needs to be done? Again, use the concepts of marginal private cost, marginal external cost, marginal social cost, and efficiency in your analysis.

13. Visit the EPA "Ground Water and Drinking Water" page.
    a. What types of externalities arise in the production of safe drinking water?
    b. Review and summarize the elements of the cost-benefit analysis that the EPA is undertaking on this issue.
    c. What do you think are the main outstanding issues to be resolved in ensuring the provision of safe drinking water in the United States? Use the concepts of marginal private cost, marginal external cost, marginal social cost, and efficiency in your analysis.

14. Visit the Cape Cod Times and read the article about wind farms off the New England coast.
    a. What types of externalities arise in the production of electricity using wind technologies?
    b. Comparing the externalities from wind technologies with those from burning coal and oil, which do you think are the more widespread and affect more people?
    c. How do you think the external costs of using wind technologies should be dealt with? Compare all the alternative methods suggested by the range of solutions considered in this chapter.
    d. Can you think of reasons why, despite the lower external costs, a campaign against the use of wind technology might be more successful than a campaign against the use of coal or oil?

15. Learn about the destruction of the habitat of the northern spotted owl.
    a. What production activity is creating problems for the northern spotted owl?
    b. What type of externalities arise from this production activity?
    c. How would you set about designing a method for dealing with this externality?

16. Visit the Global Policy site and read about the idea of introducing a carbon tax. Explain how a carbon tax might work. Would it increase or decrease the quantity of electricity consumed? How would it change the ways in which electricity is generated? Who would bear the costs of the tax and who would enjoy the benefits? Do you think such a tax is likely to be introduced? Why or why not?

CHAPTER

9

# Production and Cost

## CHAPTER CHECKLIST

When you have completed your study of this chapter,
you will be able to

**1** Explain how economists measure a firm's cost of production and profit.

**2** Explain the relationship between a firm's output and labor employed in
the short run.

**3** Explain the relationship between a firm's output and costs in the short
run.

**4** Derive and explain a firm's long-run average cost curve.

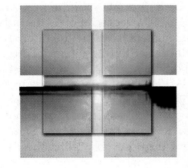

In this chapter, you're going to lay the foundation
for understanding how firms' decisions in competitive markets lead to the law of supply. We
continue to use the big ideas that define the
economic way of thinking. But we now apply
these ideas to the decisions of firms. Firms face
scarcity and make *rational* choices; the *cost* of
something is what a firm *must give up* to produce it; and firms respond to *incentives*.

You're now going to see how these principles lead firms to
make decisions that minimize the cost of producing a given
output. In this chapter, you'll learn how a firm's costs are
determined and how they vary as the firm varies its output.

What you learn in this chapter you will use again and
again in the other three chapters of this part, so it is very
important that you thoroughly understand the content of
this chapter before moving forward to Chapter 10.

## 9.1 ECONOMIC COST AND PROFIT

The 20 million firms in the United States differ in size and in what they produce. But they all perform the same basic economic function: They hire factors of production and organize them to produce and sell goods and services. To understand the behavior of a firm, we need to know its goals.

### ■ The Firm's Goal

If you asked a group of entrepreneurs what they are trying to achieve, you would get many different answers. Some would talk about making a high-quality product, others about business growth, others about market share, and others about work force job satisfaction. All of these goals might be pursued, but they are not the fundamental goal. They are a means to a deeper goal.

The firm's goal is to *maximize profit*. A firm that does not seek to maximize profit is either eliminated or bought by firms that *do* seek that goal. To calculate a firm's profit, we must determine its total revenue and total cost. Economists have a special way of defining and measuring cost and profit, which we'll explain and illustrate by looking at Sam's Smoothies, a firm that is owned and operated by Samantha.

### ■ Accounting Cost and Profit

In 2002, Sam's Smoothies' total revenue from the sale of smoothies was $150,000. The firm paid $20,000 for fruit, yogurt, and honey; $22,000 in wages for the labor it hired; and $3,000 in interest to the bank. These expenses totaled $45,000.

Sam's accountant said that the depreciation of the firm's blenders, refrigerators, and shop during 2002 was $10,000. Depreciation is the fall in the value of the firm's capital, and accountants calculate it by using the Internal Revenue Service's rules, which are based on standards set by the Financial Accounting Standards Board. So the accountant reported Sam's Smoothies' total cost for 2002 as $55,000 and the firm's profit as $95,000—$150,000 of total revenue minus $55,000 of total costs.

Sam's accountant measures cost and profit to ensure that the firm pays the correct amount of income tax and to show the bank how Sam's has used its bank loan. Economists have a different purpose: to predict the decisions that a firm makes to maximize its profit. These decisions respond to *opportunity cost* and *economic profit*.

### ■ Opportunity Cost

To produce its output, a firm employs factors of production: land, labor, capital, and entrepreneurship. Another firm could have used these same resources to produce alternative goods or services. In Chapter 3 (pp. 68–70), resources can be used to produce either bottled water or CDs, so the opportunity cost of producing a bottle of water is the number of CDs forgone. Pilots who fly passengers for United Airlines can't at the same time fly freight for Federal Express. Construction workers who are building an office tower can't simultaneously build apartments. A communications satellite operating at peak capacity can carry television signals or e-mail messages but not both at the same time. A journalist writing for the *New*

*York Times* can't at the same time create Web news reports for CNN. And Samantha can't simultaneously run her smoothies business and a flower shop.

The highest-valued alternative forgone is the opportunity cost of a firm's production. From the viewpoint of the firm, this opportunity cost is the amount that the firm must pay the owners of the factors of production it employs to attract them from their best alternative use. So a firm's opportunity cost of production is the cost of the factors of production it employs.

To determine these costs, let's return to Sam's and look at the opportunity cost of producing smoothies.

### Explicit Costs and Implicit Costs

The amount that a firm pays to attract resources from their best alternative use is either an explicit cost or an implicit cost. A cost paid in money is an **explicit cost**. Because the amount spent could have been spent on something else, an explicit cost is an opportunity cost. The wages that Samantha pays labor, the interest she pays the bank, and her expenditure on fruit, yogurt, and honey are explicit costs.

A firm incurs an **implicit cost** when it uses a factor of production but does not make a direct money payment for its use. The two categories of implicit cost are economic depreciation and the cost of the firm owner's resources.

**Economic depreciation** is the opportunity cost of the firm using capital that it owns. It is measured as the change in the *market value* of capital—the market price of the capital at the beginning of a period minus its market price at the end of a period. Suppose that Samantha could have sold her blenders, refrigerators, and shop on December 31, 2001, for $250,000. If she can sell the same capital on December 31, 2002, for $246,000, her economic depreciation during 2002 is $4,000. This is the opportunity cost of using her capital during 2002, not the $10,000 depreciation calculated by Sam's accountant.

Interest is another cost of capital. When the firm's owner provides the funds used to buy capital, the opportunity cost of those funds is the interest income forgone by not using them in the best alternative way. If Sam loaned her firm funds that could have earned her $1,000 in interest, this amount is an implicit cost of producing smoothies.

When a firm's owner supplies labor, the opportunity cost of the owner's time spent working for the firm is the wage income forgone by not working in the best alternative job. For example, instead of working at her next best job that pays $34,000 a year, Sam supplies labor to her smoothies business. This implicit cost of $34,000 is part of the opportunity cost of producing smoothies.

Finally, a firm's owner often supplies entrepreneurship, the factor of production that organizes the business and bears the risk of running it. The return to entrepreneurship is **normal profit**. Normal profit is part of a firm's opportunity cost because it is the cost of a forgone alternative—running another firm. Instead of running Sam's Smoothies, Sam could earn $16,000 a year running a flower shop. This amount is an implicit cost of production at Sam's Smoothies.

### ■ Economic Profit

A firm's **economic profit** equals total revenue minus total cost. Total revenue is the amount received from the sale of the product. It is the price of the output multiplied by the quantity sold. Total cost is the sum of the explicit costs and implicit costs and is the opportunity cost of production.

**Explicit cost**
A cost paid in money.

**Implicit cost**
An opportunity cost incurred by a firm when it uses a factor of production for which it does not make a direct money payment.

**Economic depreciation**
An opportunity cost of a firm using capital that it owns—measured as the change in the *market value* of capital over a given period.

**Normal profit**
The return to entrepreneurship. Normal profit is part of a firm's opportunity cost because it is the cost of not running another firm.

**Economic profit**
A firm's total revenue minus total cost.

■ **TABLE 9.1**
Economic Accounting

Practice Online

| Item | | |
|---|---:|---:|
| **Total Revenue** | | **$150,000** |
| *Explicit Costs* | | |
| Cost of fruit, yogurt, and honey | $20,000 | |
| Wages | $22,000 | |
| Interest | $3,000 | |
| *Implicit Costs* | | |
| Samantha's forgone wages | $34,000 | |
| Samantha's forgone interest | $1,000 | |
| Economic depreciation | $4,000 | |
| Normal profit | $16,000 | |
| **Opportunity Cost** | | **$100,000** |
| **Economic Profit** | | **$50,000** |

Because one of the firm's implicit costs is *normal profit*, the return to the entrepreneur equals normal profit plus economic profit. If a firm incurs an economic loss, the entrepreneur receives less than normal profit.

Table 9.1 summarizes the economic cost concepts, and Figure 9.1 compares the economic view and the accounting view of cost and profit. The total revenue received by Sam's Smoothies is $150,000; the opportunity cost of the resources that Sam uses is $100,000; and Sam's economic profit is $50,000.

■ **FIGURE 9.1**
Two Views of Cost and Profit

Practice Online

Economists measure economic profit as total revenue minus opportunity cost. Opportunity cost includes explicit costs and implicit costs. Normal profit is an implicit cost. Accountants measure profit as total revenue minus explicit costs—costs paid in money—and depreciation.

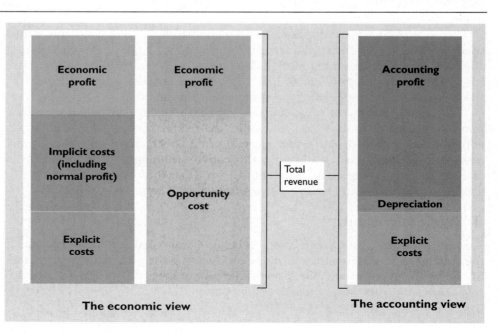

# CHECKPOINT 9.1

**1**  **Explain how economists measure a firm's cost of production and profit.**

Study Guide pp. 132–135

Practice Online 9.1

## Practice Problem 9.1

Lee is a computer programmer who earned $35,000 in 2001. But Lee loves water sports and in 2002 he opened a body board manufacturing business. At the end of the first year of operation, he submitted the following information to his accountant:

   **i.**    He stopped renting out his seaside cottage for $3,500 a year and used it as his factory. The market value of the cottage increased from $70,000 to $71,000.

  **ii.**   He spent $50,000 on materials, phone, utilities etc.

 **iii.**  He leased machines for $10,000 a year.

  **iv.**  He paid $15,000 in wages.

  **v.**   He used $10,000 from his savings account at the bank, which pays 5 percent a year interest.

  **vi.**  He borrowed $40,000 at 10 percent a year from the bank.

 **vii.**  He sold $160,000 worth of body boards.

**viii.**  Normal profit is $25,000 a year.

**a.**  Calculate Lee's explicit costs and implicit costs.

**b.**  Calculate Lee's economic profit.

**c.**  Lee's accountant recorded the depreciation on Lee's cottage during 2002 as $7,000. What did the accountant say Lee's profit or loss was for the year?

## Exercise 9.1

In 2002, Toni taught music and earned $20,000. She also earned $4,000 by renting out her basement. On January 1, 2003, she quit teaching, stopped renting out her basement, and began to use it as the office for her new Web site design business. She took $2,000 from her savings account to buy a new computer. During 2003, she paid $1,500 for the lease of a Web server and $1,750 for high-speed Internet service. She received a total revenue from Web site designing of $45,000 and earned interest at 5 percent a year on her savings account balance. The normal profit of a Web site design firm is $55,000 a year. At the end of 2003, Toni could have sold her computer for $500. For 2003, calculate Toni's

**a.**  Explicit costs.

**b.**  Implicit costs.

**c.**  Economic profit.

## Solution to Practice Problem 9.1

**a.**  Explicit costs are costs paid with money. Explicit costs are items (ii), (iii), (iv), and (vi). Explicit costs are $50,000 + $10,000 + $15,000 + $4,000, or $79,000. Implicit costs are the wages forgone and items (i), (v), and (viii) minus the increase in the market value of the cottage. That is, implicit costs are $35,000 + $3,500 + $500 + $25,000 − $1,000, or $63,000.

**b.**  Economic profit equals total revenue minus total costs. Total cost is the sum of explicit costs plus implicit costs. Total costs are $79,000 + $63,000, or $142,000. So Lee's economic profit is $160,000 − $142,000, or $18,000.

**c.**  The accountant measures Lee's profit as total revenue minus explicit costs minus depreciation. That is, profit is $160,000 − $79,000 − $7,000, or $74,000.

## SHORT RUN AND LONG RUN

The main goal of this chapter is to explore the influences on a firm's cost. The key influence on cost is the quantity of output that the firm produces per period. The greater the output rate, the higher is the total cost of production. But the effect of a change in production on cost depends on how soon the firm wants to act. A firm that plans to change its output rate tomorrow has fewer options than a firm that plans ahead and intends to change its production six months from now.

To study the relationship between a firm's output decision and its costs, we distinguish between two decision time frames:

- The short run
- The long run

### The Short Run: Fixed Plant

**Short run**

The time frame in which the quantities of some resources are fixed. In the short run, a firm can usually change the quantity of labor it uses but not its technology and quantity of capital.

The **short run** is the time frame in which the quantities of some resources are fixed. For most firms, the fixed resources are the firm's technology and capital—its equipment and buildings. The management organization is also fixed in the short run. The fixed resources that a firm uses are its *fixed factors of production* and the resources that it can vary are its *variable factors of production*. The collection of fixed resources is the firm's *plant*. So in the short run, a firm's plant is fixed.

Sam's Smoothies' plant is its blenders, refrigerators, and shop. Sam's cannot change these inputs in the short run. An electric power utility can't change the number of generators it uses in the short run. An airport can't change the number of runways, terminal buildings, and traffic control facilities in the short run.

To increase output in the short run, a firm must increase the quantity of variable factors it uses. Labor is usually the variable factor of production. To produce more smoothies, Sam must hire more labor. Similarly, to increase the production of electricity, a utility must hire more engineers and run its generators for longer hours. To increase the volume of traffic it handles, an airport must hire more check-in clerks, cargo handlers, and air-traffic controllers.

Short-run decisions are easily reversed. A firm can increase or decrease output in the short run by increasing or decreasing the labor hours it hires.

### The Long Run: Variable Plant

**Long run**

The time frame in which the quantities of *all* resources can be varied.

The **long run** is the time frame in which the quantities of *all* resources can be varied. That is, the long run is a period in which the firm can change its *plant*.

To increase output in the long run, a firm can increase the size of its plant. Sam's Smoothies can install more blenders and refrigerators and increase the size of its shop. An electric power utility can install more generators. And an airport can build more runways, terminals, and traffic-control facilities.

Long-run decisions are *not* easily reversed. Once a firm buys a new plant, its resale value is usually much less than the amount the firm paid for it. The difference between the cost of the plant and its resale value is a *sunk cost*. A sunk cost is irrelevant to the firm's decisions (see Chapter 1, p. 14). The only costs that influence the firm's decisions are the short-run cost of changing its labor inputs and the long-run cost of changing its plant.

We're going to study costs in the short run and the long run. We begin with the short run and describe the limits to the firm's production possibilities.

*He's thinking about if he wants to meet my Dad!*

## 9.2 SHORT-RUN PRODUCTION

To increase the output of a fixed plant, a firm must increase the quantity of labor it employs. We describe the relationship between output and the quantity of labor employed by using three related concepts:

- Total product
- Marginal product
- Average product

### ■ Total Product

**Total product** (*TP*) is the total quantity of a good produced in a given period. Total product is an output *rate*—the number of units produced per unit of time (for example, per hour, day, or week). Total product increases as the quantity of labor employed increases, and we illustrate this relationship as a total product schedule and total product curve like those in Figure 9.2. The total product schedule (the table below the graph) lists the maximum quantities of smoothies per hour that Sam can produce with her existing plant at each quantity of labor. Points *A* through *H* on the *TP* curve correspond to the columns in the table.

> **Total product**
> The total quantity of a good produced in a given period.

---

**■ FIGURE 9.2**

Total Product Schedule and Total Product Curve

**Practice Online**

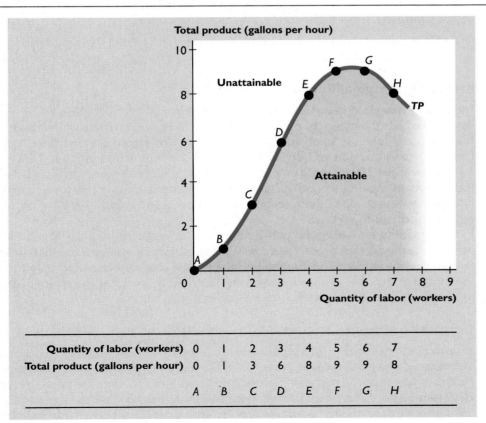

| Quantity of labor (workers) | 0 | 1 | 2 | 3 | 4 | 5 | 6 | 7 |
|---|---|---|---|---|---|---|---|---|
| Total product (gallons per hour) | 0 | 1 | 3 | 6 | 8 | 9 | 9 | 8 |
| | A | B | C | D | E | F | G | H |

The total product schedule shows how the quantity of smoothies that Sam's can produce changes as the quantity of labor employed changes. In column *C*, Sam's employs 2 workers and can produce 3 gallons of smoothies an hour.

The total product curve, *TP*, graphs the data in the table. Points *A* through *H* on the curve correspond to the columns of the table. The total product curve separates attainable outputs from unattainable outputs. Points below the *TP* curve are inefficient. Points on the *TP* curve are efficient.

Like the *production possibilities frontier* (see Chapter 3, p. 62), the total product curve separates attainable outputs from unattainable outputs. All the points that lie above the curve are unattainable. Points that lie below the curve, in the orange area, are attainable. But they are inefficient: They use more labor than is necessary to produce a given output. Only the points *on* the total product curve are efficient.

### ■ Marginal Product

**Marginal product**
The change in total product that results from a one-unit increase in the quantity of labor employed.

**Marginal product** (*MP*) is the change in total product that results from a one-unit increase in the quantity of labor employed. It tells us the contribution to total product of adding one additional worker. When the quantity of labor increases by more (or less) than one worker, we calculate marginal product as

Marginal product = Change in total product ÷ Change in quantity of labor.

Figure 9.3 shows Sam's Smoothies' marginal product curve, *MP*, and its relationship with the total product curve. You can see that as the quantity of labor increases from 1 to 3 workers, marginal product increases. But as yet more workers are employed, marginal product decreases. When the 7th worker is employed, marginal product is negative.

Notice that the steeper the slope of the total product curve in part (a), the greater is marginal product in part (b). And when the total product curve turns downward in part (a), marginal product is negative in part (b).

The total product curve and marginal product curve in Figure 9.3 incorporate a feature that is shared by all production processes in firms as different as the Ford Motor Company, Jim's Barber Shop, and Sam's Smoothies:

- Increasing marginal returns initially
- Decreasing marginal returns eventually

### Increasing Marginal Returns

**Increasing marginal returns**
When the marginal product of an additional worker exceeds the marginal product of the previous worker.

**Increasing marginal returns** occur when the marginal product of an additional worker exceeds the marginal product of the previous worker. Increasing marginal returns occur when a small number of workers are employed and arise from increased specialization and division of labor in the production process.

For example, if Samantha employs just one worker, that person must learn all the aspects of making smoothies: running the blender, cleaning it, fixing breakdowns, packaging and delivering, buying and checking the fruit. That one person must perform all these tasks.

If Samantha hires a second person, the two workers can specialize in different parts of the production process. As a result, two workers produce more than twice as much as one worker. The marginal product of the second worker is greater than the marginal product of the first worker. Marginal returns are increasing. Most production processes experience increasing marginal returns initially.

### Decreasing Marginal Returns

**Decreasing marginal returns**
When the marginal product of an additional worker is less than the marginal product of the previous worker.

All production processes eventually reach a point of *decreasing* marginal returns. **Decreasing marginal returns** occur when the marginal product of an additional worker is less than the marginal product of the previous worker. Decreasing marginal returns arise from the fact that more and more workers use the same equipment and work space. As more workers are employed, there is less and less that is productive for the additional worker to do. For example, if Samantha hires a

**■ FIGURE 9.3**
Total Product and Marginal Product

**Practice Online**

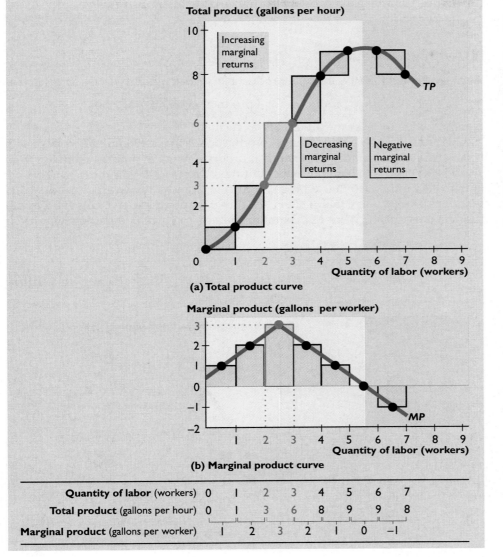

(a) Total product curve

(b) Marginal product curve

| Quantity of labor (workers) | 0 | 1 | 2 | 3 | 4 | 5 | 6 | 7 |
|---|---|---|---|---|---|---|---|---|
| Total product (gallons per hour) | 0 | 1 | 3 | 6 | 8 | 9 | 9 | 8 |
| Marginal product (gallons per worker) | | 1 | 2 | 3 | 2 | 1 | 0 | −1 |

The table calculates marginal product and the orange bars illustrate it. When labor increases from 2 to 3 workers, total product increases from 3 gallons to 6 gallons an hour. So marginal product is the orange bar whose height is 3 gallons (in both parts of the figure).

In part (b), marginal product is graphed midway between the labor inputs to emphasize that it is the result of *changing* inputs. Marginal product increases to a maximum (when 3 workers are employed in this example) and then declines—diminishing marginal product.

fourth worker, output increases but not by as much as it did when she hired the third worker. In this case, three workers exhaust all the possible gains from specialization and the division of labor. By hiring a fourth worker, Sam's produces more smoothies per hour, but the equipment is being operated closer to its limits. Sometimes the fourth worker has nothing to do because the machines are running without the need for further attention.

Hiring yet more workers continues to increase output but by successively smaller amounts until Samantha hires the sixth worker, at which point total product stops rising. Add a seventh worker and the workplace is so congested that the workers get in each other's way and total product falls.

Decreasing marginal returns are so pervasive that they qualify for the status of a law: the **law of decreasing returns**, which states that

> **As a firm uses more of a variable input, with a given quantity of fixed inputs, the marginal product of the variable input eventually decreases.**

## ■ Average Product

**Average product**
Total product divided by the quantity of an input. The average product of labor is total product divided by the quantity of labor employed.

**Average product** (*AP*) is the total product per worker employed. It is calculated as

Average product = Total product ÷ Quantity of labor.

Another name for average product is *productivity*.

Figure 9.4 shows the average product of labor, *AP*, and the relationship between average product and marginal product. Average product increases from 1 to 3 workers (its maximum value) but then decreases as yet more workers are employed. Notice also that average product is largest when average product and marginal product are equal. That is, the marginal product curve cuts the average product curve at the point of maximum average product. For employment levels

---

**FIGURE 9.4**

Average Product and Marginal Product

**Practice Online**

The table calculates average product. For example, when the quantity of labor is 3 workers, total product is 6 gallons an hour, so average product is 6 ÷ 3 = 2 gallons a worker.

The average product curve is *AP*. When marginal product exceeds average product, average product is increasing. When marginal product is less than average product, average product is decreasing.

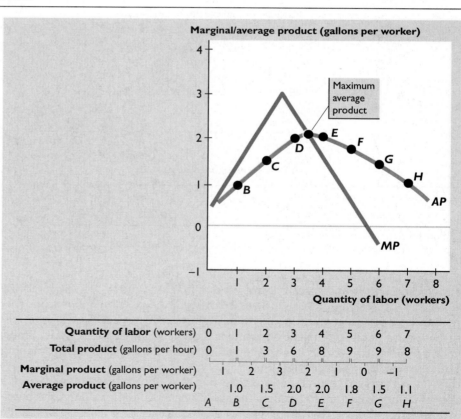

| Quantity of labor (workers) | 0 | 1 | 2 | 3 | 4 | 5 | 6 | 7 |
|---|---|---|---|---|---|---|---|---|
| Total product (gallons per hour) | 0 | 1 | 3 | 6 | 8 | 9 | 9 | 8 |
| Marginal product (gallons per worker) | | 1 | 2 | 3 | 2 | 1 | 0 | −1 |
| Average product (gallons per worker) | | 1.0 | 1.5 | 2.0 | 2.0 | 1.8 | 1.5 | 1.1 |
| | *A* | *B* | *C* | *D* | *E* | *F* | *G* | *H* |

at which marginal product exceeds average product, the average product curve slopes upward and average product increases as more labor is employed. For employment levels at which marginal product is less than average product, the average product curve is downward sloping and average product decreases as more labor is employed.

The relationship between average product and marginal product is a general feature of the relationship between the average value and the marginal value of any variable. Let's look at a familiar example.

*Marginal Grade and Grade Point Average*  Samantha is a part-time student who takes just one course each semester. To understand the relationship between average product and marginal product, think about the relationship between Sam's average grade and her marginal grade over five semesters, shown in Figure 9.5. In the first semester, Samantha takes French and her grade is a C (2). This grade is her marginal grade—the grade on the last course taken. It is also her average grade—her GPA. In the next semester, Samantha takes calculus and gets a B (3). Calculus is Sam's marginal course, and her marginal grade is 3. Her GPA rises to 2.5. Because her marginal grade exceeds her average grade, it pulls her average up. In the third semester, Samantha takes economics and gets an A (4)—her new marginal grade. Because her marginal grade exceeds her GPA, it again pulls her average up. Sam's GPA is now 3, the average of 2, 3, and 4. The fourth semester, she takes history and gets a B (3). Because her marginal grade is equal to her average, her GPA does not change. In the fifth semester, Samantha takes English and gets a D (1). Because her marginal grade of 1 is below her GPA of 3, her GPA falls.

This everyday relationship between average and marginal values is similar to the relationship between average and marginal product. Sam's GPA increases when her marginal grade exceeds her GPA. Her GPA falls when her marginal grade is below her GPA. And her GPA is constant when her marginal grade equals her GPA. The relationship between marginal product and average product is exactly the same as that between Sam's marginal and average grades.

**FIGURE 9.5**

Marginal Grade and Grade Point Average

**Practice Online**

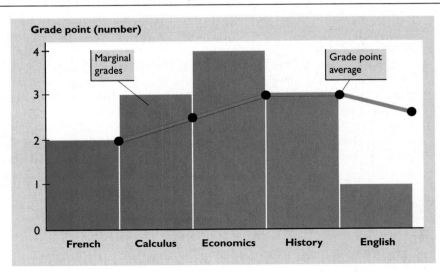

Sam's first course is French, for which she gets a C (2). Her marginal grade is 2, and her GPA is 2. She then gets a B (3) in calculus, which pulls her average up to 2.5. Next, she gets an A (4) in economics, which pulls her GPA up to 3. In her next course, history, she gets a B (3), which maintains her GPA. In her final course, English, she gets a D (1), which pulls her GPA down.

**Study Guide pp. 135–137**

**Practice Online 9.2**

**TABLE 1**

| Labor (students) | Total product (pineapples per day) |
|---|---|
| 0 | 0 |
| 1 | 100 |
| 2 | 220 |
| 3 | 300 |
| 4 | 360 |
| 5 | 400 |
| 6 | 420 |
| 7 | 430 |

**TABLE 2**

| Labor (students) | Total product (houses painted per week) |
|---|---|
| 0 | 0 |
| 1 | 2 |
| 2 | 5 |
| 3 | 9 |
| 4 | 12 |
| 5 | 14 |
| 6 | 15 |

**2** **Explain the relationship between a firm's output and labor employed in the short run.**

## Practice Problem 9.2

Tom leases a farmer's field and grows pineapples. Tom hires students to pick and pack the pineapples. Table 1 sets out Tom's total product schedule.
a. Calculate the marginal product of the third student.
b. Calculate the average product of three students.
c. Over what numbers of students does marginal product increase?
d. When marginal product increases, compare average product and marginal product.

## Exercise 9.2

Lizzie hires students in the summer to paint houses. Table 2 sets out her total product schedule.
a. Calculate the marginal product of the fourth student.
b. Calculate the average product of four students.
c. Over what numbers of students does marginal product decrease?
d. When marginal product decreases, compare average product and marginal product.

## Solution to Practice Problem 9.2

a. Marginal product of the third student is the change in total product that results from hiring the third student. When Tom hires 2 students, total product is 220 pineapples a day. When Tom hires 3 students, total product is 300 pineapples a day. Marginal product of the third worker is the total product of 3 workers minus the total product of 2 workers, which is 300 pineapples a day minus 220 pineapples a day, or 80 pineapples a day.
b. Average product equals total product divided by the number of students. When Tom hires 3 students, total product is 300 pineapples a day, so average product is 300 pineapples a day divided by 3 students, which equals 100 pineapples a day.
c. Marginal product of the first student is 100 pineapples a day, that of the second student is 120 pineapples a day, and that of the third student is 80 pineapples a day. So marginal product increases when Tom hires the first and second students.
d. When Tom hires 1 student, marginal product is 100 pineapples a day and average product is 100 pineapples a day. When Tom hires 2 students, marginal product is 120 pineapples a day and average product is 110 pineapples a day. That is, when Tom hires the second student, marginal product exceeds average product.

## 9.3 SHORT-RUN COST

To produce more output (total product) in the short run, a firm must employ more labor, which means that it must increase its costs. We describe the relationship between output and cost using three cost concepts:

- Total cost
- Marginal cost
- Average cost

### ■ Total Cost

A firm's **total cost** (TC) is the cost of all the factors of production used by the firm. Total cost divides into two parts: total fixed cost and total variable cost. **Total fixed cost** (TFC) is the cost of a firm's fixed factors of production: land, capital, and entrepreneurship. Because in the short run, the quantities of these inputs don't change as output changes, total fixed cost doesn't change as output changes. **Total variable cost** (TVC) is the cost of a firm's variable factor of production—labor. To change its output in the short run, a firm must change the quantity of labor it employs, so total variable cost changes as output changes.

Total cost is the sum of total fixed cost and total variable cost. That is,

$$TC = TFC + TVC.$$

Table 9.2 shows Sam's Smoothies' total costs. Sam's fixed costs are $10 an hour regardless of whether it operates or not—TFC is $10 an hour. To produce smoothies, Samantha hires labor, which costs $6 an hour. TVC, which increases as output increases, equals the number of workers per hour multiplied by $6. For example, to produce 6 gallons an hour, Samantha hires 3 workers, so TVC is $18 an hour. TC is the sum of TFC and TVC. So to produce 6 gallons an hour, TC is $28. Check the calculation in each row and note that to produce some quantities—2 gallons an hour, for example—Sam hires a worker for only part of the hour.

**Total cost**
The cost of all the factors of production used by a firm.

**Total fixed cost**
The cost of the fixed factors of production used by a firm—the cost of land, capital, and entrepreneurship.

**Total variable cost**
The cost of the variable factor of production used by a firm—the cost of labor.

■ **TABLE 9.2**
Sam's Smoothies' Total Costs

**Practice Online**

| Labor (workers per hour) | Output (gallons per hour) | Total fixed cost | Total variable cost | Total cost |
|---|---|---|---|---|
| | | | (dollars per hour) | |
| 0 | 0 | 10 | 0.00 | 10.00 |
| 1.00 | 1 | 10 | 6.00 | 16.00 |
| 1.60 | 2 | 10 | 9.60 | 19.60 |
| 2.00 | 3 | 10 | 12.00 | 22.00 |
| 2.35 | 4 | 10 | 14.10 | 24.10 |
| 2.70 | 5 | 10 | 16.20 | 26.20 |
| 3.00 | 6 | 10 | 18.00 | 28.00 |
| 3.40 | 7 | 10 | 20.40 | 30.40 |
| 4.00 | 8 | 10 | 24.00 | 34.00 |
| 5.00 | 9 | 10 | 30.00 | 40.00 |

Figure 9.6 illustrates Sam's total cost curves. The green total fixed cost curve (*TFC*) is horizontal because total fixed cost does not change when output changes. It is a constant at $10 an hour. The purple total variable cost curve (*TVC*) and the blue total cost curve (*TC*) both slope upward because variable cost increases as output increases. The arrows highlight total fixed cost as the vertical distance between the *TVC* and *TC* curve.

Let's now look at Sam's Smoothies' marginal cost.

### ■ Marginal Cost

In Figure 9.6, total variable cost and total cost increase at a decreasing rate at small levels of output and then begin to increase at an increasing rate as output increases. To understand these patterns in the changes in total cost, we need to use the concept of *marginal cost*.

A firm's **marginal cost** is the change in total cost that results from a one-unit increase in output. Table 9.3 calculates the marginal cost for Sam's Smoothies. When, for example, output increases from 5 gallons to 6 gallons an hour, total cost increases from $26.20 to $28. So the marginal cost of this gallon of smoothies is $1.80 ($28 − $26.20).

Marginal cost tells us how total cost changes as output changes. The final cost concept tells us what it costs, on the average, to produce a unit of output. Let's now look at Sam's average costs.

**Marginal cost**
The change in total cost that results from a one-unit increase in output.

---

### ■ FIGURE 9.6

Total Cost Curves at Sam's Smoothies

**Practice Online**

---

Total fixed cost (*TFC*) is constant—it graphs as a horizontal line—and total variable cost (*TVC*) increases as output increases. Total cost (*TC*) also increases as output increases. The vertical distance between the total cost curve and the total variable cost curve is total fixed cost, as illustrated by the two arrows.

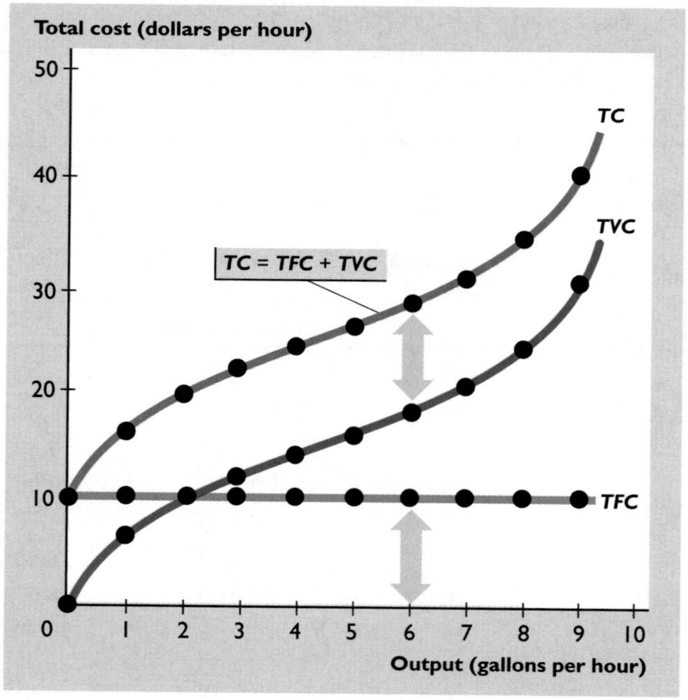

## ■ Average Cost

There are three average cost concepts:

- Average fixed cost
- Average variable cost
- Average total cost

**Average fixed cost** (*AFC*) is total fixed cost per unit of output. **Average variable cost** (*AVC*) is total variable cost per unit of output. **Average total cost** (*ATC*) is total cost per unit of output. The average cost concepts are calculated from the total cost concepts as follows:

$$TC = TFC + TVC.$$

Divide each total cost term by the quantity produced, *Q*, to give

$$\frac{TC}{Q} = \frac{TFC}{Q} + \frac{TVC}{Q},$$

or

$$ATC = AFC + AVC.$$

Table 9.3 shows these average costs. For example, when output is 3 gallons an hour, average fixed cost is ($10 ÷ 3), which equals $3.33; average variable cost is ($12 ÷ 3), which equals $4.00; and average total cost is ($22 ÷ 3), which equals $7.33. Note that average total cost ($7.33) equals average fixed cost ($3.33) plus average variable cost ($4.00).

**Average fixed cost**
Total fixed cost per unit of output.

**Average variable cost**
Total variable cost per unit of output.

**Average total cost**
Total cost per unit of output, which equals average fixed cost plus average variable cost.

---

■ **TABLE 9.3**                                                                 <u>**Practice Online**</u>

Sam's Smoothies' Marginal Cost and Average Cost

| Output (gallons per hour) | Total cost (dollars per hour) | Marginal cost (dollars per gallon) | Average fixed cost | Average variable cost | Average total cost |
|---|---|---|---|---|---|
| | | | | (dollars per gallon) | |
| 0 | 10.00 | | – | – | – |
| | | 6.00 | | | |
| 1 | 16.00 | | 10.00 | 6.00 | 16.00 |
| | | 3.60 | | | |
| 2 | 19.60 | | 5.00 | 4.80 | 9.80 |
| | | 2.40 | | | |
| 3 | 22.00 | | 3.33 | 4.00 | 7.33 |
| | | 2.10 | | | |
| 4 | 24.10 | | 2.50 | 3.53 | 6.03 |
| | | 2.10 | | | |
| 5 | 26.20 | | 2.00 | 3.24 | 5.24 |
| | | 1.80 | | | |
| 6 | 28.00 | | 1.67 | 3.00 | 4.67 |
| | | 2.40 | | | |
| 7 | 30.40 | | 1.43 | 2.91 | 4.34 |
| | | 3.60 | | | |
| 8 | 34.00 | | 1.25 | 3.00 | 4.25 |
| | | 6.00 | | | |
| 9 | 40.00 | | 1.11 | 3.33 | 4.44 |

Figure 9.7 graphs the marginal cost and average cost data in Table 9.3. The red marginal cost curve (*MC*) is U-shaped because of the way in which marginal product changes. Recall that when Samantha hires a second or a third worker, marginal product increases. Over this range, output increases and marginal cost decreases. But when Samantha hires a fourth or more workers, marginal product decreases. Over this range, output increases and marginal cost increases.

The green average fixed cost curve (*AFC*) slopes downward. As output increases, the same constant total fixed cost is spread over a larger output. The blue average total cost curve (*ATC*) and the purple average variable cost curve (*AVC*) are U-shaped. The vertical distance between the average total cost and average variable cost curves is equal to average fixed cost—as indicated by the two arrows. That distance shrinks as output increases because average fixed cost decreases with increasing output.

The marginal cost curve intersects the average variable cost curve and the average total cost curve at their minimum points. That is, when marginal cost is less than average cost, average cost is decreasing; and when marginal cost exceeds average cost, average cost is increasing. This relationship holds for both the *ATC* curve and the *AVC* curve and is another example of the relationship you saw in Figure 9.4 for average product and marginal product and in Sam's course grades.

---

■ **FIGURE 9.7**

Average Cost Curves and Marginal Cost Curve at Sam's Smoothies

<u>**Practice Online**</u>

---

Average fixed cost (*AFC*) decreases as output increases. The average total cost curve (*ATC*) and average variable cost curve (*AVC*) are U-shaped. The vertical distance between these two curves is equal to average fixed cost, as illustrated by the two arrows.

Marginal cost is the change in total cost when output increases by one unit. The marginal cost curve (*MC*) is U-shaped and intersects the average variable cost curve and the average total cost curve at their minimum points.

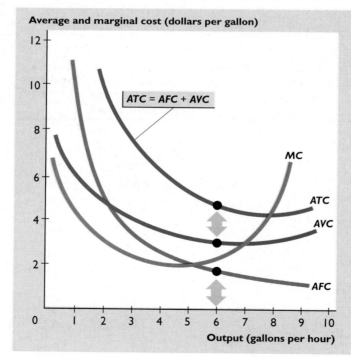

## ■ Why the Average Total Cost Curve Is U-Shaped

Average total cost, *ATC*, is the sum of average fixed cost, *AFC*, and average variable cost, *AVC*. So the shape of the *ATC* curve combines the shapes of the *AFC* and *AVC* curves. The U-shape of the average total cost curve arises from the influence of two opposing forces:

• Spreading total fixed cost over a larger output
• Decreasing marginal returns

When output increases, the firm spreads its total fixed costs over a larger output and its average fixed cost decreases—its average fixed cost curve slopes downward.

Decreasing marginal returns means that as output increases, ever larger amounts of labor are needed to produce an additional unit of output. So average variable cost eventually increases, and the *AVC* curve eventually slopes upward.

The shape of the average total cost curve combines these two effects. Initially, as output increases, both average fixed cost and average variable cost decrease, so average total cost decreases and the *ATC* curve slopes downward. But as output increases further and decreasing marginal returns set in, average variable cost begins to increase. Eventually, average variable cost increases more quickly than average fixed cost decreases, so average total cost increases and the *ATC* curve slopes upward.

All the short-run cost concepts that you've met are summarized in Table 9.4.

■ **TABLE 9.4**    Practice Online

A Compact Glossary of Costs

| Term | Symbol | Definition | Equation |
|------|--------|-----------|----------|
| Fixed cost | | The cost of a fixed factor of production that is independent of the quantity produced | |
| Variable cost | | The cost of a variable factor of production that varies with the quantity produced | |
| Total fixed cost | *TFC* | Cost of the fixed factors of production | |
| Total variable cost | *TVC* | Cost of the variable factor of production | |
| Total cost | *TC* | Cost of all factors of production | $TC = TFC + TVC$ |
| Marginal cost | *MC* | Change in total cost resulting from a one-unit increase in output (Q) | $MC = \Delta TC \div \Delta Q^*$ |
| Average fixed cost | *AFC* | Total fixed cost per unit of output | $AFC = TFC \div Q$ |
| Average variable cost | *AVC* | Total variable cost per unit of output | $AVC = TVC \div Q$ |
| Average total cost | *ATC* | Total cost per unit of output | $ATC = AFC + AVC$ |

*In this equation, the Greek letter delta ($\Delta$) stands for "change in."

## ■ Cost Curves and Product Curves

A firm's cost curves and product curves are linked, and Figure 9.8 shows how. The top figure shows the average product curve and the marginal product curve—like those in Figure 9.4. The bottom figure shows the average variable cost curve and the marginal cost curve—like those in Figure 9.7.

The figure highlights the links between the product and cost curves. At low levels of employment and output, as the firm hires more labor, marginal product and average product rise and output increases faster than costs. So marginal cost and average variable cost fall. Then, at the point of maximum marginal product, marginal cost is a minimum. As the firm hires more labor, marginal product decreases and marginal cost increases. But average product continues to rise, and average variable cost continues to fall. Then, at the point of maximum average product, average variable cost is a minimum. As the firm hires even more labor, average product decreases and average variable cost increases.

## ■ Shifts in the Cost Curves

The position of a firm's short-run cost curves in Figures 9.6 and 9.7 depend on two factors:

- Technology
- Prices of factors of production

### Technology

A technological change that increases productivity shifts the total product curve upward. It also shifts the marginal product curve and the average product curve upward. With a better technology, the same inputs can produce more output, so an advance in technology lowers the average and marginal costs and shifts the short-run cost curves downward.

For example, advances in robotic technology have increased productivity in the automobile industry. As a result, the product curves of DaimlerChrysler, Ford, and GM have shifted upward, and their average and marginal cost curves have shifted downward. But the relationships between their product curves and cost curves have not changed. The curves are still linked, as in Figure 9.8.

Often a technological advance results in a firm using more capital, a fixed input, and less labor, a variable input. For example, today telephone companies use computers to connect long-distance calls instead of the human operators they used in the 1980s. When a telephone company makes this change, total variable cost decreases and total cost decreases, but total fixed cost increases. This change in the mix of fixed cost and variable cost means that at small output levels, average total cost might increase, but at large output levels, average total cost decreases.

### Prices of Factors of Production

An increase in the price of a factor of production increases costs and shifts the cost curves. But how the curves shift depends on which resource price changes. An increase in rent or some other component of *fixed* cost shifts the fixed cost curves (*TFC* and *AFC*) upward and shifts the total cost curve (*TC*) upward but leaves the variable cost curves (*AVC* and *TVC*) and the marginal cost curve (*MC*) unchanged.

**FIGURE 9.8**

Product Curves and Cost Curves

Practice Online

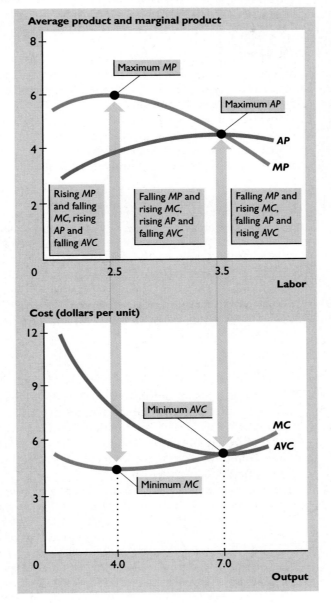

A firm's marginal cost curve is linked to its marginal product curve. If marginal product rises, marginal cost falls. If marginal product is a maximum, marginal cost is a minimum. If marginal product diminishes, marginal cost rises.

A firm's average variable cost curve is linked to its average product curve. If average product rises, average variable cost falls. If average product is a maximum, average variable cost is a minimum. If average product diminishes, average variable cost rises.

An increase in wage rates or some other component of *variable* cost shifts the variable cost curves (*TVC* and *AVC*) and the marginal cost curve (*MC*) upward but leaves the fixed cost curves (*AFC* and *TFC*) unchanged. So, for example, if the interest expense paid by a trucking company increases, the fixed cost of transportation services increases, but if the wage rate paid to truck drivers increases, the variable cost and marginal cost of transportation services increase.

Study Guide pp. 137–140

Practice Online 9.3

**3** **Explain the relationship between a firm's output and costs in the short run.**

## Practice Problem 9.3

Tom leases a farmer's field for $120 a day and grows pineapples. Tom pays students $100 a day to pick and pack the pineapples. Tom leases capital at $80 a day. Table 1 gives the daily output.

a. Construct the total cost schedule.
b. Construct the average total cost schedule.
c. Construct the marginal cost schedule.
d. At what output is Tom's average total cost a minimum?

## Exercise 9.3

Lizzie hires students at $50 a day to paint houses. She leases equipment that costs her $100 a day. Table 2 shows her total product schedule.

a. Construct the total variable cost and total cost schedules.
b. Construct the average fixed cost, average variable cost, and average total cost schedules.
c. Construct the marginal cost schedule.
d. Check that the gap between total cost and total variable cost is the same at all outputs. Explain why.

## Solution to Practice Problem 9.3

a. Total cost is the sum of total fixed cost and total variable cost. Tom leases the farmer's field for $120 a day and leases capital for $80 a day, so Tom's total fixed cost is $200 a day. Total variable cost is the wages of the students. For example, when Tom hires 3 students, the total variable cost is $300 a day. So when Tom hires 3 students, total cost is $500 a day. The *TC* column of Table 3 shows the total cost schedule.

b. Average total cost is the total cost divided by total product. For example, when Tom hires 3 students, they pick and pack 300 pineapples a day, and Tom's total cost is $500 a day. Average total cost is $1.67 a pineapple. The *ATC* column of Table 3 shows the average total cost schedule.

c. Marginal cost is the increase in total cost that results from picking and packing one additional pineapple a day. The total cost (from Table 3) of picking and packing 100 pineapples a day is $300. The total cost of picking and packing 220 pineapples a day is $400. The increase in the number of pineapples is 120, and the increase in total cost is $100. So the marginal cost is the increase in total cost divided by the increase in the number of pineapples. Marginal cost equals $100 ÷ 120 pineapples, which is $0.83 a pineapple. The *MC* column of Table 3 shows the marginal cost schedule.

d. At the minimum of average total cost, average total cost and marginal cost are equal. Minimum average total cost is $1.67 a pineapple at 330 pineapples a day.

**TABLE 1**

| Labor (students) | Output (pineapples per day) |
|---|---|
| 0 | 0 |
| 1 | 100 |
| 2 | 220 |
| 3 | 300 |
| 4 | 360 |
| 5 | 400 |
| 6 | 420 |
| 7 | 430 |

**TABLE 2**

| Labor (students) | Output (houses painted per week) |
|---|---|
| 0 | 0 |
| 1 | 2 |
| 2 | 5 |
| 3 | 9 |
| 4 | 12 |
| 5 | 14 |
| 6 | 15 |

**TABLE 3**

| Labor | TP | TC | MC | ATC |
|---|---|---|---|---|
| 0 | 0 | 200 | | – |
| | | | 1.00 | |
| 1 | 100 | 300 | | 3.00 |
| | | | 0.83 | |
| 2 | 220 | 400 | | 1.82 |
| | | | 1.25 | |
| 3 | 300 | 500 | | 1.67 |
| | | | 1.67 | |
| 4 | 360 | 600 | | 1.67 |
| | | | 2.50 | |
| 5 | 400 | 700 | | 1.75 |
| | | | 5.00 | |
| 6 | 420 | 800 | | 1.90 |
| | | | 10.00 | |
| 7 | 430 | 900 | | 2.09 |

## 9.4 LONG-RUN COST

In the long run, a firm can vary both the quantity of labor and the quantity of capital. A small firm, such as Sam's Smoothies, can increase its plant size by moving into a larger building and installing more machines. A big firm such as General Motors can decrease its plant size by closing down some production lines.

We are now going to see how costs vary in the long run when a firm varies its plant—the quantity of capital it uses—along with the quantity of labor it uses.

The first thing that happens is that the distinction between fixed cost and variable cost disappears. All costs are variable in the long run.

### ■ Plant Size and Cost

When a firm changes its plant size, its cost of producing a given output changes. In Figure 9.7, the lowest average total cost that Sam can achieve is $4.25 a gallon, which occurs when she produces 8 gallons of smoothies an hour. Samantha wonders what would happen to her average total cost if she increased the size of her plant by renting a bigger building and installing a larger number of blenders and refrigerators. Will the average total cost of producing a gallon of smoothie fall, rise, or remain the same?

Each of these three outcomes is possible, and they arise because when a firm changes the size of its plant, it might experience

- Economies of scale
- Diseconomies of scale
- Constant returns to scale

### Economies of Scale

If when a firm increases its plant size and labor employed by the same percentage, its output increases by a larger percentage, the firm's average total cost decreases. The firm experiences **economies of scale**. The main source of economies of scale is greater specialization of both labor and capital.

*Specialization of Labor*  If GM produced 100 cars a week, each production line worker would have to perform many different tasks. But if GM produces 10,000 cars a week, each worker can specialize in a small number of tasks and become highly proficient at them. The result is that the average product of labor increases and the average total cost of producing a car falls.

Specialization also occurs off the production line. For example, a small firm usually does not have a specialist sales manager, personnel manager, and production manager. One person covers all these activities. But when a firm is large enough, specialists perform these activities. Average product increases, and the average total cost falls.

*Specialization of Capital*  At a small output rate, firms often must employ general-purpose machines and tools. For example, with an output of a few gallons an hour, Sam's Smoothies uses regular blenders like the one in your kitchen. But if Sam's produces hundreds of gallons an hour, it uses custom blenders that fill, empty, and clean themselves. The result is that the output rate is larger and the average total cost of producing a gallon of smoothie is lower.

**Economies of scale**
A condition in which, when a firm increases its plant size and labor employed by the same percentage, its output increases by a larger percentage and its average total cost decreases.

## Diseconomies of Scale

If when a firm increases its plant size and labor employed by the same percentage, output increases by a smaller percentage, the firm's average total cost increases. The firm experiences **diseconomies of scale**. Diseconomies of scale arise from the difficulty of coordinating and controlling a large enterprise. The larger the firm, the greater is the cost of communicating both up and down the management hierarchy and among managers. Eventually, management complexity brings rising average cost. Diseconomies of scale occur in all production processes but in some, perhaps, only at a very large output rate.

## Constant Returns to Scale

If when a firm increases its plant size and labor employed by the same percentage, output increases by that same percentage, the firm's average total cost remains constant. The firm experiences **constant returns to scale**. Constant returns to scale occur when a firm is able to replicate its existing production facility including its management system. For example, General Motors might double its production of Cavaliers by doubling its production facility for those cars. It can build an identical production line and hire an identical number of workers. With the two identical production lines, GM produces exactly twice as many cars. The average cost of producing a Cavalier is identical in the two plants. So when production increases, average total cost remains constant.

## ■ The Long-Run Average Cost Curve

The **long-run average cost curve** shows the lowest average cost at which it is possible to produce each output when the firm has had sufficient time to change both its plant size and its labor force.

Figure 9.9 shows Sam's Smoothies' long-run average cost curve LRAC. This long-run average cost curve is derived from the short-run average total cost curves for different possible plant sizes.

With its current small plant, Sam's Smoothies operates on the average total cost curve $ATC_1$ in Figure 9.9. The other three average total cost curves are for successively bigger plants. In this example, for outputs up to 5 gallons an hour, the existing plant with average total cost curve $ATC_1$ produces smoothies at the lowest attainable average cost. For outputs between 5 and 10 gallons an hour, average total cost is lowest on $ATC_2$. For outputs between 10 and 15 gallons an hour, average total cost is lowest on $ATC_3$. And for outputs in excess of 15 gallons an hour, average total cost is lowest on $ATC_4$.

The segment of each of the four average total cost curves for which that plant has the lowest average total cost is highlighted in dark blue in Figure 9.9. The scallop-shaped curve made up of these four segments is Sam's Smoothies' long-run average cost curve.

### Economies and Diseconomies of Scale

When economies of scale are present, the LRAC curve slopes downward. The LRAC curve in Figure 9.9 shows that Sam's Smoothies experiences economies of scale for output rates up to 9 gallons an hour. At output rates between 9 and 12 gallons an hour, the firm experiences constant returns to scale. And at output rates that exceed 12 gallons an hour, the firm experiences diseconomies of scale.

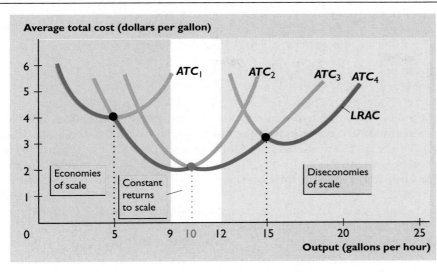

In the long run, Samantha can vary both capital and labor inputs. The long-run average cost curve traces the lowest attainable average total cost of producing each output.

Sam's experiences economies of scale as output increases to 9 gallons an hour, constant returns to scale for outputs between 9 gallons and 12 gallons an hour, and diseconomies of scale for outputs that exceed 12 gallons an hour.

# Eye on the U.S. Economy

## The ATM and the Cost of Getting Cash

Most banks use automated teller machines—ATMs—to dispense cash. But small credit unions don't have ATMs. Instead, they employ tellers.

Gemini Consulting of Morristown, New Jersey, estimates that the average total cost of a transaction is $1.07 for a teller and 27¢ for an ATM. Given these numbers, why don't small credit unions install ATMs and lay off their tellers?

The answer is scale. At a small number of transactions per month, it costs less to use a teller than an ATM. In the figure, the average total cost

curve for transactions done with a teller is $ATC_T$. The average total cost curve for transactions done with an ATM is $ATC_A$. You can see that if the number of transactions is $Q$ a month, the average total cost per transaction is the same for both methods. For a

bank that does more than $Q$ transactions per month, the least-cost method is the ATM. For a credit union that does fewer than $Q$ transactions a month, its least-cost method is the teller. More technology is not always more efficient.

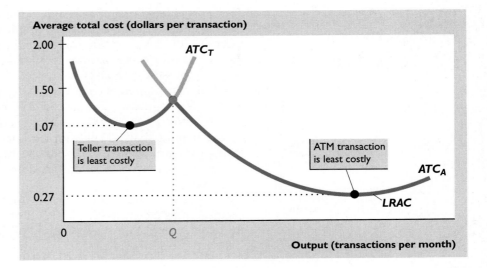

Study Guide **pp. 141–143**

Practice Online **9.4**

**4** **Derive and explain a firm's long-run average cost curve.**

**TABLE 1**

| Labor (students per day) | Output with 1 field | Output with 2 fields |
|---|---|---|
| | (pineapples per day) | |
| 0 | 0 | 0 |
| 1 | 100 | 220 |
| 2 | 220 | 460 |
| 3 | 300 | 620 |
| 4 | 360 | 740 |
| 5 | 400 | 820 |
| 6 | 420 | 860 |
| 7 | 430 | 880 |

**TABLE 2**

| TP (1 field) | ATC (1 field) | TP (2 fields) | ATC (2 fields) |
|---|---|---|---|
| 100 | 3.00 | 220 | 2.27 |
| 220 | 1.82 | 460 | 1.30 |
| 300 | 1.67 | 620 | 1.13 |
| 360 | 1.67 | 740 | 1.08 |
| 400 | 1.75 | 820 | 1.10 |
| 420 | 1.90 | 860 | 1.16 |
| 430 | 2.09 | 880 | 1.25 |

**FIGURE 1**

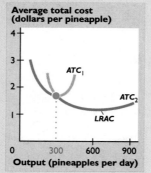

Average total cost (dollars per pineapple)

$ATC_1$

$ATC_2$

LRAC

Output (pineapples per day)

## Practice Problem 9.4

Tom grows pineapples. He leases a farmer's field for $120 a day and capital for $80 a day. He hires students at $100 a day. Suppose that Tom now leases two fields for $240 a day and twice as much capital for $160 a day. Tom discovers that his output is the numbers in the third column of Table 1. The numbers in the second column are his output with 1 field and the original amount of capital.

a. Find Tom's average total cost curve schedule when he operates with two fields.

b. Make a graph of Tom's average total cost curves using 1 field and 2 fields, and show on the graph Tom's long-run average cost curve.

c. Over what output range will Tom operate with 1 field and at what output rate will he operate with 2 fields?

d. What happens to Tom's average total cost curve if he farms 2 fields and doubles his capital?

e. Does Tom experience economies of scale or diseconomies of scale?

## Exercise 9.4

Lizzie hires students at $50 a day to paint houses. She leases equipment that costs her $100 a day. Suppose that Lizzie doubles the number of students she hires and doubles the amount of equipment that she leases. If Lizzie experiences diseconomies of scale, explain

a. What has happened to her average total cost curve.

b. What might be the source of those diseconomies of scale.

## Solution to Practice Problem 9.4

a. Total cost is fixed cost of $400 a day plus $100 a day for each student hired. Average total cost is the total cost divided by output. The "$ATC$ (2 fields)" column of Table 2 shows Tom's average total cost schedule.

b. Figure 1 shows Tom's average total cost curves using 1 field as $ATC_1$. This curve graphs the data on $ATC$ and total product in Table 3 on p. 310. Using 2 fields, the average total cost curve is $ATC_2$. Tom's long-run average cost curve is the lower segments of these two $ATC$ curves, highlighted in Figure 1.

c. If Tom produces up to 300 pineapples a day, he will operate with 1 field. If he produces more than 300 pineapples a day, he will operate with 2 fields.

d. When Tom farms 2 fields and doubles his capital, average total cost increases at low outputs (up to 300 a day) and decreases at high outputs (greater than 300 a day).

e. Tom experiences economies of scale up to an output of 740 pineapples a day, because as he increases his plant and produces up to 740 pineapples a day, the average total cost of picking and packing a pineapple decreases.

# CHAPTER CHECKPOINT

## Key Points

**1** **Explain how economists measure a firm's cost of production and profit.**

- Firms seek to maximize economic profit, which is total revenue minus total cost.
- Total cost equals opportunity cost—the sum of explicit costs plus implicit costs and includes normal profit.

**2** **Explain the relationship between a firm's output and labor employed in the short run.**

- In the short run, the firm can change the output it produces by changing labor only.
- A total product curve shows the limits to the output that the firm can produce with a given quantity of capital and different quantities of labor.
- As the quantity of labor increases, the marginal product of labor increases initially but eventually decreases—the law of decreasing returns.

**3** **Explain the relationship between a firm's output and costs in the short run.**

- As total product increases, total fixed cost is constant, and total variable cost and total cost increase.
- As total product increases, average fixed cost decreases and average variable cost, average total cost, and marginal cost decrease at small outputs and increase at large outputs. Their curves are U-shaped.

**4** **Derive and explain a firm's long-run average cost curve.**

- In the long run, the firm can change the size of its plant.
- Long-run cost is the cost of production when all inputs have been adjusted to produce at the lowest attainable cost.
- The long-run average cost curve traces out the lowest attainable average total cost at each output when both capital and labor inputs can be varied.
- The long-run average cost curve slopes downward with economies of scale and upward with diseconomies of scale.

## Key Terms

Average fixed cost, 231
Average product, 226
Average total cost, 231
Average variable cost, 231
Constant returns to scale, 238
Decreasing marginal returns, 224
Diseconomies of scale, 238
Economic depreciation, 219

Economic profit, 219
Economies of scale, 237
Explicit cost, 219
Implicit cost, 219
Increasing marginal returns, 224
Law of decreasing returns, 226
Long run, 222
Long-run average cost curve, 238

Marginal cost, 230
Marginal product, 224
Normal profit, 219
Short run, 222
Total cost, 229
Total fixed cost, 229
Total product, 223
Total variable cost, 229

## Exercises

1. Joe runs a shoeshine stand at the airport. With no skills and no job experience, Joe has no alternative employment. The other shoeshine stand operators that Joe knows earn $10,000 a year. Joe pays the airport $2,000 a year for the space he uses, and his total revenue from shining shoes is $15,000 a year. He spent $1,000 on a chair, polish, and brushes and paid for these items using his credit card. The interest on his credit card balance is 20 percent a year. At the end of the year, Joe was offered $500 for his business and all its equipment. Calculate Joe's
   a. Explicit costs.
   b. Implicit costs.
   c. Economic profit.

2. Sonya used to sell real estate and earn $25,000 a year, but she now sells greeting cards. Normal profit for the retailers of greeting cards is $14,000. Over the past year, Sonya bought $10,000 worth of cards from manufacturers of cards. She sold these cards for $58,000. Sonya rents a shop for $5,000 a year and spends $1,000 on utilities and office expenses. Sonya owns a cash register, which she bought for $2,000 with her savings account. Her bank pays 3 percent a year on savings accounts. At the end of the year, Sonya was offered $1,600 for her cash register. Calculate Sonya's
   a. Explicit costs.
   b. Implicit costs.
   c. Economic profit.

**TABLE I**

| Labor (workers per day) | Total product (body boards per day) |
|---|---|
| 0 | 0 |
| 1 | 20 |
| 2 | 44 |
| 3 | 60 |
| 4 | 72 |
| 5 | 80 |
| 6 | 84 |
| 7 | 86 |

3. Len's body board factory rents equipment for shaping boards and hires students. Table 1 sets out Len's total product schedule.
   a. Construct Len's marginal product and average product schedules.
   b. Over what range of workers do marginal returns increase?
   c. After how many workers employed do marginal returns decrease?

4. Yolanda runs a bullfrog farm in Yuma, Arizona. When Yolanda employed one person, she produced 1,000 bullfrogs a week. When she hired a second worker, her total product doubled. Her total product doubled again when she hired a third worker. When she hired a fourth worker, her total product increased, but by only 1,000 bullfrogs.
   a. Construct Yolanda's marginal product and average product schedules.
   b. Over what range of workers do marginal returns increase?
   c. After how many workers employed do marginal returns decrease?

5. Len, in exercise 3, pays $300 a week for equipment and $1,000 a week to each student he hires. Given his total product schedule in Table 1,
   a. Construct Len's total variable cost and total cost schedules.
   b. Calculate total cost minus total variable cost at each output rate. What does this quantity equal? Why?
   c. Construct the average fixed cost, average variable cost, and average total cost schedules.
   d. Construct the marginal cost schedule.
   e. Calculate the output at which Len's average total cost is a minimum.
   f. Calculate the output at which Len's average variable cost is a minimum.
   g. Explain why the output at which average variable cost is a minimum is smaller than the output at which average total cost is a minimum.

6. Yolanda, in exercise 4, pays $1,000 a week for equipment and $500 a week to each worker she hires. Given her description of how her total product changes as she hires more labor,
   a. Construct Yolanda's total variable cost and total cost schedules.
   b. Calculate total cost minus total variable cost at each output rate. What does this quantity equal? Why?
   c. Construct the average fixed cost, average variable cost, and average total cost schedules.
   d. Construct the marginal cost schedule.
   e. Calculate the output at which Yolanda's average total cost is a minimum.
   f. Calculate the output at which Yolanda's average variable cost is a minimum.
   g. Explain why the output at which average total cost is a minimum is larger than the output at which average variable cost is a minimum.

7. Table 2 shows the costs incurred at Pete's peanut farm. Complete the table.

**TABLE 2**

| L | TP | TVC | TC | AFC | AVC | ATC | MC |
|---|-----|-----|-----|-----|-----|-----|-----|
| 0 | 0 | 0 | 100 | | | | |
| 1 | 10 | 35 | | | | | |
| 2 | 24 | 70 | | | | | |
| 3 | 38 | 105 | | | | | |
| 4 | 44 | 140 | | | | | |
| 5 | 47 | 175 | | | | | |

8. Table 3 shows some of the costs incurred at Bill's Bakery. Calculate the values of A, B, C, D, and E. Show your work.

**TABLE 3**

| L | TP | TVC | TC | AFC | AVC | ATC | MC |
|---|-----|-----|-----|-----|-----|-----|-----|
| 1 | 100 | 350 | 850 | C | 3.50 | D | 2.50 |
| 2 | 240 | 700 | B | 2.08 | 2.92 | 5.00 | E |
| 3 | 380 | A | 1,550 | 1.32 | 2.76 | 4.08 | 5.83 |
| 4 | 440 | 1,400 | 1,900 | 1.14 | 3.18 | 4.32 | 11.67 |
| 5 | 470 | 1,750 | 2,250 | 1.06 | 3.72 | 4.79 | |

9. Explain what the long-run average cost curve shows and how it is derived.

10. Can a firm that produces at the lowest possible average cost lower its average cost further by increasing production? Explain using the long-run average cost curve.

11. Explain the sources of economies of scale and diseconomies of scale and illustrate these two situations in a graph.

12. Provide examples of industries in which you think economies of scale exist and explain why you think they are present in these industries.

13. Provide examples of industries in which you think diseconomies of scale exist and explain why you think they are present in these industries.

## Critical Thinking

14. MCI, a global communications company, spent billions of dollars laying fiber-optic cables under the oceans. Is the cost of this communications network a short-run cost or a long-run cost? Is it a sunk cost or an opportunity cost? Explain your answer.

15. Study *Eye on the U.S. Economy* on p. 313 and then answer the following questions:
    a. What is the main difference, from a cost point of view, between human tellers and ATMs?
    b. Why do you think ATMs have become so popular?
    c. Would it ever make sense for a bank in the United States not to use ATMs?
    d. Do you think that ATMs are as common in China as they are in the United States? Explain why or why not.

16. Suppose the government put a tax on banks for each ATM transaction but did not put a similar tax on human teller transactions.
    a. How would the tax affect a bank's costs and cost curves?
    b. Would the tax change the number of ATMs and the number of tellers that banks hire? If so, explain how. If not, why not?

## Practice Online   Web Exercises

**Use the links on your Foundations Web site to work the following exercises.**

17. Visit the Bullfrogs and check out the prices of bullfrogs of various sizes. Assume that prices reflect the cost of production and answer the following questions:
    a. Does farming bullfrogs appear to display increasing marginal cost? Explain why or why not.
    b. Does farming bullfrogs appear to display decreasing marginal returns? Explain why or why not.
    c. Why might someone pay $20 for a large (6 inches plus) bullfrog when the price of a smaller (4 to 6 inch) bullfrog is only $12?

18. Visit the Federal Reserve Bank of St. Louis and read the article "Do Economies of Scale Exist in the Banking Industry?"
    a. What is the survivor technique for identifying whether the firms in an industry experience economies of scale?
    b. Why does the survivor technique work?
    c. What does the survivor technique imply about economies of scale in the banking industry?
    d. Sketch the long-run average cost curve of a bank that is consistent with what the survivor technique implies about economies of scale.

19. Obtain information about the cost of producing pumpkins.
    a. List all the costs referred to on the Web site.
    b. For each item, classify it as a fixed cost, a variable cost, or perhaps a combination of the two.
    c. Make some assumptions and sketch the average cost curves (*AFC*, *AVC*, and *ATC*) and the marginal cost curve.
    d. Identify the minimum points of the *AVC* and *ATC* curves in your graph.

# Perfect Competition

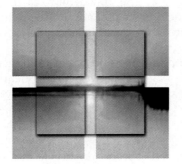

Some markets are highly competitive, and firms find it hard to earn profits. Other markets appear to be almost free from competition, and firms earn large profits. Some markets are dominated by fierce advertising campaigns in which each firm seeks to persuade buyers that it has the best products. And some markets display a warlike character. In this chapter, we study the first of the above market types, known as perfect competition.

What you learned in the previous chapter gets its first big workout in this chapter. If your understanding of a firm's cost curves is still a bit shaky, check back to Chapter 9 when you need to.

You're going to see how the principles of rational choice, balancing costs and benefits at the margin, and responding to incentives enable us to understand and predict the decisions that firms make in competitive markets.

## MARKET TYPES

The four market types are

- Perfect competition
- Monopoly
- Monopolistic competition
- Oligopoly

### ■ Perfect Competition

**Perfect competition**
A market in which there are many firms, each selling an identical product; many buyers; no restrictions on the entry of new firms into the industry; no advantage to established firms; and buyers and sellers are well informed about prices.

**Perfect competition** exists when

- Many firms sell an identical product to many buyers.
- There are no restrictions on entry into (or exit from) the market.
- Established firms have no advantage over new firms.
- Sellers and buyers are well informed about prices.

These conditions that define perfect competition arise when the market demand for the product is large relative to the output of a single producer. And this situation arises when economies of scale are absent so the efficient scale of each firm is small. But a large market and the absence of economies of scale are not sufficient to create perfect competition. In addition, each firm must produce a good or service that has no characteristics that are unique to that firm so that consumers don't care from which firm they buy. Firms in perfect competition all look the same to the buyer.

Wheat farming, fishing, wood pulping and paper milling, the manufacture of paper cups and plastic shopping bags, lawn service, dry cleaning, and the provision of laundry services are all examples of highly competitive industries.

### ■ Other Market Types

**Monopoly**
A market for a good or service that has no close substitutes and in which there is one supplier that is protected from competition by a barrier preventing the entry of new firms.

**Monopoly** arises when one firm sells a good or service that has no close substitutes and a barrier blocks the entry of new firms. In some places, the phone, gas, electricity, and water suppliers are local monopolies—monopolies that are restricted to a given location. For many years, a global firm called DeBeers had a near international monopoly in diamonds.

**Monopolistic competition**
A market in which a large number of firms compete by making similar but slightly different products.

**Monopolistic competition** arises when a large number of firms compete by making similar but slightly different products. Each firm is the sole producer of the particular version of the good in question. For example, in the market for running shoes, Nike, Reebok, Fila, Asics, New Balance, and many others make their own versions of the perfect shoe. The term "monopolistic competition" reminds us that each firm has a monopoly on a particular brand of shoe but the firms compete with each other.

**Oligopoly**
A market in which a small number of firms compete.

**Oligopoly** arises when a small number of firms compete. Airplane manufacture is an example of oligopoly. Oligopolies might produce almost identical products, such as Kodak and Fuji film. Or they might produce differentiated products such as the colas produced by Coke and Pepsi.

We study perfect competition in this chapter, monopoly in Chapter 11, and monopolistic competition and oligopoly in Chapter 12.

## 10.1 A FIRM'S PROFIT-MAXIMIZING CHOICES

A firm's objective is to maximize *economic profit*, which is equal to *total revenue* minus the *total cost* of production. *Normal profit*, the return that the firm's entrepreneur can obtain in the best alternative business, is part of the firm's cost.

In the short run, a firm achieves its objective by deciding the quantity to produce. This quantity influences the firm's total revenue, total cost, and economic profit. In the long run, a firm achieves its objective by deciding whether to enter or exit a market.

These are the key decisions that a firm in perfect competition makes. Such a firm does *not* choose the price at which to sell its output. The firm in perfect competition is a **price taker**—it cannot influence the price of its product.

**Price taker**
A firm that cannot influence the price of the good or service that it produces.

### ■ Price Taker

To see why a firm in perfect competition is a price taker, imagine that you are a wheat farmer in Kansas. You have a thousand acres under cultivation—which sounds like a lot. But then you go on a drive through Colorado, Oklahoma, Texas, and back up to Nebraska and the Dakotas. You find unbroken stretches of wheat covering millions of acres. And you know that there are similar vistas in Canada, Argentina, Australia, and Ukraine. Your thousand acres are a drop in the ocean. Nothing makes your wheat any better than any other farmer's, and all the buyers of wheat know the price they must pay. If the going price of wheat is $4 a bushel, you are stuck with that price. You can't get a higher price than $4, and you have no incentive to offer it for less than $4 because you can sell your entire output at that price.

The producers of most agricultural products are price takers. We'll illustrate perfect competition with another agriculture example: the market for maple syrup. The next time you pour syrup on your pancakes, think about the competitive market that gets this product from the sap of the maple tree to your table!

Dave's Maple Syrup is one of the more than 10,000 similar firms in the maple syrup market of North America. Dave is a price taker. Like the Kansas wheat farmer, he can sell any quantity he chooses at the going price but none above that price. Dave faces a *perfectly elastic* demand. The demand for Dave's syrup is perfectly elastic because syrup from Casper Sugar Shack and all the other maple farms in the United States and Canada are *perfect substitutes* for Dave's syrup.

We'll explore Dave's decisions and their implications for the way a competitive market works. We begin by defining some revenue concepts.

*Wheat farmers and maple syrup farmers are price takers.*

### ■ Revenue Concepts

In perfect competition, market demand and market supply determine the price. A firm's *total revenue* equals this given price multiplied by the quantity sold. A firm's **marginal revenue** is the change in total revenue that results from a one-unit increase in the quantity sold. In perfect competition, marginal revenue equals price. The reason is that the firm can sell any quantity it chooses at the going market price. So if the firm sells one more unit, it sells it for the market price and total revenue increases by that amount. But this increase in total revenue is marginal revenue. So marginal revenue equals price.

The table in Figure 10.1 illustrates the equality of marginal revenue and price. The price of syrup is $8 a can. Total revenue is equal to the price multiplied by the quantity sold. So if Dave sells 10 cans, his total revenue is $10 \times \$8 = \$80$. If the

**Marginal revenue**
The change in total revenue that results from a one-unit increase in the quantity sold.

quantity sold increases from 10 cans to 11 cans, total revenue increases from $80 to $88, so marginal revenue is $8 a can, the same as the price.

Figure 10.1 illustrates price determination and revenue in the perfectly competitive market. Market demand and market supply in part (a) determine the market price. Dave is a price taker, so he sells his syrup for the market price. The demand curve for Dave's syrup is the horizontal line at the market price in part (b). Because price equals marginal revenue, the demand curve for Dave's syrup is Dave's marginal revenue curve (*MR*). The total revenue curve (*TR*), in part (c), shows the total revenue at each quantity sold. Because he sells each can for the market price, the total revenue curve is an upward-sloping straight line.

## ■ Profit-Maximizing Output

As output increases, total revenue increases. But total cost also increases. And because of *decreasing marginal returns* (see pp. 298–300), total cost eventually increases faster than total revenue. There is one output level that maximizes economic profit, and a perfectly competitive firm chooses this output level.

---

### ▓ FIGURE 10.1

Demand, Price, and Revenue in Perfect Competition

**Practice Online**

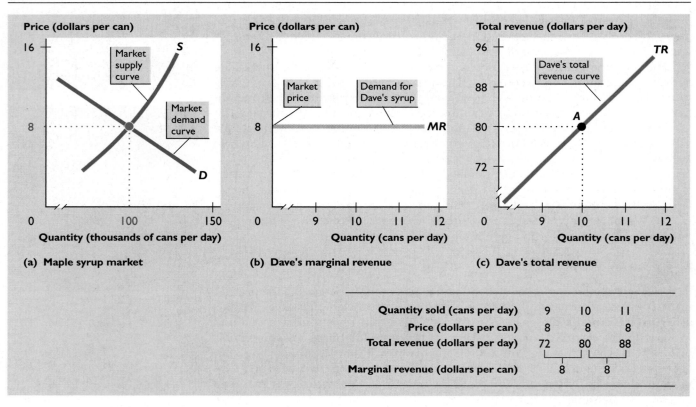

| Quantity sold (cans per day) | 9 | 10 | 11 |
|---|---|---|---|
| Price (dollars per can) | 8 | 8 | 8 |
| Total revenue (dollars per day) | 72 | 80 | 88 |
| Marginal revenue (dollars per can) | 8 | 8 | |

Part (a) shows the market for maple syrup. The market price is $8 a can. The table calculates total revenue and marginal revenue.

Part (b) shows the demand curve for Dave's syrup, which is Dave's marginal revenue curve (*MR*).

Part (c) shows Dave's total revenue curve (*TR*). Point A corresponds to the second column of the table.

One way to find the profit-maximizing output is to use a firm's total revenue and total cost curves. Profit is maximized at the output level at which total revenue exceeds total cost by the largest amount. Figure 10.2 shows how to do this for Dave's Maple Syrup.

The table lists Dave's total revenue, total cost, and economic profit at different output levels. Figure 10.2(a) shows the total revenue and total cost curves. These curves are graphs of the numbers shown in the first three columns of the table. The total revenue curve (*TR*) is the same as that in Figure 10.1(c). The total cost curve (*TC*) is similar to the one that you met in Chapter 9 (p. 230). Figure 10.2(b) is an economic profit curve.

Dave makes an economic profit on outputs between 4 and 13 cans a day. At outputs of less than 4 cans a day and more than 13 cans a day, he incurs an economic loss. At outputs of 4 cans and 13 cans a day, total cost equals total revenue and Dave's economic profit is zero—Dave's *break-even points*.

The profit curve is at its highest when the vertical distance between the *TR* and *TC* curves is greatest. In this example, profit maximization occurs at an output of 10 cans a day. At this output, Dave's economic profit is $29 a day.

*Economic Profit =*
*TR − TC*

---

**FIGURE 10.2**

Total Revenue, Total Cost, and Economic Profit

<u>**Practice Online**</u>

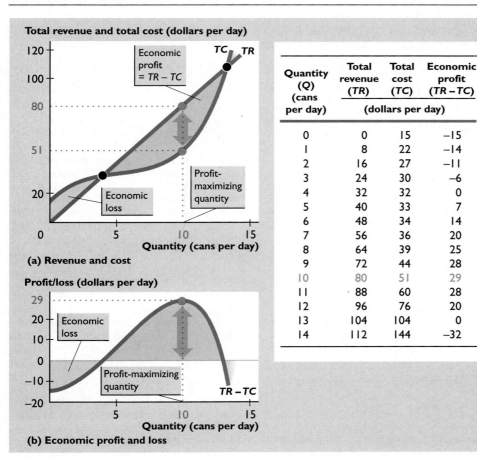

| Quantity (Q) (cans per day) | Total revenue (TR) | Total cost (TC) | Economic profit (TR − TC) |
|---|---|---|---|
| | (dollars per day) | | |
| 0 | 0 | 15 | −15 |
| 1 | 8 | 22 | −14 |
| 2 | 16 | 27 | −11 |
| 3 | 24 | 30 | −6 |
| 4 | 32 | 32 | 0 |
| 5 | 40 | 33 | 7 |
| 6 | 48 | 34 | 14 |
| 7 | 56 | 36 | 20 |
| 8 | 64 | 39 | 25 |
| 9 | 72 | 44 | 28 |
| 10 | 80 | 51 | 29 |
| 11 | 88 | 60 | 28 |
| 12 | 96 | 76 | 20 |
| 13 | 104 | 104 | 0 |
| 14 | 112 | 144 | −32 |

In part (a), economic profit is the vertical distance between the total cost and total revenue curves. Dave's maximum economic profit is $29 a day ($80 − $51) when output is 10 cans a day.

In part (b), economic profit is the height of the profit curve.

### ■ Marginal Analysis and the Supply Decision

Another way to find the profit-maximizing output is to use *marginal analysis*, which compares marginal revenue, *MR*, with marginal cost, *MC*. As output increases, marginal revenue is constant but marginal cost eventually increases.

If marginal revenue exceeds marginal cost (if *MR > MC*), then the extra revenue from selling one more unit exceeds the extra cost incurred to produce it. Economic profit increases if output *increases*. If marginal revenue is less than marginal cost (if *MR < MC*), then the extra revenue from selling one more unit is less than the extra cost incurred to produce it. Economic profit increases if output *decreases*. If marginal revenue equals marginal cost (if *MR = MC*), economic profit is maximized. The rule *MR = MC* is a prime example of marginal analysis.

Figure 10.3 illustrates these propositions. The table records Dave's marginal revenue and marginal cost. If Dave increases output from 9 cans to 10 cans a day, marginal revenue is $8 and marginal cost is $7. Because marginal revenue exceeds marginal cost, economic profit increases. The last column of the table shows that economic profit increases from $28 to $29. The blue area in the figure shows this economic profit from the tenth can.

If Dave increases output from 10 cans to 11 cans a day, marginal revenue is still $8 but marginal cost is $9. Because marginal revenue is less than marginal cost, economic profit decreases. The last column of the table shows that economic profit decreases from $29 to $28. The red area in the figure shows this economic loss from the eleventh can.

Dave maximizes economic profit by producing 10 cans a day, the quantity at which marginal revenue equals marginal cost.

### ■ FIGURE 10.3
Profit-Maximizing Output

**Practice Online**

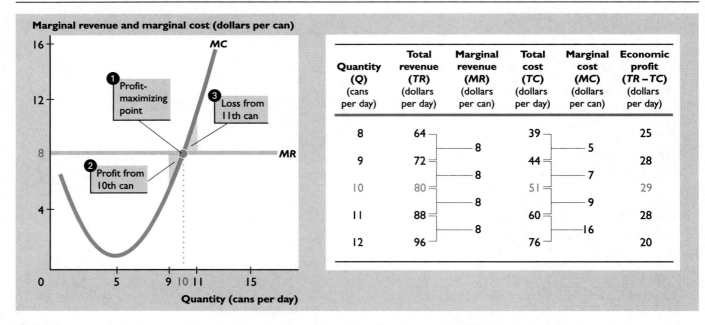

| Quantity (Q) (cans per day) | Total revenue (TR) (dollars per day) | Marginal revenue (MR) (dollars per can) | Total cost (TC) (dollars per day) | Marginal cost (MC) (dollars per can) | Economic profit (TR – TC) (dollars per day) |
|---|---|---|---|---|---|
| 8 | 64 |  | 39 |  | 25 |
|  |  | 8 |  | 5 |  |
| 9 | 72 |  | 44 |  | 28 |
|  |  | 8 |  | 7 |  |
| 10 | 80 |  | 51 |  | 29 |
|  |  | 8 |  | 9 |  |
| 11 | 88 |  | 60 |  | 28 |
|  |  | 8 |  | 16 |  |
| 12 | 96 |  | 76 |  | 20 |

**①** Profit is maximized when marginal revenue equals marginal cost at 10 cans a day. **②** If output increases from 9 to 10 cans a day, marginal cost is $7, which is less than the marginal revenue of $8, and profit increases. **③** If output increases from 10 to 11 cans a day, marginal cost is $9, which exceeds the marginal revenue of $8, and profit decreases.

In the example that we've just worked through, Dave's profit-maximizing output is 10 cans a day. This quantity is Dave's *quantity supplied* at a price of $8 a can. If the price were higher than $8 a can, he would increase production. If the price were lower than $8 a can, he would decrease production. These profit-maximizing responses to different prices are the foundation of the law of supply: *Other things remaining the same, the higher the price of a good, the greater is the quantity supplied of that good.*

## ■ Exit and Temporary Shutdown Decisions

Sometimes, the price falls so low that a firm cannot cover its costs. What does the firm do in such a situation? The answer depends on whether the firm expects the low price to be permanent or temporary.

If a firm is incurring an economic loss that it believes is permanent and sees no prospect of ending, the firm exits the market. We'll study the consequences of this action later in this chapter where we look at the long run (pp. 260–261).

If a firm is incurring an economic loss that it believes is temporary, it will remain in the market, and it might produce some output or temporarily shut down. To decide whether to produce or to shut down, the firm compares the loss it would incur in the two situations.

If the firm shuts down, it incurs an economic loss equal to total fixed cost. If the firm produces some output, it incurs an economic loss equal to total fixed cost *plus* total variable cost *minus* total revenue. If total revenue exceeds total variable cost, the firm's economic loss is less than total fixed cost. So it pays the firm to produce. But if total revenue were less than total variable cost, the firm's economic loss would exceed total fixed cost. So the firm would shut down temporarily. Total fixed cost is the largest economic loss that the firm will incur.

The firm's economic loss equals total fixed cost when price equals average variable cost. So the firm produces if price exceeds average variable cost and shuts down if average variable cost exceeds price.

## ■ The Firm's Short-Run Supply Curve

A perfectly competitive firm's short-run supply curve shows how the firm's profit-maximizing output varies as the price varies, other things remaining the same. This supply curve is based on the marginal analysis and shutdown decision that we've just explored.

Figure 10.4 derives Dave's supply curve. Part (a) shows the marginal cost and average variable cost curves, and part (b) shows the supply curve. There is a direct link between the marginal cost and average variable cost curves and the supply curve. Let's see what that link is.

If the price is above minimum average variable cost, Dave maximizes profit by producing the output at which marginal cost equals price. We can determine the quantity produced at each price from the marginal cost curve. At a price of $8 a can, the marginal revenue curve is $MR_1$ and Dave maximizes profit by producing 10 cans a day. If the price rises to $12 a can, the marginal revenue curve is $MR_2$ and Dave increases production to 11 cans a day.

The firm shuts down if the price falls below minimum average variable cost. The **shutdown point** is the output and price at which the firm just covers its total variable cost. In Figure 10.4(a), if the price is $3 a can, the marginal revenue curve is $MR_0$, and the profit-maximizing output is 7 cans a day at the shutdown point.

**Shutdown point**
The output and price at which the firm just covers its total variable cost.

But both price and average variable cost equal $3 a can, so total revenue equals total variable cost and Dave incurs an economic loss equal to total fixed cost. At a price below $3 a can, if Dave produces any positive quantity, average *variable* cost exceeds price and the firm's loss exceeds total fixed cost. So at a price below $3 a can, Dave shuts down and produces nothing.

Dave's short-run supply curve, shown in Figure 10.4(b), has two separate parts: First, at prices that exceed minimum average variable cost, the supply curve is the same as the marginal cost curve above the shutdown point (*T*). Second, at prices below minimum average variable cost, Dave shuts down and produces nothing. His supply curve runs along the vertical axis. At a price of $3 a can, Dave is indifferent between shutting down and producing 7 cans a day. Either way, he incurs a loss of $15 a day, which equals his total fixed cost.

So far, we have studied one firm in isolation. We have seen that the firm's profit-maximizing actions depend on the price, which the firm takes as given. In the next section, you'll learn how market supply is determined.

## FIGURE 10.4
Dave's Supply Curve

**Practice Online**

Part (a) shows that at $8 a can, Dave produces 10 cans a day; at $12 a can, he produces 11 cans a day; and at $3 a can, he produces either 7 cans a day or nothing. At any price below $3 a can, Dave produces nothing. The minimum average variable cost is the shutdown point.

Part (b) shows Dave's supply curve, which is made up of the marginal cost curve (part a) at all points *above* the shutdown point *T* (minimum average variable cost) and the vertical axis at all prices *below* the shutdown point.

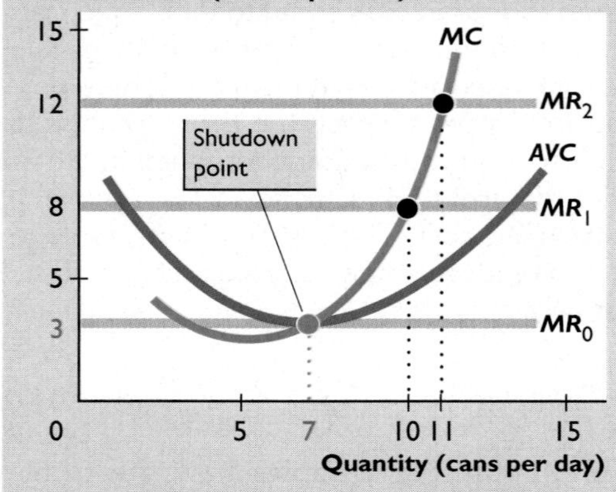

(a) Marginal cost and average variable cost

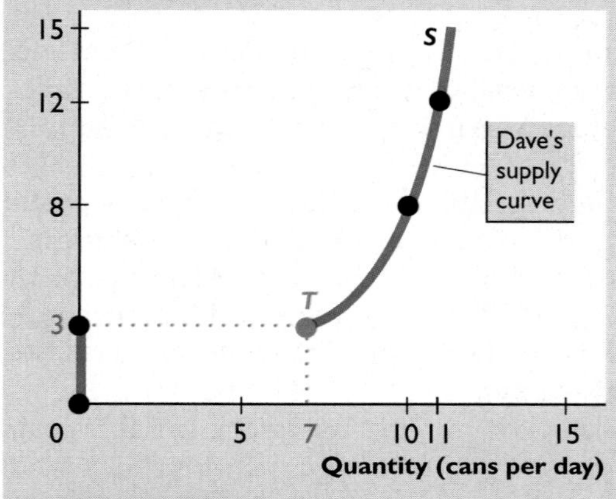

(b) Dave's supply curve

# CHECKPOINT 10.1

**1** Explain a perfectly competitive firm's profit-maximizing choices and derive its supply curve.

**Study Guide pp. 150–154**

**Practice Online 10.1**

## Practice Problems 10.1

1. Sarah's Salmon Farm produces 1,000 fish a week. The marginal cost is $30 a fish, average variable cost is $20 a fish, and the market price is $25 a fish. Is Sarah maximizing profit? Explain why or why not. If Sarah is not maximizing profit, to do so, will she increase or decrease the number of fish she produces in a week?

2. Trout farming is a perfectly competitive industry, and all trout farms have the same cost curves. The market price is $25 a fish. To maximize profit, each farm produces 200 fish a week. Average total cost is $20 a fish, and average variable cost is $15 a fish. Minimum average variable cost is $12 a fish.
   a. If the price falls to $20 a fish, will trout farms continue to produce 200 fish a week? Explain why or why not.
   b. If the price falls to $12 a fish, what will the trout farmer do?
   c. What is one point on the trout farm's supply curve?

## Exercise 10.1

Paula is an asparagus farmer, and the world asparagus market is perfectly competitive. The market price is $15 a box. Paula sells 800 boxes a week, and her marginal cost is $18 a box.
a. Calculate Paula's total revenue.
b. Calculate Paula's marginal revenue.
c. Is Paula maximizing profit? Explain your answer.
d. The price falls to $12 a box, and Paula cuts her output to 500 boxes a week. Her average variable cost and marginal cost fall to $12 a box. Is Paula maximizing profit? Is she earning an economic profit or incurring an economic loss?
e. What is one point on Paula's supply curve?

## Solutions to Practice Problems 10.1

1. Profit is maximized when marginal cost equals marginal revenue. In perfect competition, marginal revenue equals the market price and is $25 a fish. Because marginal cost exceeds marginal revenue, Sarah is not maximizing profit. To maximize profit, she will decrease her output until marginal cost falls to $25 a fish (Figure 1).

2a. The farm will produce fewer than 200 fish a week. The marginal cost increases as the farm produces more fish. So to reduce its marginal cost from $25 to $20, the farm cuts production.

2b. If the price falls to $12 a fish, farms cut production to the quantity where marginal cost equals $12. But because $12 is minimum average variable cost, this price puts farms at the shutdown point. Farms will be indifferent between producing the profit-maximizing output and producing nothing. Either way, they incur an economic loss equal to total fixed cost.

2c. At $25 a fish, the quantity supplied is 200 fish; at $12 a fish, the quantity supplied might be zero; at a price below $12 a fish, the quantity supplied is zero.

**FIGURE 1**

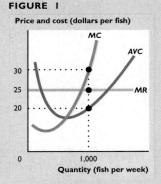

## 10.2 OUTPUT, PRICE, AND PROFIT IN THE SHORT RUN

To determine the price and quantity in a perfectly competitive market, we need to know how market demand and supply interact. We begin by studying a perfectly competitive market in the short run when the number of firms is fixed.

### ■ Market Supply in the Short Run

The market supply curve in the short run shows the quantity supplied at each price by a fixed number of firms. The quantity supplied at a given price is the sum of the quantities supplied by all firms at that price.

Figure 10.5 shows the supply curve for the competitive syrup market. In this example, the market consists of 10,000 firms exactly like Dave's Maple Syrup. The table shows how the market supply schedule is constructed. At prices below $3, every firm in the market shuts down; the quantity supplied is zero. At a price of $3, each firm is indifferent between shutting down and producing nothing or operating and producing 7 cans a day. The quantity supplied by each firm is *either* 0 or 7 cans, and the quantity supplied in the market is *between* 0 (all firms shut down) and 70,000 (all firms produce 7 cans a day each). At prices above $3, we sum the quantities supplied by the 10,000 firms, so the quantity supplied in the market is 10,000 times the quantity supplied by one firm.

At prices below $3, the market supply curve runs along the price axis. Supply is perfectly inelastic. At a price of $3, the market supply curve is horizontal. Supply is perfectly elastic. At prices above $3, the supply curve is upward sloping.

---

■ **FIGURE 10.5**

The Market Supply Curve

**Practice Online**

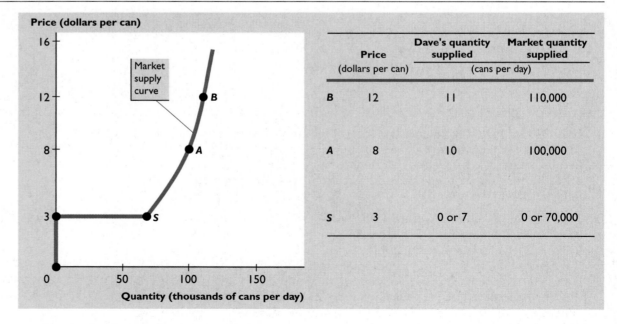

| | Price | Dave's quantity supplied | Market quantity supplied |
|---|---|---|---|
| | (dollars per can) | (cans per day) | |
| B | 12 | 11 | 110,000 |
| A | 8 | 10 | 100,000 |
| S | 3 | 0 or 7 | 0 or 70,000 |

A market with 10,000 identical firms has a supply schedule similar to that of the individual firm, but the quantity supplied is 10,000 times greater. At the shutdown price of $3 a can, each firm produces either 0 or 7 cans a day, but the market supply curve is perfectly elastic at that price.

## ■ Short-Run Equilibrium in Good Times

Market demand and market supply determine the price and quantity bought and sold. Figure 10.6(a) shows a short-run equilibrium in the syrup market. The supply curve $S$ is the same as that in Figure 10.5.

If the demand curve $D_1$ shows market demand, the equilibrium price is $8 a can. Although market demand and market supply determine this price, each firm takes the price as given and produces its profit-maximizing output, which is 10 cans a day. Because the market has 10,000 firms, market output is 100,000 cans a day.

Figure 10.6(b) shows the situation that Dave faces. The price is $8 a can, so Dave's marginal revenue is constant at $8 a can. Dave maximizes profit by producing 10 cans a day.

Figure 10.6(b) also shows Dave's average total cost curve ($ATC$). Recall that average total cost is the cost per unit produced. It equals total cost divided by the quantity of output produced.

Here, when Dave produces 10 cans a day, his average total cost is $5.10 a can. So the price of $8 a can exceeds average total cost by $2.90 a can. This amount is Dave's economic profit per can.

If we multiply the economic profit per can of $2.90 by the number of cans, 10 a day, we arrive at Dave's economic profit, which is $29 a day.

The blue rectangle shows this economic profit. The height of that rectangle is the profit per can, $2.90, and the length is the quantity of cans, 10 a day, so the area of the rectangle (height × length) measures Dave's economic profit of $29 a day.

---

■ **FIGURE 10.6**
Economic Profit in the Short Run

**Practice Online**

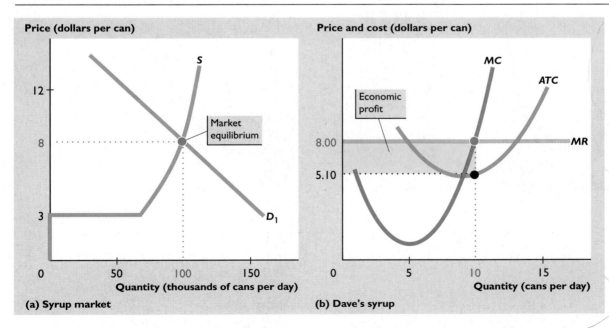

(a) Syrup market

(b) Dave's syrup

In part (a), with market demand curve $D_1$ and market supply curve $S$, the equilibrium market price is $8 a can.

In part (b), Dave's marginal revenue is $8 a can, so he produces 10 cans a day. At this quantity, price ($8) exceeds average total cost ($5.10), so Dave makes an economic profit shown by the blue rectangle.

## ■ Short-Run Equilibrium in Bad Times

In the short-run equilibrium that we've just examined, Dave is enjoying an economic profit. But such an outcome is not inevitable. Figure 10.7 shows the syrup market in a less happy state. The market demand curve is now $D_2$. The market still has 10,000 firms, and the costs of these firms are the same as before. So the market supply curve, $S$, is the same as before.

With the demand and supply curves shown in Figure 10.7(a), the equilibrium price of syrup is $3 a can and the equilibrium quantity is 70,000 cans a day.

Figure 10.7(b) shows the situation that Dave faces. The price is $3 a can, so Dave's marginal revenue is constant at $3 a can. Dave maximizes profit by producing 7 cans a day.

Figure 10.7(b) also shows Dave's average total cost curve (*ATC*), and you can see that when Dave produces 7 cans a day, his average total cost is $5.14 a can. So the price of $3 a can is less than average total cost by $2.14 a can. This amount is Dave's economic loss per can.

If we multiply the economic loss per can of $2.14 by the number of cans, 7 a day, we arrive at Dave's economic loss, which is $14.98 a day.

The red rectangle shows this economic loss. The height of that rectangle is the loss per can, $2.14, and the length is the quantity of cans, 7 a day, so the area of the rectangle measures Dave's economic loss of $14.98 a day.

---

■ **FIGURE 10.7**                                                    **Practice Online**
Economic Loss in the Short Run

---

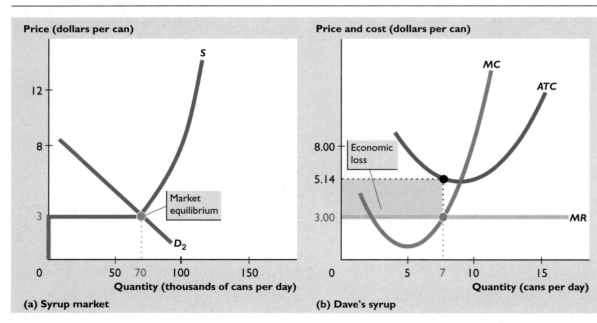

**(a) Syrup market**

**(b) Dave's syrup**

In part (a), with market demand curve $D_2$ and market supply curve $S$, the equilibrium market price is $3 a can.

In part (b), Dave's marginal revenue is $3 a can, so he produces 7 cans a day. At this quantity, price ($3) is less than average total cost ($5.14), so Dave incurs an economic loss shown by the red rectangle.

# CHECKPOINT 10.2

**2** Explain how output, price, and profit are determined in the short run.

Study Guide pp. 154–157

Practice Online 10.2

## Practice Problem 10.2

Tulip growing is a perfectly competitive industry, and all tulip growers have the same cost curves. The market price of tulips is $25 a bunch, and each grower maximizes profit by producing 2,000 bunches a week. The average total cost of producing tulips is $20 a bunch, and the average variable cost is $15 a bunch. Minimum average variable cost is $12 a bunch.
a. What is the economic profit that each grower is making in the short run?
b. What is the price at the grower's shutdown point?
c. What is each grower's profit at the shutdown point?

## Exercises 10.2

1. Tom's Tattoos is a tattooing business in a perfectly competitive market. The market price of a tattoo is $20. Table 1 shows Tom's total costs.
   a. How many tattoos an hour does Tom's Tattoos sell?
   b. What is Tom's Tattoos' economic profit in the short run?

2. In exercise 1, if the market price of a tattoo falls to $15,
   a. How many tattoos an hour does Tom's Tattoos sell?
   b. What is Tom's Tattoos' economic profit in the short run?

3. In exercise 1,
   a. At what market price will Tom's Tattoos shut down?
   b. At the shutdown point, what is Tom's Tattoos' economic loss?

TABLE 1

| Quantity (tattoos per hour) | Total cost (dollars per hour) |
|---|---|
| 0 | 30 |
| 1 | 50 |
| 2 | 65 |
| 3 | 75 |
| 4 | 90 |
| 5 | 110 |
| 6 | 140 |

## Solution to Practice Problem 10.2

a. The market price ($25) exceeds the average total cost ($20), so tulip growers are making an economic profit of $5 a bunch. Each grower produces 2,000 bunches a week, so each grower makes an economic profit of $10,000 a week (Figure 1).
b. The price at which a grower will shut down is equal to minimum average variable cost—$12 a bunch (Figure 1).
c. At the shutdown point, the grower incurs an economic loss equal to total fixed cost. $ATC = AFC + AVC$. When 2,000 bunches a week are grown, $ATC$ is $20 a bunch and $AVC$ is $15 a bunch, so $AFC$ is $5 a bunch. Total fixed cost equals $10,000 a week—$5 a bunch × 2,000 bunches a week. So at the shutdown point, the grower incurs an economic loss equal to $10,000 a week.

FIGURE 1

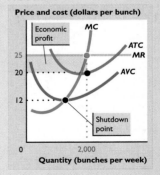

## 10.3 OUTPUT, PRICE, AND PROFIT IN THE LONG RUN

Neither good times nor bad times last forever in perfect competition. In the long run, a firm in perfect competition earns normal profit. It earns zero economic profit and incurs no economic loss.

Figure 10.8 shows the syrup market in a long-run equilibrium. The market demand curve is now $D_3$. The market still has 10,000 firms, and the costs of these firms are the same as before. So the market supply curve, $S$, is the same as before.

With the demand and supply curves shown in Figure 10.8(a), the equilibrium price of syrup is $5 a can and the equilibrium quantity is 90,000 cans a day.

Figure 10.8(b) shows the situation that Dave faces. The price is $5 a can, so Dave's marginal revenue is constant at $5 a can and Dave maximizes profit by producing 9 cans a day.

Figure 10.8(b) also shows Dave's average total cost curve ($ATC$), and you can see that when Dave produces 9 cans a day, his average total cost is $5 a can, which is also the minimum average total cost. That is, Dave can't produce syrup at an average total cost that is less than $5 a can no matter what his output is.

The price of $5 a can equals average total cost, so Dave has neither an economic profit nor an economic loss. He breaks even. But because his average total cost includes normal profit, Dave earns normal profit.

---

**■ FIGURE 10.8**
Long-run Equilibrium

**Practice Online**

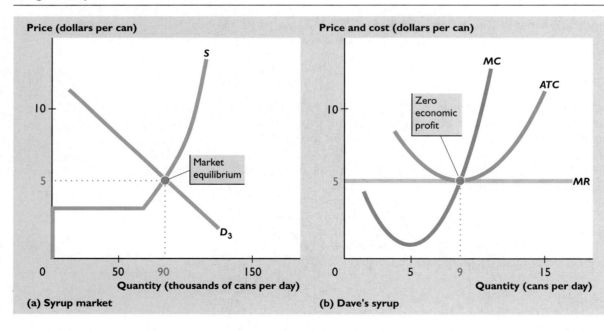

(a) Syrup market

(b) Dave's syrup

In part (a), with market demand curve $D_3$ and market supply curve $S$, the equilibrium market price is $5 a can.

In part (b), Dave's marginal revenue is $5 a can, so he produces 9 cans a day, where marginal cost equals marginal revenue. At this profit-maximizing quantity, price equals average total cost ($5), so Dave earns no economic profit. He earns normal profit.

## ■ Entry and Exit

In the short run, a perfectly competitive firm might make an economic profit (Figure 10.6) or incur an economic loss (Figure 10.7). But in the long run, a firm earns normal profit (Figure 10.8).

In the long run, firms respond to economic profit and economic loss by either entering or exiting a market. New firms enter a market in which the existing firms are making an economic profit. And existing firms exit a market in which they are incurring an economic loss. Temporary economic profit or temporary economic loss, like a win or loss at a casino, does not trigger entry and exit. But the prospect of persistent economic profit or loss does.

Entry and exit influence price, the quantity produced, and economic profit. The immediate effect of the decision to enter or exit is to shift the market supply curve. If more firms enter a market, supply increases and the market supply curve shifts rightward. If firms exit a market, supply decreases and the market supply curve shifts leftward.

Let's see what happens when new firms enter a market.

### The Effects of Entry

Figure 10.9 shows the effects of entry. Initially, the market is in long-run equilibrium. Demand is $D_0$, supply is $S_0$, the price is $5 a can, and the quantity is 90,000 cans a day. A surge in the popularity of syrup increases demand, and the demand curve shifts to $D_1$. The price rises to $8 a can, and the firms in the syrup market increase output to 100,000 cans a day and make an economic profit.

Times are good for syrup producers like Dave, so other potential syrup producers want some of the action. New firms begin to enter the market. As they do so, supply increases and the market supply curve shifts rightward to $S_1$. With the

### ■ FIGURE 10.9
The Effects of Entry

**Practice Online**

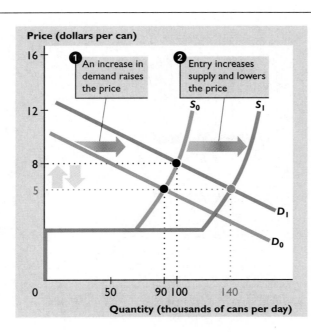

Starting in long-run equilibrium, ❶ demand increases and the demand curve shifts from $D_0$ to $D_1$. The price rises from $5 to $8 a can.

Economic profit brings entry. ❷ As firms enter the market, the supply curve shifts rightward, from $S_0$ to $S_1$. The equilibrium price falls from $8 to $5 a can, and the quantity produced increases from 100,000 to 140,000 cans a day.

greater supply and unchanged demand, the price falls from $8 to $5 a can and the quantity increases to 140,000 cans a day.

Market output increases, but because the price falls, Dave and the other producers decrease output, back to its original level. But because the number of firms in the market increases, the market as a whole produces more.

As the price falls, each firm's economic profit decreases. When the price falls to $5, economic profit disappears and each firm makes a normal profit. The entry process stops, and the market is again in long-run equilibrium.

You have just discovered a key proposition:

> **Economic profit is an incentive for new firms to enter a market, but as they do so, the price falls and the economic profit of each existing firm decreases.**

### The Effects of Exit

Figure 10.10 shows the effects of exit. Again we begin on demand curve $D_0$ and supply curve $S_0$ in long-run equilibrium. Now suppose that the development of a new high-nutrition, low-fat breakfast food decreases the demand for pancakes, and as a result, the demand for maple syrup decreases. The demand curve shifts from $D_0$ to $D_2$. Firms' costs are the same as before, so the market supply curve is $S_0$.

With demand at $D_2$ and supply at $S_0$, the price falls to $3 a can and 70,000 cans a day are produced. The firms in the syrup market incur economic losses.

Times are tough for syrup producers, and Dave must seriously think about leaving his dream business and finding some other way of making a living. But other producers are in the same situation as Dave. And some start to exit the market while Dave is still thinking through his options.

---

**FIGURE 10.10**
The Effects of Exit

**Practice Online**

Starting in long-run equilibrium, ❶ demand decreases and the demand curve shifts from $D_0$ to $D_2$. The price falls from $5 to $3 a can.

Economic loss brings exit. ❷ As firms exit the market, the supply curve shifts leftward, from $S_0$ to $S_2$. The equilibrium price rises from $3 to $5 a can, and the quantity produced decreases from 70,000 to 40,000 cans a day.

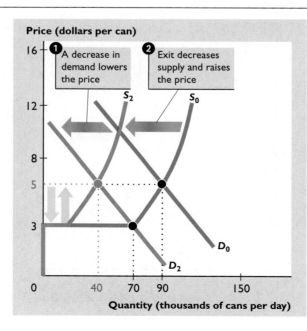

As firms exit, the market supply curve shifts leftward to $S_2$. With the decrease in supply, output decreases from 70,000 to 40,000 cans and the price rises from $3 to $5 a can.

As the price rises, Dave and each other firm that remains in the market move up along their supply curves and increase output. That is, for each firm that remains in the market, the profit-maximizing output *increases*. As the price rises and each firm sells more, economic loss decreases. When the price rises to $5, each firm makes a normal profit. Dave is happy that he can still make a living producing syrup.

You have just discovered a second key proposition:

**Economic loss is an incentive for firms to exit a market, but as they do so, the price rises and the economic loss of each remaining firm decreases.**

## Eye on the U.S. Economy

### Entry in Personal Computers, Exit in Farm Machines

An example of entry and falling prices occurred during the 1980s and 1990s in the personal computer market. When IBM introduced its first PC in 1981, there was little competition; the price was $7,000 (a bit more than $14,000 in today's money), and IBM earned a large economic profit on the new machine. But new firms such as Compaq, NEC, Dell, and a host of others entered the market with machines that were technologically identical to IBM's. In fact, they were so similar that they came to be called "clones." The massive wave of entry into the personal computer market shifted the supply curve rightward and lowered the price and the economic profit for all firms. Today, a $1,000 computer is much more powerful

than its 1981 ancestor that cost 14 times as much.

An example of a firm leaving a market is International Harvester, a manufacturer of farm equipment. For decades, people associated the name "International Harvester" with tractors, combines, and other farm machines. But International Harvester wasn't the only maker of farm equipment. The market became intensely competitive, and the firm began to incur an economic loss. Now the

company has a new name, Navistar International, and it doesn't make tractors any more. After years of economic losses and shrinking revenues, it got out of the farm-machine business in 1985 and started to make trucks.

International Harvester exited because it was incurring an economic loss. Its exit decreased supply and made it possible for the remaining firms in the market to earn a normal profit.

## ■ A Permanent Change in Demand

The long-run adjustments in the maple syrup market that we've just explored apply to all competitive markets. The market begins in long-run equilibrium. Price equals minimum average total cost, and firms are making normal profit. Then demand increases permanently. The increase in demand raises the price above average total cost, so firms make economic profits. To maximize profit, firms increase output to keep marginal cost equal to price.

The market is now in short-run equilibrium but not long-run equilibrium. It is in short-run equilibrium because the number of firms is fixed. But it is not in long-run equilibrium because each firm is making an economic profit.

The economic profit is an incentive for new firms to enter the market. As they do so, market supply starts to increase and the price starts to fall. At each lower price, a firm's profit-maximizing output is less, so each firm decreases its output. That is, as firms enter the market, market output increases but the output of each firm decreases. Eventually, enough firms enter for market supply to have increased by enough to return the price to its original level. At this price, the firms produce the same quantity that they produced before the increase in demand and they earn normal profit again. The market is again in long-run equilibrium.

The difference between the initial long-run equilibrium and the final long-run equilibrium is the number of firms in the market. A permanent increase in demand increases the number of firms. Each firm produces the same output in the new long-run equilibrium as initially and earns a normal profit. In the process of moving from the initial equilibrium to the new one, firms make economic profits.

The demand for airline travel in the world economy has increased permanently in recent years, and the deregulation of the airlines has freed up firms to seek profit opportunities in this market. The result was a massive rate of entry of new airlines. The process of competition and change in the airline market, although not a perfectly competitive market, is similar to what we have just studied.

A permanent decrease in demand triggers a similar response, except in the opposite direction. The decrease in demand brings a lower price, economic loss, and exit. Exit decreases market supply and eventually raises the price to its original level.

One feature of the predictions that we have just generated seems odd: In the long run, regardless of whether demand increases or decreases, the price returns to its original level. Is this outcome inevitable? In fact, it is not. It is possible for the long-run equilibrium price to remain the same, rise, or fall.

## ■ External Economies and Diseconomies

**External economies**
Factors beyond the control of an individual firm that lower its costs as the *market* output increases.

**External diseconomies**
Factors outside the control of a firm that raise the firm's costs as *market* output increases.

The change in the long-run equilibrium price depends on external economies and external diseconomies. **External economies** are factors beyond the control of an individual firm that lower its costs as the *market* output increases. **External diseconomies** are factors outside the control of a firm that raise the firm's costs as *market* output increases. With no external economies or external diseconomies, a firm's costs remain constant as the *market* output changes.

Figure 10.11 illustrates these three cases and introduces a new supply concept: the long-run market supply curve.

■ **FIGURE 10.11**

Long-run Changes in Price and Quantity

**Practice Online**

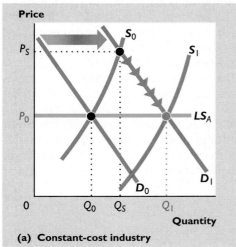

**(a) Constant-cost industry**

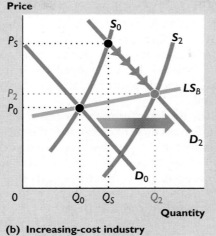

**(b) Increasing-cost industry**

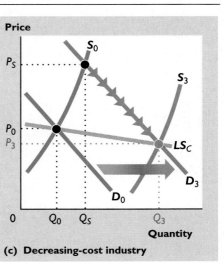

**(c) Decreasing-cost industry**

When demand increases from $D_0$ to $D_1$, entry occurs and the market supply curve shifts from $S_0$ to $S_1$. The long-run market supply curve, $LS_A$, is horizontal.

The long-run market supply curve is $LS_B$; the price rises to $P_2$, and the quantity increases to $Q_2$. This case occurs in industries with external diseconomies.

The long-run market supply curve is $LS_C$; the price falls to $P_3$, and the quantity increases to $Q_3$. This case occurs in an industry with external economies.

A **long-run market supply curve** shows the relationship between the quantity supplied and the price when the number of firms changes so that each firm earns zero economic profit.

Figure 10.11(a) shows the case we have just studied: no external economies or diseconomies. The long-run market supply curve ($LS_A$) is perfectly elastic. In this case, a permanent increase in demand from $D_0$ to $D_1$ has no effect on the price in the long run. The increase in demand initially increases the price to $P_S$ and increases the quantity to $Q_S$. Entry increases supply from $S_0$ to $S_1$, which lowers the price to its original level, $P_0$, and increases the quantity to $Q_1$.

Figure 10.11(b) shows the case of external diseconomies. The long-run market supply curve ($LS_B$) slopes upward. A permanent increase in demand from $D_0$ to $D_2$ increases the price in both the short run and the long run. As in the previous case, the increase in demand initially increases the price to $P_S$ and increases the quantity to $Q_S$. Entry increases supply from $S_0$ to $S_2$, which lowers the price to $P_2$ and increases the quantity to $Q_2$.

One source of external diseconomies is congestion. The airline market provides a good example. With bigger airline market output, there is more congestion of airports and airspace, which results in longer delays and extra waiting time for passengers and airplanes. These external diseconomies mean that as the output of air transportation services increases (in the absence of technological advances), average cost increases. As a result, the long-run supply curve is upward sloping. So a permanent increase in demand brings an increase in quantity and a rise in the price.

Figure 10.11(c) shows the case of external economies. In this case, the long-run market supply curve ($LS_C$) slopes downward. A permanent increase in demand from $D_0$ to $D_3$ increases the price in the short run and lowers it in the long run.

**Long-run market supply curve**
A curve that shows the relationship between the quantity supplied and the price when the number of firms changes so that each firm earns zero economic profit.

Again, the increase in demand initially increases the price to $P_S$, and increases the quantity to $Q_S$. Entry increases supply from $S_0$ to $S_3$, which lowers the price to $P_3$ and increases the quantity to $Q_3$.

One of the best examples of external economies is the growth of specialist support services for a market as it expands. As farm output increased in the nineteenth and early twentieth centuries, the services available to farmers expanded and average farm costs fell. For example, new firms specialized in the development and marketing of farm machinery and fertilizers. As a result, average farm costs decreased. Farms enjoyed the benefits of external economies. As a consequence, as the demand for farm products increased, the output increased but the price fell.

Over the long term, the prices of many goods and services have fallen. Some have fallen because of external economies. But prices in markets with external diseconomies have also fallen. The reason in both cases is that technological advances increase supply and shift the long-run supply curve rightward. Let's now study this influence on a competitive market.

## ■ Technological Change

Firms are constantly discovering lower-cost techniques of production. For example, the cost of producing personal computers has tumbled. So have the costs of producing CD players, DVD players, and most other electronic products. Most cost-saving production techniques cannot be implemented without investing in new plants. Consequently, it takes time for a technological advance to spread through a market. Some firms whose plants are on the verge of being replaced will be quick to adopt the new technology, while other firms whose plants have recently been replaced will continue to operate with an old technology until they can no longer cover their average variable cost. Once average variable cost cannot be covered, a firm will scrap even a relatively new plant (embodying an old technology) in favor of a plant with a new technology.

New technology allows firms to produce at a lower cost. As a result, as firms adopt a new technology, their cost curves shift downward. With lower costs, firms are willing to supply a given quantity at a lower price or, equivalently, they are willing to supply a larger quantity at a given price. In other words, market supply increases, and the market supply curve shifts rightward. With a given demand, the quantity produced increases and the price falls.

Two forces are at work in a market undergoing technological change. Firms that adopt the new technology make an economic profit. So new-technology firms have an incentive to enter. Firms that stick with the old technology incur economic losses. They either exit the market or switch to the new technology.

As old-technology firms exit and new-technology firms enter, the price falls and the quantity produced increases. Eventually, the market arrives at a long-run equilibrium in which all the firms use the new technology and each firm makes zero economic profit (a normal profit). Because competition eliminates economic profit in the long run, technological change brings only temporary gains to firms. But the lower prices and better products that technological advances bring are permanent gains for consumers.

The process that we've just described is one in which some firms experience economic profits and others experience economic losses—a period of dynamic change for a market. Some firms do well, and others do badly. Often, the process has a geographical dimension: The expanding new-technology firms bring prosperity to what was once the boondocks, and with old-technology firms going out of business, traditional industrial regions decline. Sometimes, the new-technology firms are in a foreign country, while the old-technology firms are in the domestic economy. The information revolution of the 1990s has produced many examples of changes like these. Commercial banking (a competitive but less than perfectly competitive industry), which was traditionally concentrated in New York, San Francisco, and other large cities, now flourishes in Charlotte, North Carolina, which has become the nation's number three commercial banking city. Television shows and movies, traditionally made in Los Angeles and New York, are now made in large numbers in Orlando and Toronto.

Technological advances are not confined to the information and entertainment market. Food production is undergoing a major technological change because of genetic engineering.

## Eye on the Global Economy

### The North American Market in Maple Syrup

North American maple syrup production runs at about 8 million gallons a year. Most of this syrup is produced in Canada, but farms in Vermont, New York, Maine, Wisconsin, New Hampshire, Ohio, and Michigan together produce close to 20 percent of the total output.

The number of firms that produce maple syrup can only be estimated, because some are tiny and sell their output to a small local market. But there are around 9,500 producers in Canada and approaching 2,000 in the United States.

The syrup of each producer is not quite identical. And at the retail level, people have preferences about brands and sources of supply. But at the wholesale level, the market is highly competitive and a good example of perfect competition.

All of the events that can occur in a perfectly competitive market and that we've studied in this chapter have actually occurred in the maple syrup market over the past 20 years.

During the 1980s, the technology for extracting sap advanced as more taps were installed that use a plastic tube vacuum technology. During this period, farms exited the market and the average farm increased in scale. In 1980, the average farm had 1,400 taps; by 1990, this number was 2,000; and by 1996, the number of taps had increased to 2,400.

During the 1990s, with a steady growth in the demand for maple syrup, new farms entered the market.

Through the past 20 years, total production has increased and the price has held remarkably stable at around $8 per half-gallon can. So increasing demand has brought economic profit, which in turn has brought entry and an increase in supply.

Study Guide pp. 157–160

Practice Online 10.3

**3** Explain how output, price, and profit are determined in the long run.

## Practice Problem 10.3

Tulip growing is a perfectly competitive industry, and all tulip growers have the same cost curves. The market price of tulips is $15 a bunch, and each grower maximizes profit by producing 1,500 bunches a week. The average total cost of producing tulips is $21 a bunch. Minimum average variable cost is $12 a bunch, and the minimum average total cost is $18 a bunch. Tulip growing is a constant cost industry.

a. What is a tulip grower's economic profit in the short run?
b. How does the number of tulip growers change in the long run?
c. What is the price in the long run?
d. What is the economic profit in the long run?

## Exercise 10.3

Tom's Tattoos is a tattooing business in a perfectly competitive market. Table 1 shows Tom's total costs.

a. If the market price is $20 per tattoo, what is Tom's economic profit?
b. If the market price is $20 per tattoo, do new firms enter or do existing firms exit the industry in the long run?
c. What is the price of a tattoo in the long run?
d. How many tattoos per hour does Tom sell in the long run?
e. What is Tom's economic profit in the long run?

## Solution to Practice Problem 10.3

a. The price is less than average total cost, so the tulip grower is incurring an economic loss in the short run. Because the price exceeds minimum average variable cost, the tulip grower continues to produce. The economic loss equals the loss per bunch ($21 minus $15) multiplied by the number of bunches (1,500), which equals $9,000 (Figure 1).
b. Because firms in the industry are incurring a loss, some firms will exit in the long run. So the number of tulip growers will decrease.
c. The price in the long run will be such that economic profit is zero. That is, as tulip growers exit, the price will rise until it equals minimum average total cost. Because tulip growing is a constant cost industry, the long-run price will be $18 a bunch (Figure 2).
d. Economic profit in the long run will be zero. Tulip growers will make normal profit (Figure 2).

**TABLE 1**

| Quantity (tattoos per hour) | Total cost (dollars per hour) |
| --- | --- |
| 0 | 30 |
| 1 | 50 |
| 2 | 65 |
| 3 | 75 |
| 4 | 90 |
| 5 | 110 |
| 6 | 140 |

**FIGURE 1**

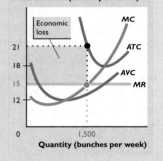

Price and cost (dollars per bunch)

**FIGURE 2**

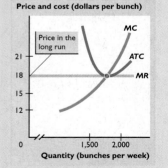

Price and cost (dollars per bunch)

# CHAPTER CHECKPOINT

## Key Points

**1** **Explain a perfectly competitive firm's profit-maximizing choices and derive its supply curve.**

- A perfectly competitive firm is a price taker.
- Marginal revenue equals price.
- The firm produces the output at which price equals marginal cost.
- If price is less than minimum average variable cost, the firm temporarily shuts down.
- A firm's supply curve is the upward-sloping part of its marginal cost curve above minimum average variable cost and the vertical axis at all prices below minimum average variable cost.

**2** **Explain how output, price, and profit are determined in the short run.**

- Market demand and market supply determine price.
- Firms choose the quantity to produce that maximizes profit, which is the quantity at which marginal cost equals price.
- In short-run equilibrium, a firm can make an economic profit or incur an economic loss.

**3** **Explain how output, price, and profit are determined in the long run.**

- Economic profit induces entry, which increases supply and lowers price and profit. Economic loss induces exit, which decreases supply, raises price, and lowers the losses.
- In the long run, economic profit is zero and there is no entry or exit.
- The long-run effect of a permanent increase in demand on price depends on whether there are external economies (price falls) or external diseconomies (price rises) or neither (price remains constant).
- New technologies increase supply and in the long run lower the price and increase the quantity.

## Key Terms

External diseconomies, 262
External economies, 262
Long-run market supply curve, 263
Marginal revenue, 247
Monopolistic competition, 246

Monopoly, 246
Oligopoly, 246
Perfect competition, 246
Price taker, 247
Shutdown point, 251

# Exercises

1. In what type of market is each of the following goods and services sold? Explain your answers.
   a. Wheat
   b. Jeans
   c. Camera film
   d. Toothpaste
   e. Taxi rides in a town with one taxi company

2. Explain why in a perfectly competitive market, the firm is a price taker. Why can't the firm choose the price at which it sells its good?

3. Table 1 shows the demand schedule for Lin's Fortune Cookies.
   a. In what type of market does Lin's Fortune Cookies operate? How can you tell?
   b. Calculate Lin's marginal revenue for each quantity demanded.
   c. Why does Lin's marginal revenue equal price?

4. Table 2 shows some cost data for Lin's Fortune Cookies, which operates in the market described in exercise 3. To answer these questions, draw Lin's short-run cost curves.

**TABLE 1**

| Price (dollars per batch) | Quantity demanded (batches of fortune cookies per day) |
|---|---|
| 50 | 0 |
| 50 | 1 |
| 50 | 2 |
| 50 | 3 |
| 50 | 4 |
| 50 | 5 |
| 50 | 6 |

**TABLE 2**

| Total product (batches of cookies per day) | Average fixed cost | Average variable cost | Average total cost | Marginal cost |
|---|---|---|---|---|
| | | (dollars per batch) | | |
| 1 | 84.00 | 51.00 | 135 | |
| | | | | 37 |
| 2 | 42.00 | 44.00 | 86 | |
| | | | | 29 |
| 3 | 28.00 | 39.00 | 67 | |
| | | | | 27 |
| 4 | 21.00 | 36.00 | 57 | |
| | | | | 32 |
| 5 | 16.80 | 35.20 | 52 | |
| | | | | 40 |
| 6 | 14.00 | 36.00 | 50 | |
| | | | | 57 |
| 7 | 12.00 | 39.00 | 51 | |
| | | | | 83 |
| 8 | 10.50 | 44.50 | 55 | |

   a. At a price of $50 per batch of cookies, what quantity does Lin produce and what is the firm's economic profit? Do firms enter or exit the industry?
   b. At a price of $35.20 per batch, what quantity does Lin produce and what is the firm's economic profit? Do firms enter or exit the industry?
   c. At a price of $83 per batch, what quantity does Lin produce and what is the firm's economic profit? Do firms enter or exit the industry?

5. Use the data in Table 2 to create Lin's short-run supply schedule and make a graph of Lin's short-run supply curve.

6. Explain why Lin's supply curve is only part of his marginal cost curve. Why will Lin never consider producing 2 batches of fortune cookies a day?

7. Suppose there are 1,000 fortune cookie producers that are exactly like Lin's Fortune Cookies. Table 3 shows the demand schedule for fortune cookies.
   a. What is the short-run equilibrium price of fortune cookies?
   b. What is the short-run equilibrium quantity of fortune cookies?
   c. What is the economic profit earned or loss incurred by each firm?
   d. Do firms enter or exit the industry? Why?
   e. What is the price in long-run equilibrium?
   f. Approximately how many firms are in the industry in long-run equilibrium?

8. Suppose that the restaurant industry is perfectly competitive. Joe's Diner is always packed in the evening but rarely has a customer at lunchtime. Why doesn't Joe's Diner close—temporarily shut down—at lunchtime?

9. 3M created the sticky note, which 3M called the Post-it note. Soon many other firms entered the sticky note market and started to produce sticky notes.
   a. What was the incentive for these firms to enter the sticky note market?
   b. As time goes by, do you expect more firms to enter this market? Explain why or why not.
   c. Can you think of any reason why any of these firms might exit the sticky note market?

10. In 1969, when Rod Laver completed his tennis grand slam, all tennis rackets were made of wood. Today, tennis players use graphite rackets.
   a. Draw two graphs of the market for wooden tennis rackets in 1969: one that shows the market as a whole and one that shows an individual producer of rackets.
   b. Show in the graphs the effect of a permanent decrease in the demand for wooden rackets.
   c. How did the economic profit from producing wooden rackets change and what effects did the change in profit have on the number of producers of wooden rackets?

11. During the 1980s and 1990s, the cost of producing a personal computer decreased.
   a. Draw two graphs of the market for personal computers: one that shows the market as a whole and one that shows an individual producer.
   b. Show in the graphs the effect of a decrease in the cost of producing a computer on the price of a computer, the quantity of computers bought, and the economic profit of producers in the short run and in the long run.

12. Small aluminum scooters became popular during 2000. Sketch the cost and revenue curves of a typical firm in the scooter industry when
   a. The scooter fashion began.
   b. The scooter fashion was two years old.
   c. The scooter fashion faded.

**TABLE 3**

| Price (dollars per batch) | Quantity demanded (batches per day) |
|---|---|
| 92 | 4,000 |
| 85 | 4,500 |
| 78 | 5,000 |
| 71 | 5,500 |
| 64 | 6,000 |
| 57 | 6,500 |
| 50 | 7,000 |
| 43 | 7,500 |
| 36 | 8,000 |

## Critical Thinking

13. Airport security has been stepped up in the period since the attacks on September 11, 2001, and much of the additional security service is provided by private firms that operate in a competitive market. Use the perfect competition model to answer the following questions.
    a. Do you think that airport security providers earned an economic profit or incurred an economic loss during 2002? Explain your answer.
    b. Do you predict that the price of airport security services will increase or decrease in the near future? Why?
    c. Do you think that airport security services are subject to increasing cost or decreasing cost in the long run? Why?

14. Review *Eye on the Global Economy* on p. 265.
    a. List the features of the maple syrup market that make it an example of perfect competition.
    b. Draw a graph to describe the maple syrup market and the cost and revenue of an individual firm in 1980, assuming that the industry was in long-run equilibrium.
    c. Use your answer to part b to explain the effects of the technological changes in maple syrup farming during the 1980s.
    d. Suppose that Aunt Jemima invents a new maple-flavored syrup that no one can distinguish, in a blind test, from the real thing and can produce it for $5 a gallon. What effect would this invention have on the market for real maple syrup? Illustrate the effects graphically.

15. The combination of the DVD player, the flat plasma screen, and surround sound has revolutionized watching a movie at home. At the same time, advances in technology in the movie theater have raised the standard that the home entertainment alternative must achieve. Think about the effects of these technological changes on competitive markets for goods and services that are influenced by movie going and home movie watching. Identify the market for one related good or service that will expand and one that will contract. Describe in detail the sequence of events as the two markets you've identified respond to the new technologies.

**Practice Online**     ## Web Exercise

**Use the links on your Foundations Web site to work the following exercise.**

16. Open the spreadsheet that provides information about the world market for wheat and then answer the following questions:
    a. Is the world market for wheat perfectly competitive? Why or why not?
    b. What happened to the price of wheat during the 1990s?
    c. What happened to the quantity of wheat produced during the 1990s?
    d. What do you think were the main influences on the demand for wheat during the 1990s?
    e. What do you think were the main influences on the supply of wheat during the 1990s?
    f. Do you think farmers entered or exited the wheat market during the 1990s? Explain your answer.

# Monopoly

If you live in University City, Missouri, you buy your electricity from Union Electric or light your home with candles. If you live in Gainesville, Florida, and want cable TV service, you have only one option: buy from Cox Cable. These are examples of monopoly. Such firms can choose their own price. How do such firms choose the quantity to produce and the price at which to sell it? Do they charge too much?

Some firms—hairdressers, museums, and movie theaters are examples—give discounts to students. Are these firms run by generous folk to whom the model of profit-maximizing firms doesn't apply? Aren't these firms throwing profit away by cutting ticket prices and offering discounts?

In this chapter, we study monopoly. We learn how a monopoly behaves, and we discover whether monopoly is efficient and fair.

## 11.1 MONOPOLY AND HOW IT ARISES

A *monopoly* is a market with a single supplier of a good or service that has no close substitutes and in which natural or legal barriers to entry prevent competition.

Markets for local telephone service, gas, electricity, and water are examples of local monopoly. GlaxoSmithKline has a monopoly on AZT, a drug that is used to treat AIDS. DeBeers, a South African firm, controls 80 percent of the world's production of raw diamonds—close to being a monopoly but not quite one.

### ■ How Monopoly Arises

Monopoly arises when there are

- No close substitutes
- Barriers to entry

### No Close Substitutes

If a good has a close substitute, even though only one firm produces it, that firm effectively faces competition from the producers of substitutes. Water supplied by a local public utility is an example of a good that does not have close substitutes. While it does have a close substitute for drinking—bottled spring water—it has no effective substitutes for doing the laundry, taking a shower, or washing a car.

Sometimes the arrival of a new product weakens a monopoly. For example, Federal Express, UPS, the fax machine, and e-mail have weakened the monopoly of the U.S. Postal Service; broadband fiber-optic phone lines and the satellite dish have weakened the monopoly of cable television companies.

The arrival of a new product can also create a monopoly. For example, the IBM PC of the early 1980s gave a monopoly in PC operating systems to Microsoft's DOS.

### Barriers to Entry

Anything that protects a firm from the arrival of new competitors is a **barrier to entry**. There are two types of barrier to entry:

- Natural
- Legal

***Natural Barriers to Entry*** A **natural monopoly** exists when the technology for producing a good or service enables one firm to meet the entire market demand at a lower price than two or more firms could. One electric power distributor can meet the market demand for electricity at a lower cost than two or more firms could. Imagine two or more sets of wires running to your home so that you could choose your electric power supplier.

Figure 11.1 illustrates a natural monopoly in the distribution of electric power. Here, the demand curve for electric power is *D* and the long-run average cost curve is *LRAC*. Economies of scale prevail over the entire length of this *LRAC* curve, indicated by the fact that the curve slopes downward. One firm can produce 4 million kilowatt-hours at 5 cents a kilowatt-hour. At this price, the quantity demanded is 4 million kilowatt-hours. So if the price was 5 cents, one firm could supply the entire market. If two firms shared the market, it would cost each

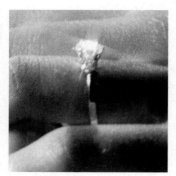

*The market for diamonds is close to being a monopoly.*

**Barrier to entry**
A natural or legal constraint that protects a firm from competitors.

**Natural monopoly**
A monopoly that arises because one firm can meet the entire market demand at a lower price than two or more firms could.

**■ FIGURE 11.1**
Natural Monopoly

**Practice Online**

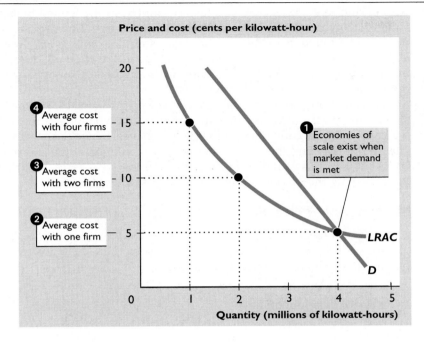

**Price and cost (cents per kilowatt-hour)**

**4** Average cost with four firms

**3** Average cost with two firms

**2** Average cost with one firm

**1** Economies of scale exist when market demand is met

LRAC

D

**Quantity (millions of kilowatt-hours)**

The demand curve for electric power is *D*, and the long-run average cost curve is *LRAC*.

**1** Economies of scale exist over the entire *LRAC* curve. One firm can distribute 4 million kilowatt-hours at a **2** cost of 5 cents a kilowatt-hour. This same total output **3** costs 10 cents a kilowatt-hour with two firms and **4** 15 cents a kilowatt-hour with four firms. So one firm can meet the market demand at a lower cost than two or more firms can, and the market is a natural monopoly.

of them 10 cents a kilowatt-hour to produce a total of 4 million kilowatt-hours. If four firms shared the market, it would cost each of them 15 cents a kilowatt-hour to produce a total of 4 million kilowatt-hours. So in conditions like those shown in Figure 11.1, one firm can supply the entire market at a lower cost than two or more firms can.

The distribution of water and natural gas are two other examples of natural monopoly.

***Legal Barriers to Entry***    Legal barriers to entry create a legal monopoly. A **legal monopoly** is a market in which competition and entry are restricted by the concentration of ownership of a natural resource or by the granting of a public franchise, government license, patent, or copyright.

A firm can create its own barrier to entry by buying up a significant portion of a natural resource. DeBeers, which controls more than 80 percent of the world's production of raw diamonds, is an example of this type of monopoly. There is no natural barrier to entry in diamonds. Even though the diamond is a relatively rare mineral, its sources of supply could have many owners who compete in a global competitive auction market. DeBeers was able to prevent such competition by being a dominant player and effectively controlling entry.

A *public franchise* is an exclusive right granted to a firm to supply a good or service, an example of which is the U.S. Postal Service's exclusive right to deliver first-class mail. A *government license* controls entry into particular occupations, professions, and industries. An example is Michael's Texaco in Charleston, Rhode Island, which is the only firm in the area licensed to test for vehicle emissions.

**Legal monopoly**
A market in which competition and entry are restricted by the concentration of ownership of a natural resource or by the granting of a public franchise, government license, patent, or copyright.

A *patent* is an exclusive right granted to the inventor of a product or service. A *copyright* is an exclusive right granted to the author or composer of a literary, musical, dramatic, or artistic work. Patents and copyrights are valid for a limited time period that varies from country to country. In the United States, a patent is valid for 20 years. Patents are designed to encourage the *invention* of new products and production methods. They also stimulate *innovation*—the use of new inventions—by encouraging inventors to publicize their discoveries and offer them for use under license. Patents have stimulated innovations in areas as diverse as soybean seeds, pharmaceuticals, memory chips, and video games.

Most monopolies are regulated by government agencies. We can better understand why governments regulate monopolies and what effects regulations have if we know how an unregulated monopoly behaves. So we'll first study an unregulated monopoly and then look at monopoly regulation at the end of this chapter.

A monopoly sets its own price, but in doing so, it faces a market constraint. Let's see how the market limits a monopoly's pricing choices.

### ■ Monopoly Price-Setting Strategies

A monopolist faces a tradeoff between price and the quantity sold. To sell a larger quantity, the monopolist must set a lower price. But there are two price-setting possibilities that create different tradeoffs:

- Single price
- Price discrimination

### Single Price

**Single-price monopoly**
A monopoly that must sell each unit of its output for the same price to all its customers.

A **single-price monopoly** is a firm that must sell each unit of its output for the same price to all its customers. DeBeers sells diamonds (of a given size and quality) for the same price to all its customers. If it tried to sell at a higher price to some customers than to others, only the low-price customers would buy from DeBeers. Others would buy from DeBeers's low-price customers. So DeBeers is a *single-price* monopoly.

### Price Discrimination

**Price-discriminating monopoly**
A monopoly that is able to sell different units of a good or service for different prices.

A **price-discriminating monopoly** is a firm that is able to sell different units of a good or service for different prices. Many firms price discriminate. Airlines offer a dizzying array of different prices for the same trip. Pizza producers charge one price for a single pizza and almost give away a second one. Different customers might pay different prices (like airfares), or one customer might pay different prices for different quantities bought (like the bargain price for a second pizza).

When a firm price discriminates, it appears to be doing its customers a favor. In fact, it is charging the highest possible price for each unit sold and making the largest possible profit.

Not all monopolies can price discriminate. The main obstacle to the practice of price discrimination is resale by the customers who buy for a low price. Because of resale possibilities, price discrimination is limited to monopolies that sell services that cannot be resold.

# CHECKPOINT 11.1

**1** Explain how monopoly arises and distinguish between single-price monopoly and price-discriminating monopoly.

Study Guide pp. 166–168

Practice Online 11.1

## Practice Problems 11.1

1. Monopoly arises in which of the following situations?
   a. Coca-Cola cuts its price below that of Pepsi-Cola in an attempt to increase its market share.
   b. A single firm, protected by a barrier to entry, produces a personal service that has no close substitutes.
   c. A barrier to entry exists, but some close substitutes for the good exist.
   d. A firm offers discounts to students and seniors.
   e. A firm can sell any quantity it chooses at the going price.
   f. The government issues Tiger Woods, Inc. an exclusive license to produce golf balls.
   g. A firm experiences economies of scale even when it produces the quantity that meets the entire market demand.

2. Which of the cases **a** to **f** in problem 1 are natural monopolies and which are legal monopolies? Which can price discriminate, which cannot, and why?

## Exercises 11.1

1. Which of the following are monopolies?
   a. A large shopping mall in downtown Houston
   b. Tiffany, the upscale jeweler
   c. Wal-Mart
   d. The Grand Canyon mule train
   e. The only shoe-shine stand licensed to operate in an airport
   f. The U.S. Postal Service

2. Which of the monopolies in exercise 1 are natural monopolies and which are legal monopolies? Which can price discriminate, which cannot, and why?

## Solutions to Practice Problems 11.1

1. Monopoly arises when a single firm produces a good or service that has no close substitutes and a barrier to entry exists. Monopoly arises in **b**, **f**, and **g**. In **a**, there is more than one firm. In **c**, the good has some close substitutes. In **d**, a monopoly might be able to price discriminate, but other types of firms (for example, pizza producers and art museums) price discriminate and they are not monopolies. In **e**, the demand for the good that the firm produces is perfectly elastic and there is no limit to what the firm could sell if it wished. Such a firm is in perfect competition.

2. Natural monopoly exists when one firm can meet the entire market demand at a lower price than two or more firms could. So **g** is a natural monopoly, but **b** could be also. Legal monopoly exists when the granting of a right creates a barrier to entry. So **f** is a legal monopoly, but **b** could be also. Monopoly **b** could price discriminate because a personal service cannot be resold. Monopoly **f** could not price discriminate because golf balls can be resold.

## 11.2 SINGLE-PRICE MONOPOLY

To understand how a single-price monopoly makes its output and price decisions, we must first study the link between price and marginal revenue.

### ■ Price and Marginal Revenue

Because in a monopoly there is only one firm, the firm's demand curve is the market demand curve. Let's look at Bobbie's Barbershop, the sole supplier of haircuts in Cairo, Nebraska. The table in Figure 11.2 shows the demand schedule for Bobbie's haircuts. For example, at $12, consumers demand 4 haircuts an hour (row *E*).

*Total revenue* is the price multiplied by the quantity sold. For example, in row *D*, Bobbie sells 3 haircuts at $14 each, so total revenue is $42. *Marginal revenue* is the change in total revenue resulting from a one-unit increase in the quantity sold. For example, if the price falls from $16 (row *C*) to $14 (row *D*), the quantity sold increases from 2 to 3 haircuts. Total revenue rises from $32 to $42, so the change in total revenue is $10. Because the quantity sold increases by 1 haircut, marginal revenue equals the change in total revenue and is $10. Marginal revenue is placed between the two rows to emphasize that marginal revenue relates to the *change* in the quantity sold.

Figure 11.2 shows Bobbie's demand curve and marginal revenue curve (*MR*) and also illustrates the calculation that we've just made. Notice that at each output, marginal revenue is less than price—the marginal revenue curve lies below the demand curve. Why is marginal revenue less than price? It is because when the price is lowered to sell one more unit, two opposing forces affect total revenue.

---

### ■ FIGURE 11.2
Demand and Marginal Revenue

**Practice Online**

The table shows Bobbie's demand, total revenue, and marginal revenue schedules.

If the price falls from $16 to $14, the quantity sold increases from 2 to 3. ❶ Total revenue lost on 2 haircuts is $4; ❷ total revenue gained on 1 haircut is $14; and ❸ marginal revenue is $10.

| | Price (dollars per haircut) | Quantity demanded (haircuts per hour) | Total revenue (dollars per hour) | Marginal revenue (dollars per haircut) |
|---|---|---|---|---|
| **A** | 20 | 0 | 0 | |
| | | | | 18 |
| **B** | 18 | 1 | 18 | |
| | | | | 14 |
| **C** | 16 | 2 | 32 | |
| | | | | 10 |
| **D** | 14 | 3 | 42 | |
| | | | | 6 |
| **E** | 12 | 4 | 48 | |
| | | | | 2 |
| **F** | 10 | 5 | 50 | |

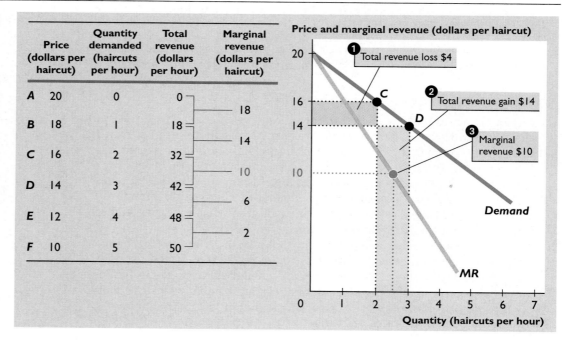

The lower price results in a revenue loss, and the increased quantity sold results in a revenue gain. For example, at a price of $16, Bobbie sells 2 haircuts (point C). If she lowers the price to $14 a haircut, she sells 3 haircuts and has a revenue gain of $14 on the third haircut. But she now receives only $14 a haircut on the first two—$2 less than before. As a result, she loses $4 of revenue on the first 2 haircuts. To calculate marginal revenue, she must deduct this amount from the revenue gain of $14. So her marginal revenue is $10, which is less than the price.

## ■ Marginal Revenue and Elasticity

In Chapter 5 (p. 126), you learned about the *total revenue test*, which determines whether demand is elastic or inelastic. Recall that if a price fall increases total revenue, demand is elastic, but if it decreases total revenue, demand is inelastic.

We can use the total revenue test to see the relationship between marginal revenue and elasticity. Figure 11.3 illustrates this relationship. As the price falls from $20 to $10, the quantity demanded increases from 0 to 5 an hour. Total revenue increases (part b), so demand is elastic and marginal revenue is positive (part a). As the price falls from $10 to $0, the quantity demanded increases from 5 to 10 an hour. Total revenue decreases (part b), so demand is inelastic and marginal revenue is

---

**■ FIGURE 11.3**
Marginal Revenue and Elasticity

**Practice Online**

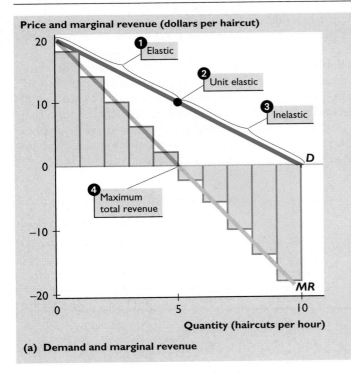

**(a) Demand and marginal revenue**

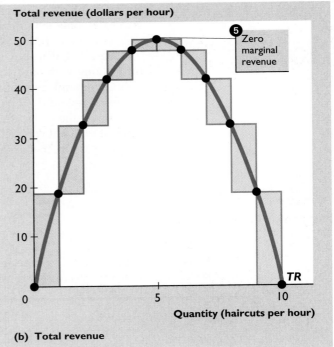

**(b) Total revenue**

Over the range from 0 to 5 haircuts an hour, marginal revenue is positive and **❶** demand is elastic. At 5 haircuts an hour, marginal revenue is zero and **❷** demand is unit elastic. Over the range 5 to 10 haircuts an hour, marginal revenue is negative and **❸** demand is inelastic. At zero marginal revenue in part (a), **❹** total revenue is maximized. And at maximum total revenue in part (b), **❺** marginal revenue is zero.

negative (part a). When the price is $10, total revenue is at a maximum, demand is unit elastic, and marginal revenue is zero.

The relationship between marginal revenue and elasticity implies that a monopoly never profitably produces an output in the inelastic range of its demand curve. It could charge a higher price, produce a smaller quantity, and increase its profit. Let's look at a monopoly's output and price decision.

### ■ Output and Price Decision

To determine the output level and price that maximize a monopoly's profit, we study the behavior of both revenue and costs as output varies.

Table 11.1 summarizes the information we need about Bobbie's revenue, costs, and economic profit. Economic profit, which equals total revenue minus total cost, is maximized at $12 an hour when Bobbie sells 3 haircuts an hour for $14 each. If she sold 2 haircuts for $16 each, her economic profit would be only $9. And if she sold 4 haircuts for $12 each, her economic profit would be only $8.

You can see why 3 haircuts is Bobbie's profit-maximizing output by looking at the marginal revenue and marginal cost. When Bobbie increases output from 2 to 3 haircuts, her marginal revenue is $10 and her marginal cost is $7. Profit increases by the difference, $3 an hour. If Bobbie increases output yet further, from 3 to 4 haircuts, her marginal revenue is $6 and her marginal cost is $10. In this case, marginal cost exceeds marginal revenue by $4, so profit decreases by $4 an hour.

Figure 11.4 shows the information contained in Table 11.1 graphically. Part (a) shows Bobbie's total revenue curve (TR) and her total cost curve (TC). It also shows Bobbie's economic profit as the vertical distance between the TR and TC curves. Bobbie maximizes her profit at 3 haircuts an hour and earns an economic profit of $12 an hour ($42 of total revenue minus $30 of total cost).

Figure 11.4(b) shows Bobbie's demand curve (D) and marginal revenue curve (MR) along with her marginal cost curve (MC) and average total cost curve (ATC). Bobbie maximizes profit by producing the output at which marginal cost equals marginal revenue—3 haircuts an hour. But what price does she charge for a haircut? To set the price, the monopoly uses the demand curve and finds the highest price at which it can sell the profit-maximizing output. In Bobbie's case, the highest price at which she can sell 3 haircuts an hour is $14 a haircut.

■ **TABLE 11.1**

A Monopoly's Output and Price Decision

**Practice Online**

| | Price (dollars per haircut) | Quantity demanded (haircuts per hour) | Total revenue (dollars per hour) | Marginal revenue (dollars per haircut) | Total cost (dollars per hour) | Marginal cost (dollars per haircut) | Profit (dollars per hour) |
|---|---|---|---|---|---|---|---|
| A | 20 | 0 | 0 | | 12 | | −12 |
| | | | | 18 | | 5 | |
| B | 18 | 1 | 18 | | 17 | | 1 |
| | | | | 14 | | 6 | |
| C | 16 | 2 | 32 | | 23 | | 9 |
| | | | | 10 | | 7 | |
| D | 14 | 3 | 42 | | 30 | | 12 |
| | | | | 6 | | 10 | |
| E | 12 | 4 | 48 | | 40 | | 8 |
| | | | | 2 | | 15 | |
| F | 10 | 5 | 50 | | 55 | | −5 |

When Bobbie produces 3 haircuts an hour, her average total cost is $10 (read from the *ATC* curve) and her price is $14 (read from the *D* curve). Her profit per haircut is $4 ($14 minus $10). Bobbie's economic profit is shown by the blue rectangle, which equals the profit per haircut ($4) multiplied by the number of haircuts (3 an hour), for a total of $12 an hour.

A positive economic profit is an incentive for firms to enter a market. But barriers to entry prevent that from happening in a monopoly. So in a monopoly, the firm can make a positive economic profit and continue to do so indefinitely.

A monopoly charges a price that exceeds marginal cost, but does it always make an economic profit? The answer is no! Bobbie makes a positive economic profit in Figure 11.4. But suppose that Bobbie's landlord increases the rent she pays for her barbershop. If Bobbie pays an additional $12 an hour in shop rent, her fixed cost increases by that amount. Her marginal cost and marginal revenue don't change, so her profit-maximizing output remains at 3 haircuts an hour. Her profit decreases by $12 an hour to zero. If Bobbie pays more than an additional $12 an hour for her shop rent, she incurs an economic loss. If this situation were permanent, Bobbie would go out of business. But monopoly entrepreneurs are creative, and Bobbie might find another shop at a lower rent.

---

■ **FIGURE 11.4**

**Practice Online**

A Monopoly's Profit-Maximizing Output and Price

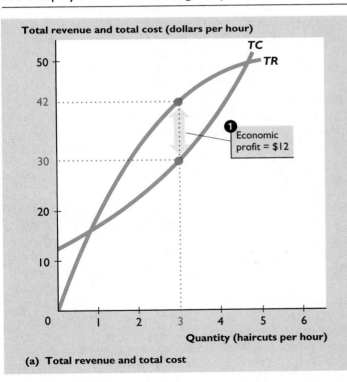

**(a) Total revenue and total cost**

**(b) Demand, marginal revenue, and marginal cost**

In part (a) economic profit is maximized when total revenue (*TR*) minus total cost (*TC*) is greatest. ❶ Economic profit, the vertical distance between *TR* and *TC*, is $12 an hour at 3 haircuts an hour.

In part (b), economic profit is maximized when marginal cost (*MC*) equals marginal revenue (*MR*). The price is determined by the demand curve (*D*) and is $14. ❷ Economic profit, the blue rectangle, is $12—the profit per haircut ($4) multiplied by 3 haircuts.

**2** Explain how a single-price monopoly determines its output and price.

**TABLE 1**

| Price (dollars per bottle) | Quantity (bottles per hour) | Total cost (dollars per hour) |
|---|---|---|
| 10 | 0 | 1.0 |
| 9 | 1 | 1.5 |
| 8 | 2 | 2.5 |
| 7 | 3 | 5.5 |
| 6 | 4 | 10.5 |
| 5 | 5 | 17.5 |

**TABLE 2**

| Price (thousands of dollars per ride) | Quantity (rides per month) | Total cost (thousands of dollars per month) |
|---|---|---|
| 220 | 0 | 80 |
| 200 | 1 | 160 |
| 180 | 2 | 260 |
| 160 | 3 | 380 |
| 140 | 4 | 520 |
| 120 | 5 | 680 |

**TABLE 3**

| Quantity (bottles per hour) | Total revenue (dollars per hour) | Marginal revenue (dollars per bottle) |
|---|---|---|
| 0 | 0 | |
| | | 9 |
| 1 | 9 | |
| | | 7 |
| 2 | 16 | |
| | | 5 |
| 3 | 21 | |
| | | 3 |
| 4 | 24 | |
| | | 1 |
| 5 | 25 | |

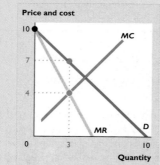

**FIGURE 1**

## Practice Problem 11.2

Minnie's Mineral Springs is a single-price monopoly. The first two columns of Table 1 show the demand schedule for Minnie's spring water, and the middle and third columns show the firm's total cost schedule.

a. Calculate Minnie's total revenue schedule and marginal revenue schedule.
b. Sketch Minnie's demand curve and marginal revenue curve.
c. Calculate Minnie's profit-maximizing output, price, and economic profit.
d. If the owner of the water source that Minnie uses increases the fee that Minnie pays by $15.50 an hour, what are Minnie's new profit-maximizing output, price, and economic profit?
e. If instead of increasing the fee that Minnie pays by $15.50 an hour, the owner of the water source increases the fee that Minnie pays by $4 a bottle, what are Minnie's new profit-maximizing output, price, and economic profit?

## Exercise 11.2

Fossett's Round-the-World Balloon Rides is a single-price monopolist. The first two columns of Table 2 show the demand schedule for Fossett's rides, and the middle and third column show the firm's total cost schedule.

a. Calculate Fossett's total revenue schedule and marginal revenue schedule.
b. Sketch Fossett's demand curve and marginal revenue curve.
c. Calculate Fossett's profit-maximizing output, price, and economic profit.
d. If the government places a fixed tax on Fossett's of $60,000 a month, what are the new profit-maximizing output, price, and economic profit?
e. If instead of imposing a fixed tax on Fossett's, the government taxes Fossett's by $30,000 per ride, what are the new profit-maximizing output, price, and economic profit?

## Solution to Practice Problem 11.2

a. Total revenue equals price multiplied by quantity sold, and marginal revenue equals the change in total revenue when the quantity sold increases by one unit (Table 3).
b. Figure 1 shows Minnie's demand curve and marginal revenue curve.
c. The profit-maximizing output is 3 bottles an hour, where marginal revenue equals marginal cost. To calculate Minnie's marginal cost, find the change in total cost when the quantity produced increases by 1 bottle. Then plot marginal cost on Figure 1. Minnie's profit-maximizing price is $7 a bottle, and Minnie's economic profit is $15.50 an hour.
d. If the owner of the water source that Minnie uses increases the fee that Minnie pays by $15.50 an hour, Minnie's fixed cost increases but her marginal cost doesn't change. Her profit-maximizing output and price are unchanged, but she now earns no economic profit.
e. If Minnie pays an extra $4 a bottle, her marginal cost increases by this amount. Her new profit-maximizing output is 2 bottles an hour; the price is $8 a bottle; and economic profit is $5.50 an hour.

## 11.3  MONOPOLY AND COMPETITION COMPARED

Imagine a market in which many small firms operate in perfect competition. Then a single firm buys out all these small firms and creates a monopoly. What happens in this market to the quantity produced, the price, and efficiency?

### ■ Output and Price

Figure 11.5 shows the market that we'll study. The market demand curve is $D$. Initially, with many small firms in the market, the market supply curve is $S$, which is the sum of the supply curves—and marginal cost curves—of the individual firms. The equilibrium price is $P_C$, which makes the quantity demanded equal the quantity supplied. The equilibrium quantity is $Q_C$. Each firm takes the price $P_C$ and maximizes its profit by producing the output at which its own marginal cost equals the price.

A single firm now buys all the firms in this market. Consumers don't change, so the demand curve doesn't change. But the monopoly recognizes this demand curve as a constraint on its sales and knows that its marginal revenue curve is $MR$.

The market supply curve in perfect competition is the sum of the marginal cost curves of the firms in the industry. So the monopoly's marginal cost curve is the market supply curve of perfect competition—labeled $S = MC$. The monopoly maximizes profit by producing the quantity at which marginal revenue equals marginal cost, which is $Q_M$. This output is smaller than the competitive output, $Q_C$. And the monopoly charges the price $P_M$, which is higher than $P_C$. So

> **Compared to perfect competition, a single-price monopoly produces a smaller output and charges a higher price.**

---

■ **FIGURE 11.5**

Monopoly's Smaller Output and Higher Price

**Practice Online**

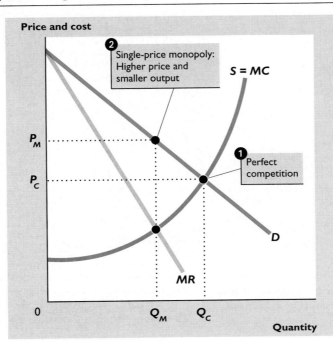

Price and cost

**2** Single-price monopoly: Higher price and smaller output

$S = MC$

**1** Perfect competition

$P_M$

$P_C$

$D$

$MR$

$0$      $Q_M$    $Q_C$

**Quantity**

**1** A competitive industry produces the quantity $Q_C$ at price $P_C$.

**2** A single-price monopoly produces the quantity $Q_M$ at which marginal revenue equals marginal cost and sells that quantity for the price $P_M$. Compared to perfect competition, a single-price monopoly restricts output and raises the price.

## ■ Is Monopoly Efficient?

You learned in Chapter 6 that resources are used efficiently when marginal benefit equals marginal cost. Figure 11.6(a) shows that perfect competition achieves this efficient use of resources. The demand curve ($D = MB$) shows the marginal benefit to consumers. The supply curve ($S = MC$) shows the marginal cost (opportunity cost) to producers. At the competitive equilibrium, the price is $P_C$ and the quantity is $Q_C$. Marginal benefit equals marginal cost and resource use is efficient. The sum of *consumer surplus* (Chapter 6, p. 145), the green triangle, and *producer surplus* (Chapter 6, p. 148), the blue area, is maximized.

Figure 11.6(b) shows that monopoly is inefficient. Monopoly output is $Q_M$ and price is $P_M$. Price (marginal benefit) exceeds marginal cost and the underproduction creates a *deadweight loss* (Chapter 6, p. 154), shown by the gray area. Consumers lose partly by getting less of the good, shown by the gray triangle above $P_C$, and partly by paying more for the good. Consumer surplus shrinks to the smaller green triangle. Producers lose by selling less of the good, shown by the part of the gray area below $P_C$, but gain by selling their output for a higher price, shown by the dark blue rectangle. Producer surplus expands and is larger in monopoly than in perfect competition.

### FIGURE 11.6
The Inefficiency of Monopoly

**Practice Online**

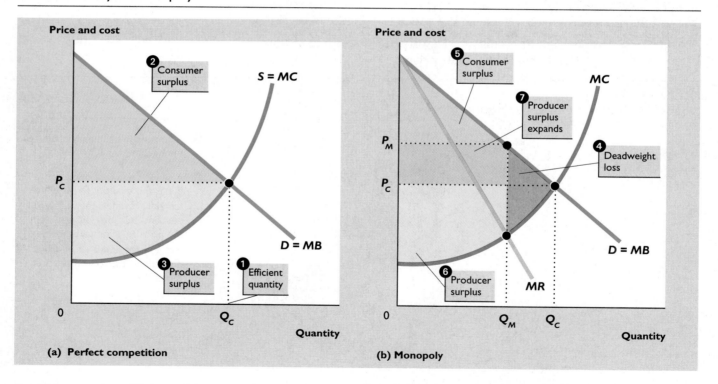

(a) **Perfect competition**

(b) **Monopoly**

In perfect competition, ❶ the equilibrium quantity is the efficient quantity, $Q_C$, because at that quantity, the price, $P_C$, equals marginal benefit and marginal cost. The sum of ❷ consumer surplus and ❸ producer surplus is maximized.

In a single-price monopoly, the equilibrium quantity, $Q_M$, is inefficient because the price, $P_M$, which equals marginal benefit, exceeds marginal cost. Underproduction creates a ❹ deadweight loss. ❺ Consumer surplus shrinks and ❻ producer surplus ❼ expands.

## ■ Is Monopoly Fair?

Monopoly is inefficient because it creates a deadweight loss. But monopoly also *redistributes* consumer surplus. The producer gains, and the consumers lose.

Figure 11.6 shows this redistribution. The monopoly gets the difference between the higher price, $P_M$, and the competitive price, $P_C$, on the quantity sold, $Q_M$. So the dark blue rectangle shows the part of the consumer surplus taken by the monopoly. This portion of the loss of consumer surplus is not a loss to society. It is redistribution from consumers to the monopoly producer.

Are the gain for the monopoly and loss for consumers fair? You learned about two standards of fairness in Chapter 6: fair *results* and fair *rules*. Redistribution from the rich to the poor is consistent with the fair results view. So on this view of fairness, whether monopoly redistribution is fair or unfair depends on who is richer: the monopolist or the consumers of its product. It might be either. Whether the *rules* are fair depends on whether the monopoly has benefited from a protected position that is not available to anyone else. If everyone is free to acquire the monopoly, then the rules are fair. So monopoly is inefficient and it might be, but is not always, unfair.

The pursuit of monopoly profit leads to an additional costly activity that we'll now describe: rent seeking.

## ■ Rent Seeking

**Rent seeking** is the act of obtaining special treatment by the government to create economic profit or to divert consumer surplus or producer surplus away from others. ("Rent" is a general term in economics that includes all forms of surplus such as consumer surplus, producer surplus, and economic profit.) Rent seeking does not always create a monopoly, but it always restricts competition and often creates a monopoly.

**Rent seeking**
The act of obtaining special treatment by the government to create economic profit or to divert consumer surplus or producer surplus away from others.

Scarce resources can be used to produce the goods and services that people value or they can be used in rent seeking. Rent seeking is potentially profitable for the rent seeker but costly to society because it uses scarce resources purely to transfer wealth from one person or group to another person or group rather than to produce the things that people value.

To see why rent seeking occurs, think about the two ways that a person might become the owner of a monopoly:

- Buy a monopoly
- Create a monopoly by rent seeking

### Buy a Monopoly

A person might try to earn a monopoly profit by buying a firm (or a right) that is protected by a barrier to entry. Buying a taxicab medallion in New York is an example. The number of medallions is restricted, so their owners are protected from unlimited entry into the industry. A person who wants to operate a taxi must buy a medallion from someone who already has one. But anyone is free to enter the bidding for a medallion. So competition among buyers drives the price up to the point at which they earn only normal profit. For example, competition for the right to operate a taxi in New York City has led to a price of more than $165,000 for a taxi medallion, which is sufficiently high to eliminate economic profit for taxi operators and leave them with normal profit.

## Create a Monopoly by Rent Seeking

Because buying a monopoly means paying a price that soaks up the economic profit, creating a monopoly by rent seeking is an attractive alternative to buying one. Rent seeking is a political activity. It takes the form of lobbying and trying to influence the political process to get laws that create legal barriers to entry. Such influence might be sought by making campaign contributions in exchange for legislative support or by indirectly seeking to influence political outcomes through publicity in the media or by direct contacts with politicians and bureaucrats. An example of a rent created in this way is the law that restricts the quantities of textiles that can be imported into the United States. Another is a law that limits the quantity of tomatoes that can be imported in the United States. These laws restrict competition, which decreases the quantity for sale and increases prices.

## Rent Seeking Equilibrium

Rent seeking is a competitive activity. If an economic profit is available, a rent seeker will try to get some of it. Competition among rent seekers pushes up the cost of rent seeking until it leaves the monopoly earning only a normal profit after paying the rent-seeking costs.

Figure 11.7 shows a rent-seeking equilibrium. The cost of rent seeking is a fixed cost that must be added to a monopoly's other costs. The average total cost curve, which includes the fixed cost of rent seeking, shifts upward until it just touches the demand curve. Consumer surplus is unaffected. But the deadweight loss of monopoly now includes the original deadweight loss triangle plus the economic profit consumed by rent seeking, which the enlarged gray area shows.

---

■ **FIGURE 11.7**

Rent-Seeking Equilibrium

**Practice Online**

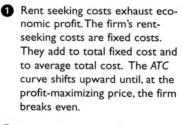

❶ Rent seeking costs exhaust economic profit. The firm's rent-seeking costs are fixed costs. They add to total fixed cost and to average total cost. The *ATC* curve shifts upward until, at the profit-maximizing price, the firm breaks even.

❷ Consumer surplus shrinks.

❸ The deadweight loss increases.

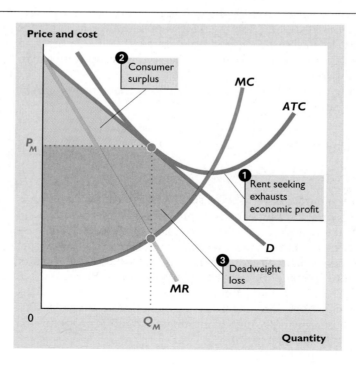

# CHECKPOINT 11.3

**3**  **Compare the performance of a single-price monopoly with that of perfect competition.**

Study Guide pp. 172–174

Practice Online 11.3

## Practice Problem 11.3

Township is a small isolated community served by one newspaper that can meet the market demand at a lower cost than two or more newspapers could. There is no local radio or TV station and no Internet access. The *Township Gazette* is the only source of news. Figure 1 shows the marginal cost of printing the *Township Gazette* and the demand for it. The *Township Gazette* is a profit-maximizing, single-price monopoly.

a. How many copies of the *Township Gazette* are printed each day?
b. What is the price of the *Township Gazette*?
c. What is the efficient number of copies of the *Township Gazette*?
d. What is the price at which the efficient number of copies could be sold?
e. Is the number of copies printed the efficient quantity? Explain why or why not.
f. On the graph, show the consumer surplus that is redistributed from consumers to the *Township Gazette*.
g. On the graph, show the deadweight loss that arises from the monopoly of the *Township Gazette*.

**FIGURE 1**

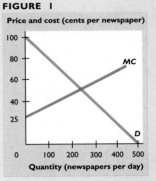

## Exercise 11.3

Is Bobbie's Barbershop in Cairo, Nebraska, (on pp. 350–353) efficient? What is the consumer surplus that is transferred to Bobbie? What is the deadweight loss that she generates? How much would someone be willing to pay to buy Bobbie's monopoly?

## Solution to Practice Problem 11.3

a. The profit-maximizing quantity of newspapers for the *Township Gazette* is 150 a day, where marginal revenue equals marginal cost (Figure 2).
b. The price is 70¢ a copy (Figure 2).
c. The efficient quantity of copies is 250, where demand (marginal benefit) equals marginal cost (Figure 2).
d. The efficient quantity would be bought at 50¢ a copy (Figure 2).
e. The number of copies printed is not efficient because the marginal benefit of the 150th copy exceeds its marginal cost (Figure 2).
f. The blue rectangle ❶ in Figure 2 shows the consumer surplus transferred from the consumers to the *Township Gazette*.
g. The gray triangle ❷ in Figure 2 shows the deadweight loss.

**FIGURE 2**

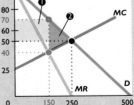

## 11.4 PRICE DISCRIMINATION

Price discrimination—selling a good or service at a number of different prices—is widespread. You encounter it when you travel, go to the movies, get your hair cut, buy pizza, or visit an art museum. At first sight, it appears that price discrimination contradicts the assumption of profit maximization. Why would a movie operator allow children to see movies at half price? Why would a hairdresser charge students and senior citizens less? Aren't these firms losing profit by being nice to their customers?

Deeper investigation shows that far from lowering profit, price discriminators make a bigger profit than they would otherwise. So a monopoly has an incentive to find ways of discriminating and charging each buyer the highest possible price. Some people pay less with price discrimination, but others pay more.

Most price discriminators are *not* monopolies, but monopolies do price discriminate when they can. To be able to price discriminate, a firm must

- Identify and separate different types of buyers.
- Sell a product that cannot be resold.

Price discrimination is charging different prices for a single good or service because the willingness to pay varies across buyers. Not all price *differences* are price *discrimination*. Some goods that are similar but not identical have different prices because they have different production costs. For example, the cost of producing electricity depends on time of day. If an electric power company charges a higher price for consumption between 7:00 and 9:00 in the morning and between 4:00 and 7:00 in the evening than it does at other times of the day, it is not price discriminating.

### ■ Price Discrimination and Consumer Surplus

The key idea behind price discrimination is to convert consumer surplus into economic profit. To extract every dollar of consumer surplus from every buyer, the monopoly would have to offer each individual customer a separate price schedule based on that customer's own willingness to pay. Such price discrimination cannot be carried out in practice because a firm does not have enough information about each consumer's demand curve. But firms try to extract as much consumer surplus as possible, and to do so, they discriminate in two broad ways:

- Among groups of buyers
- Among units of a good

#### Discriminating Among Groups of Buyers

To price discriminate among groups of buyers, the firm offers different prices to different types of buyers, based on things like age, employment status, or some other easily distinguished characteristic. This type of price discrimination works when each group has a different average willingness to pay for the good or service.

For example, a face-to-face sales meeting with a customer might bring a large and profitable order. For salespeople and other business travelers, the marginal benefit from an airplane trip is large and the price that such a traveler will pay for a trip is high. In contrast, for a vacation traveler, any of several different trips or even no vacation trip are options. So for vacation travelers, the marginal benefit of a trip is small and the price that such a traveler will pay for a trip is low. Because business travelers are willing to pay more than vacation travelers are, it is possible for an airline to profit by price discriminating between these two groups.

## Discriminating Among Units of a Good

To price discriminate among units of a good, the firm charges the same prices to all its customers but offers a lower price per unit for a larger number of units bought. When Pizza Hut charges $10 for one home-delivered pizza and $14 for two, it is using this type of price discrimination. In this example, the price of the second pizza is only $4.

Let's see how an airline exploits the differences in demand by business and vacation travelers and increases its profit by price discriminating.

## ■ Profiting by Price Discriminating

Global Air has a monopoly on an exotic route. Figure 11.8 shows the demand curve (*D*) for travel on this route and Global Air's marginal revenue curve (*MR*). It also shows Global Air's marginal cost (*MC*) and average total cost (*ATC*) curves.

Initially, Global is a single-price monopoly and maximizes its profit by producing 8,000 trips a year (the quantity at which *MR* equals *MC*). The price is $1,200 a trip. The average total cost of a trip is $600, so economic profit is $600 a trip. On 8,000 trips, Global's economic profit is $4.8 million a year, shown by the blue rectangle. Global's customers enjoy a consumer surplus shown by the green triangle.

---

■ **FIGURE 11.8**

A Single Price of Air Travel

**Practice Online**

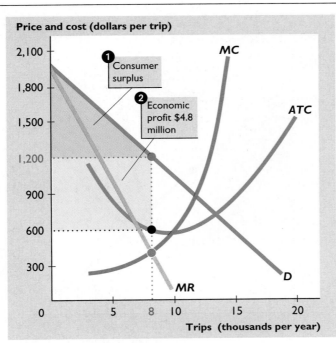

Global Air has a monopoly on an air route. The demand curve for travel on this route is *D*, and Global's marginal revenue curve is *MR*. Its marginal cost curve is *MC*, and its average total cost curve is *ATC*.

As a single-price monopoly, Global maximizes profit by selling 8,000 trips a year at $1,200 a trip. ❶ Global's customers enjoy a consumer surplus—the green triangle—and ❷ Global's economic profit is $4.8 million a year—the blue rectangle.

Global is struck by the fact that many of its customers are business travelers, and Global suspects that they are willing to pay more than $1,200 a trip. So Global does some market research, which tells Global that some business travelers are willing to pay as much as $1,800 a trip. Also, these customers almost always make their travel plans at the last moment. Another group of business travelers is willing to pay $1,600. These customers know a week ahead when they will travel and they never want to stay over a weekend. Yet another group is willing to pay up to $1,400. These travelers know two weeks ahead when they will travel and they don't want to stay away over a weekend.

So Global announces a new fare schedule. No restrictions, $1,800; 7-days advance purchase, no cancellation, $1,600; 14-days advance purchase, no cancellation, $1,400; 14-days advance purchase, must stay over weekend, $1,200.

Figure 11.9 shows the outcome with this new fare structure and also shows why Global is pleased with its new fares. It sells 2,000 trips at each of its four prices. Global's economic profit increases by the blue steps in the figure. Its economic profit is now its original $4.8 million a year plus an additional $2.4 million from its new higher fares. Consumer surplus has shrunk to the smaller green area.

## ■ Perfect Price Discrimination

**Perfect price discrimination**
Price discrimination that extracts the entire consumer surplus by charging the highest price that consumers are willing to pay for each unit.

But Global reckons that it can do even better. It plans to achieve **perfect price discrimination**, which extracts the entire consumer surplus. To do so, Global must get creative and come up with a host of additional business fares ranging between $2,000 and $1,200, each one of which appeals to a small segment of the business market and that together extract the entire consumer surplus from the business travelers.

---

### ■ FIGURE 11.9
Price Discrimination

**Practice Online**

Global revises its fare structure. It now offers no restrictions at $1,800, 7-day advance purchase at $1,600, 14-day advance purchase at $1,400, and 14-day advance purchase, must stay over the weekend at $1,200.

Global sells 2,000 units at each of its four new fares. It economic profit increases by $2.4 million a year to $7.2 million a year, which is shown by the original blue rectangle plus the blue steps. Global's customers' consumer surplus shrinks.

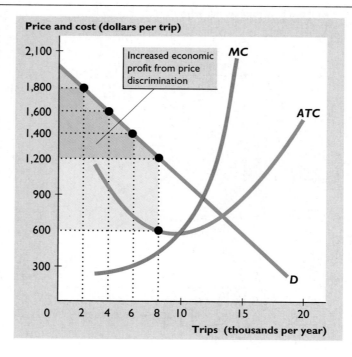

Once Global is discriminating finely between different customers and getting from each the maximum they are willing to pay, something special happens to marginal revenue. Recall that for the single-price monopoly, marginal revenue is less than price. The reason is that when the price is cut to sell a larger quantity, the price is lower on all units sold. But with perfect price discrimination, Global sells only the marginal seat at the lower price. All the other customers continue to buy for the highest price they are willing to pay. So for the perfect price discriminator, marginal revenue equals price and the demand curve becomes the marginal revenue curve.

With marginal revenue equal to price, Global can obtain yet greater profit by increasing output up to the point at which price (and marginal revenue) is equal to marginal cost.

So Global now seeks additional travelers who will not pay as much as $1,200 a trip but who will pay more than marginal cost. More creative pricing comes up with vacation specials and other fares that have combinations of advance reservation, minimum stay, and other restrictions that make these fares unattractive to its existing customers but attractive to a further group of travelers. With all these fares and specials, Global extracts the entire consumer surplus and maximizes economic profit.

Figure 11.10 shows the outcome with perfect price discrimination. The dozens of fares paid by the original travelers who are willing to pay between $1,200 and $2,000 have extracted the entire consumer surplus from this group and converted it into economic profit for Global. The new fares between $900 and $1,200 have attracted 3,000 additional travelers but have taken their entire consumer surplus also. Global is earning an economic profit of more than $9 million a year.

**FIGURE 11.10**

Perfect Price Discrimination

**Practice Online**

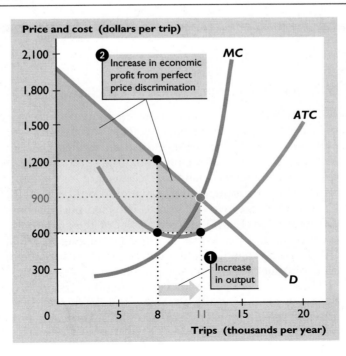

With perfect price discrimination, the demand curve becomes Global's marginal revenue curve. Economic profit is maximized when the lowest price equals marginal cost.

❶ Output increases to 11,000 passengers a year, and ❷ Global's economic profit increases to $9.35 million a year.

## Airline Price Discrimination

The normal coach fare from San Francisco to Washington, D.C., is $1,200. Book 14 days in advance, and this fare is $500. On a typical flight, United Airlines or American Airlines might have passengers paying as many as 20 different fares.

The airlines sort their customers according to their willingness to pay by offering a maze of advance-purchase and stayover restrictions that attract price-sensitive leisure travelers but don't get bought by business travelers.

Despite the sophistication of the airlines' pricing schemes, about 30 percent of seats fly empty. The marginal cost of filling an empty seat is close to zero, so a ticket sold at a few dollars would be profitable.

Extremely low prices are now feasible, thanks to Priceline.com. Shopping around airlines with bids from travelers, Priceline brokers about 1,000 tickets a day and gets the lowest possible fares.

Would it bother you to hear how little I paid for this flight?

From William Hamilton, "Voodoo Economics," © 1992 by the Chronicle Publishing Company, p. 3. Reprinted with permission of Chronicle Books.

## ■ Price Discrimination and Efficiency

With perfect price discrimination, the monopoly increases output to the point at which price equals marginal cost. This output is identical to that of perfect competition. Perfect price discrimination pushes consumer surplus to zero but increases producer surplus to equal the sum of consumer surplus and producer surplus in perfect competition. Deadweight loss with perfect price discrimination is zero. So perfect price discrimination produces the efficient quantity.

But there are two differences between perfect competition and perfect price discrimination. First, the distribution of the surplus is different. It is shared by consumers and producers in perfect competition while the producer gets it all with perfect price discrimination. Second, because the producer grabs all the surplus, rent seeking becomes profitable.

Rent seekers use resources in pursuit of monopoly, and the bigger the rents, the greater is the incentive to use resources to pursue those rents. With free entry into rent seeking, the long-run equilibrium outcome is that rent seekers use up the entire producer surplus.

# CHECKPOINT 11.4

**4**  **Explain how price discrimination increases profit.**

**Study Guide pp. 174–176**

**Practice Online  11.4**

## Practice Problem 11.4

Village, a small isolated town, has one doctor. For a 30-minute consultation, the doctor charges a rich person twice as much as a poor person.
a.  Does the doctor practice price discrimination?
b.  Does the doctor's pricing system redistribute consumer surplus? If so, explain how.
c.  Is the doctor using resources efficiently? Explain your answer.
d.  If the doctor decided to charge everyone the maximum price that he or she would be willing to pay, what would be the consumer surplus?
e.  In part **d**, is the market for medical service in Village efficient?

## Exercises 11.4

1.  Under what conditions is price discrimination possible?

2.  Which of the following is *not* an example of price discrimination?
    a.  A diner offers senior citizens a discount on Tuesday lunches.
    b.  An airline offers stand-by fares at a 75 percent discount.
    c.  An airline offers a 25 percent discount on a round-trip ticket for a week-end stay.
    d.  A supermarket sells water for $2 a bottle or $18 for a box of 12 bottles.
    e.  A bank charges a higher interest rate on a loan to buy a motorbike than the rate it charges the same person on a student loan.
    f.  A California car wash pays a higher price for water than a California farmer pays.
    g.  A cell phone company offers free calls on the weekend.
    h.  A museum offers discounts to students and senior citizens.
    i.  A power utility charges a steel smelter a higher price for electricity between 6:00 A.M. and 9:00 A.M. than it charges between midnight and 6:00 A.M.

## Solution to Practice Problem 11.4

a.  The doctor practices price discrimination because rich people and poor people pay a different price for the same service: a 30-minute consultation.
b.  With price discrimination, the doctor takes some of the consumer surplus. So yes, consumer surplus is reduced and redistributed to the doctor as economic profit.
c.  No, the doctor creates a deadweight loss and so is not using resources efficiently.
d.  The doctor now practices perfect price discrimination. To maximize profit, the doctor increases the number of consultations to make the lowest price charged equal to marginal cost. The doctor takes the entire consumer surplus. So consumer surplus is zero.
e.  The doctor no longer creates a deadweight loss, so resources are being used efficiently.

## 11.5 MONOPOLY POLICY ISSUES

The comparison of monopoly and competition makes monopoly look bad. Monopoly is inefficient, and it captures consumer surplus and converts it into economic profit or pure waste in the form of rent-seeking costs. If monopoly is so bad, why do we put up with it? Why don't we have laws that crack down on monopoly so hard that it never rears its head? We do indeed have laws that limit monopoly and regulate the prices that monopolies are permitted to charge. But monopoly also brings some benefits. We begin this review of monopoly policy issues by looking at the benefits of monopoly. We then look at the regulation of monopoly.

### ■ Gains from Monopoly

The main reason why monopoly exists is that it has potential advantages over a competitive alternative. These advantages arise from

- Economies of scale
- Incentives to innovate

#### Economies of Scale

Economies of scale can lead to *natural monopoly*—a situation in which a single firm can produce at a lower average total cost than a larger number of smaller firms can. Examples of industries in which economies of scale are so significant that they lead to a natural monopoly are becoming more rare. Public utilities such as gas, electric power, local telephone service, and garbage collection once were natural monopolies. But technological advances now enable us to separate the *production* of electric power and natural gas from their *distribution*. The provision of water though, remains a natural monopoly. Where significant economies of scale exist, it would be wasteful not to have a monopoly. So creating competition in a market that is a natural monopoly would be wasteful.

#### Incentives to Innovate

Invention leads to a wave of innovation as new knowledge is applied to the production process. Do large firms with monopoly power or small competitive firms lacking monopoly power innovate most? The evidence is mixed. Large firms do more research and development than do small firms, and they are usually the first to use a new technology. But their rate of productivity growth is no greater than that of small firms.

### ■ Regulating Natural Monopoly

Figure 11.11 shows the demand curve, $D$, the marginal revenue curve, $MR$, the long-run average cost curve, $LRAC$, and the marginal cost curve, $MC$, for a gas distribution company. The firm's marginal cost is constant at 10 cents a cubic foot. Average cost decreases as output increases. This firm is a natural monopoly.

If the firm is not regulated and maximizes profit, it produces only 2 million cubic feet a day, the quantity at which marginal cost equals marginal revenue. The firm prices gas at 20 cents a cubic foot and makes an economic profit of 2 cents a cubic foot, or $40,000 a day. This outcome is inefficient. Gas costs 20 cent a cubic

■ **FIGURE 11.11**

**Practice Online**

Regulating a Natural Monopoly

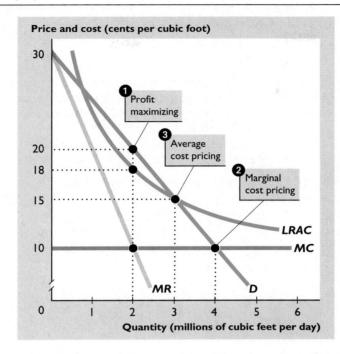

**Price and cost (cents per cubic foot)**

The demand curve for gas is the curve *D*. The natural monopoly's marginal cost, *MC*, is constant at 10 cents a cubic foot and its long-run average cost curve is *LRAC*.

**❶** The unregulated natural monopoly produces 2 million cubic feet and sets the price at 20 cents a cubic foot.

**❷** With a marginal cost pricing rule, the price is 10 cents a cubic foot and the quantity produced is 4 million cubic feet a day. The firm incurs an economic loss.

**❸** With an average cost pricing rule, the price is 15 cents a cubic foot and the quantity produced is 3 million cubic feet a day. The firm makes a normal profit.

foot when marginal cost is only 10 cents a cubic foot. Also, the gas company is making an economic profit. What can regulation do to change this outcome?

An efficient use of resources is achieved when marginal benefit equals marginal cost. You can see in Figure 11.11 that this outcome occurs if the price is regulated at 10 cents a cubic foot and if 4 million cubic feet a day are produced. A **marginal cost pricing rule** that sets price equal to marginal cost achieves this outcome.

The marginal cost pricing rule is efficient, but it leaves the natural monopoly incurring an economic loss. How can a firm cover its costs and, at the same time, obey a marginal cost pricing rule? One possibility is to use a two-part price (called a two-part tariff). For example, the gas company might charge a monthly fixed fee that covers its fixed cost and then charge for gas consumed at marginal cost. But a natural monopoly cannot always cover its costs in this way.

Regulators almost never use marginal cost pricing because of its consequences for the firm's profit. Instead, they use an **average cost pricing rule**, which sets the price equal to average cost and enables the firm to cover its costs and earn a normal profit.

Figure 11.11 shows the average cost pricing outcome. The firm charges 15 cents a cubic foot and sells 3 million cubic feet a day. This outcome is better for consumers than the unregulated profit-maximizing outcome. The price is 5 cents a cubic foot lower, and the quantity consumed is 1 million cubic feet a day more. And the outcome is better for the producer than the marginal cost pricing rule outcome. The firm earns normal profit. The outcome is inefficient but less so than the unregulated profit-maximizing outcome.

**Marginal cost pricing rule**
A price rule for a natural monopoly that sets price equal to marginal cost.

**Average cost pricing rule**
A price rule for a natural monopoly that sets the price equal to average cost and enables the firm to cover its costs and earn a normal profit.

**Study Guide pp. 176–178**

**Practice Online 11.5**

**5** **Explain how monopoly regulation influences output, price, economic profit, and efficiency.**

## Practice Problem 11.5

The local water company is a natural monopoly. Figure 1 shows the demand for water and the water company's cost of providing water.

a. If the company is an unregulated profit-maximizer:
   i. What is the price of water?
   ii. What quantity of water would be supplied?
   iii. What would be the deadweight loss?

b. If the company is regulated to make normal profit:
   i. What is the price of water?
   ii. What quantity of water would be supplied?
   iii. What would be the deadweight loss?

c. If the company is regulated to be efficient:
   i. What is the price of water?
   ii. What quantity of water would be supplied?
   iii. What would be the deadweight loss?

**FIGURE 1**

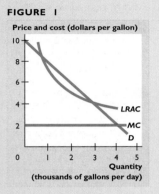

Price and cost (dollars per gallon)

## Exercise 11.5

Cox Cable has a monopoly in the provision of cable television service in many regions. If Cox Cable were regulated so that

a. Cable television service was efficient,
   i. Would the price of cable service change? If so, explain how and why.
   ii. Would Cox Cable make an economic profit, a normal profit, or an economic loss?
   iii. Would the consumer surplus change? If so, explain how and why.

b. Cox Cable made normal profit,
   i. Would the price of cable service change? If so, explain how and why.
   ii. Would the deadweight loss created by Cox Cable change? If so, explain how and why.
   iii. Would the consumer surplus change? If so, explain how and why.

**FIGURE 2**

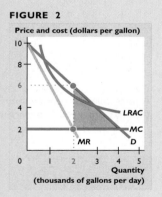

Price and cost (dollars per gallon)

## Solution to Practice Problem 11.5

a. The price of water is $6 a gallon, the quantity produced is 2,000 gallons a day, and the deadweight loss is $4,000 a day (the shaded triangle in Figure 2).

b. To make normal profit, the monopoly is regulated to set the price equal to average cost. Water is $4 a gallon, the quantity produced is 3,000 gallons a day, and the deadweight loss is $1,000 a day (the shaded triangle in Figure 3).

c. To be efficient, the monopoly is regulated to set the price (marginal benefit) equal to marginal cost. Water is $2 a gallon, the quantity produced is 4,000 gallons a day, and the deadweight loss is zero (Figure 4.)

**FIGURE 3**

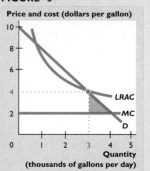

Price and cost (dollars per gallon)

**FIGURE 4**

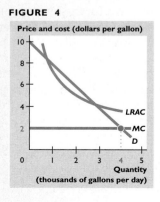

Price and cost (dollars per gallon)

# CHAPTER CHECKPOINT

## Key Points

**1**  **Explain how monopoly arises and distinguish between single-price monopoly and price-discriminating monopoly.**

* A monopoly is a market with a single supplier of a good or service that has no close substitutes and in which legal or natural barriers to entry prevent competition.
* A monopoly can price discriminate when there is no resale possibility.
* Where resale is possible, a firm charges a single price.

**2**  **Explain how a single-price monopoly determines its output and price.**

* The demand for a monopoly's output is the market demand, and a single-price monopoly's marginal revenue is less than price.
* A monopoly maximizes profit by producing the output at which marginal revenue equals marginal cost and by charging the maximum price that consumers are willing to pay for that output.

**3**  **Compare the performance of a single-price monopoly with that of perfect competition.**

* A single-price monopoly charges a higher price and produces a smaller quantity than does a perfectly competitive market and creates a deadweight loss.
* Monopoly imposes a loss on society that equals its deadweight loss plus the cost of the resources devoted to rent seeking.

**4**  **Explain how price discrimination increases profit.**

* Perfect price discrimination charges a different price for each unit sold, obtains the maximum price that each consumer is willing to pay for each unit, and redistributes the entire consumer surplus to the monopoly.
* With perfect price discrimination, the monopoly produces the same output as would a perfectly competitive market, but rent seeking uses some of the surplus.

**5**  **Explain how monopoly regulation influences output, price, economic profit, and efficiency.**

* Natural monopolies can produce at a lower price than competitive firms can, and monopolies might be more innovative than competitive firms.
* Efficient regulation requires that price equal marginal cost, but for a natural monopoly, such a price is less than average cost.
* Average cost pricing is a rule that covers a firm's costs and provides a normal profit but is inefficient.

## Key Terms

# Exercises

1. What are the two types of barrier to entry that can create a monopoly? Provide an example of each type. Why can't barriers to entry simply be torn down so that all markets become competitive?

2. Technological change is constantly creating and destroying barriers to entry and is changing the competitive and monopoly landscapes.
   a. Provide three examples of technological changes that have occurred during the past 20 years that have created a new barrier to entry and resulted in monopoly.
   b. Provide three examples of technological changes that have occurred during the past 20 years that have destroyed a barrier to entry and resulted in competition where previously monopoly was present.

3. Why isn't the demand for a monopoly's product perfectly elastic like that for the product of a firm in perfect competition?

4. Elixir Spring produces a unique and highly prized mineral water. The firm's total fixed cost is $5,000 a day, and its marginal cost is zero. Table 1 shows the demand schedule for Elixir water.
   a. Construct Elixir's total revenue schedule and marginal revenue schedule and make a graph of the demand and marginal revenue curves.
   b. Calculate and illustrate in a graph Elixir's profit-maximizing price, output, and economic profit.
   c. What is the elasticity of demand for Elixir water at the profit-maximizing quantity?

5. The Blue Rose Company is the only flower grower to have cracked the secret of making a blue rose. The first two columns of Table 2 show the demand schedule for blue roses, and the middle and third column show the total cost schedule for producing them.
   a. Construct Blue Rose's total revenue and marginal revenue schedule and make a graph of the demand and marginal revenue curves.
   b. Calculate Blue Rose's marginal cost schedule and add it to your graph.
   c. Calculate Blue Rose's profit-maximizing price, output, and economic profit.

6. Use the demand schedule for Elixir water in Table 1. Suppose that there are 1,000 springs, all able to produce this water at zero marginal cost. Suppose that for these firms, total fixed cost is also zero.
   a. What are the equilibrium price and quantity of Elixir water?
   b. Compare this equilibrium with the monopoly equilibrium in exercise 4.
   c. What is the consumer surplus if Elixir water is produced in perfect competition?
   d. What is the producer surplus if Elixir water is produced in perfect competition?
   e. What are the consumer surplus and producer surplus from Elixir water if a monopoly produces it?
   f. When the Elixir monopoly maximizes profit, what is the deadweight loss?

**TABLE 1**

| Price (dollars per bottle) | Quantity (bottles per day) |
| --- | --- |
| 10 | 0 |
| 9 | 1,000 |
| 8 | 2,000 |
| 7 | 3,000 |
| 6 | 4,000 |
| 5 | 5,000 |
| 4 | 6,000 |
| 3 | 7,000 |
| 2 | 8,000 |
| 1 | 9,000 |
| 0 | 10,000 |

**TABLE 2**

| Price (dollars per bunch) | Quantity (bunches per day) | Total cost (dollars per day) |
| --- | --- | --- |
| 80 | 0 | 80 |
| 72 | 1 | 82 |
| 64 | 2 | 88 |
| 56 | 3 | 100 |
| 48 | 4 | 124 |
| 40 | 5 | 160 |
| 32 | 6 | 208 |
| 24 | 7 | 268 |
| 16 | 8 | 340 |

7. Suppose that 1,000 competitive firms produce Elixir water and that one of these firms begins quietly to buy the others.
   a. What is the most that a firm would be willing to pay to obtain a monopoly in Elixir water?
   b. Illustrate this maximum amount in a graph.
   c. If a firm pays the maximum amount it is willing to pay for a monopoly in Elixir water, what is the firm's economic profit? Explain.

8. Bobbie's Hair Care is a natural monopoly in a small isolated town. The first two columns of Table 3 show the demand schedule for Bobbie's haircuts, and the middle and third column show Bobbie's total cost. Bobbie has done a survey and discovered that she gets four types of customer each hour—one woman who is willing to pay $18, one senior citizen who is willing to pay $16, one student who is willing to pay $14, and one boy who is willing to pay $12.
   a. If Bobbie charges just a single price for haircuts, what is that price, how many haircuts per hour does she do, and what is her economic profit?
   b. If Bobbie price discriminates among the four types of customer she has identified, what is the price she charges to each type of customer?
   c. How many haircuts an hour does Bobbie sell?
   d. What is Bobbie's economic profit?
   e. Is the quantity of haircuts efficient? Explain why or why not.
   f. What are the consumer surplus and producer surplus?
   g. Who benefits from Bobbie's price discrimination?

**TABLE 3**

| Price (dollars per haircut) | Quantity (haircuts per hour) | Total cost (dollars per hour) |
|---|---|---|
| 20 | 0 | 20 |
| 18 | 1 | 21 |
| 16 | 2 | 24 |
| 14 | 3 | 30 |
| 12 | 4 | 40 |
| 10 | 5 | 54 |

9. A city art museum, which is a local monopoly, is worried that it is not generating enough revenue to cover its costs, and the city government is cutting its budget. The museum charges $1 admission and $5 for special exhibitions. The museum director asks you to help him solve his problem. Can you suggest a pricing scheme that will bring in more revenue? At the same time, can you help the museum get even more people to visit it?

10. A global telephone company has large fixed costs, but its marginal cost of a call, whether local, long-distance, or international, is almost zero.
    a. If this firm is a profit-maximizing monopoly, how does it determine the price of a call and the number of calls to carry?
    b. If this firm is a regulated monopoly that is required to produce the efficient number of calls, what is the price of a call?
    c. Can you suggest a scheme that enables the firm to earn an economic profit and at the same time produce the efficient quantity of calls?
    d. Why is average cost pricing not a way of achieving the efficient quantity of calls?

11. Someone suggests that the way to deal with a natural monopoly is to permit it to maximize profit and then tax its profit at a very high rate. If a monopoly faces a tax on its economic profit,
    a. What happens to the profit-maximizing price and quantity?
    b. What happens to the producer surplus, consumer surplus, and deadweight loss?
    c. Can you suggest an alternative tax that brings output closer to the efficient level?

*FOMC meeting*

## ■ The Fed's Power Center

A description of the formal structure of the Fed gives the impression that power in the Fed resides with the Board of Governors. In practice, it is the chairman of the Board of Governors who has the largest influence on the Fed's monetary policy actions. Some remarkable people have been Fed chairmen.

The current chairman of the Board of Governors (in 2003) is Alan Greenspan, who was appointed by President Reagan in 1987 and reappointed by President Bush in 1992 and by President Clinton in 1996 and 2000. Alan Greenspan succeeded another influential chairman, Paul Volcker, who was appointed in 1979 by President Carter and reappointed in 1983 by President Reagan. Volcker ended the 1970s inflation but helped to create one of the most severe post–World War II recessions.

The chairman's power and influence stem from three sources. First, it is the chairman who controls the agenda and who dominates the meetings of the FOMC. Second, day-to-day contact with a large staff of economists and other technical experts provides the chairman with detailed background briefings on monetary policy issues. Third, the chairman is the spokesperson for the Fed and the main point of contact of the Fed with the President and government and with foreign central banks and governments.

## ■ The Fed's Policy Tools

The Federal Reserve has many responsibilities, but we'll examine its single most important one: regulating the amount of money floating around in the United States. How does the Fed control the quantity of money? It does so by adjusting the reserves of the banking system. Also, by adjusting the reserves of the banking system and standing ready to make loans to banks, the Fed is able to prevent bank failures. The Fed uses three main policy tools to achieve its objectives:

- Required reserve ratios
- Discount rate
- Open market operations

**TABLE 17.2 REQUIRED RESERVE RATIOS**

| Type of Deposit | Percent |
|---|---|
| Checkable deposits up to $41.3 million | 3 |
| Checkable deposits above $41.3 million | 10 |
| All other deposits | 0 |

SOURCE: Federal Reserve.

**Discount rate**
The interest rate at which the Fed stands ready to lend reserves to commercial banks.

**Open market operation**
The purchase or sale of government securities—U.S. Treasury bills and bonds—by the Federal Reserve in the open market.

**Monetary base**
The sum of coins, Federal Reserve notes, and banks' reserves at the Fed.

### Required Reserve Ratios

Banks hold reserves. These reserves are currency in the institutions' vaults and ATMs plus deposits held with other banks or with the Fed itself. Banks and thrifts are required to hold a minimum percentage of deposits as reserves. This minimum percentage is known as a *required reserve ratio*. The Fed determines a required reserve ratio for each type of deposit. In 2002, banks were required to hold minimum reserves equal to 3 percent of checkable deposits up to $41.3 million and 10 percent of these deposits in excess of this amount. The required reserves on other types of deposits were zero—see Table 17.2.

### Discount Rate

The **discount rate** is the interest rate at which the Fed stands ready to lend reserves to commercial banks. A change in the discount rate begins with a proposal to the FOMC by at least one of the 12 Federal Reserve Banks. If the FOMC agrees that a change is required, it proposes the change to the Board of Governors for its approval.

### Open Market Operations

An **open market operation** is the purchase or sale of government securities—U.S. Treasury bills and bonds—by the Federal Reserve in the open market. When the Fed conducts an open market operation, it makes a transaction with a bank or some other business but it does not transact with the federal government.

To understand how the Fed's policy tools work, you need to know about the monetary base.

### ■ The Monetary Base

The **monetary base** is the sum of coins, Federal Reserve notes, and banks' reserves at the Fed. The monetary base is so called because it acts like a base that supports the nation's money. The larger the monetary base, the greater is the quantity of money that it can support. Chapter 18 explains how a change in the monetary base leads to a change in the quantity of money.

In September 2002, the monetary base was $670 billion. Figure 17.9 shows how this amount was distributed among its three components: Coins were $30 billion; banks' deposits at the Fed were $10 billion; and the bulk of the monetary base, $630 billion, was made up of Federal Reserve notes.

Federal reserve notes and banks' reserves at the Fed are *liabilities* of the Fed. The Fed's *assets* are

- Gold and deposits in other central banks
- U.S. government securities
- Loans to banks

The Fed holds gold that it could sell if it needed or wished to. It also has deposits in other central banks such as the Bank of Japan and the Bank of England that it can withdraw if it needs to. The Fed holds U.S. government securities that it can sell. Finally, the Fed makes loans to banks, which it can call in. (These loans are usually very small). The Fed charges the banks the discount rate on these loans.

**FIGURE 17.9**

The Monetary Base and Its Composition

**Practice Online**

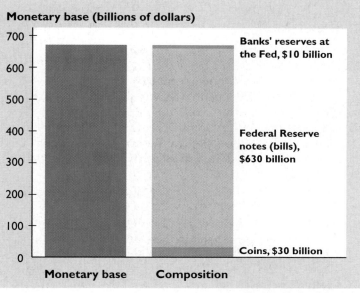

The monetary base is the sum of banks' reserves at the Fed, coins, and Federal Reserve notes (bills). Most of the monetary base consists of Federal Reserve notes.

SOURCE: Federal Reserve.

### Why Are Dollar Notes a Liability of the Fed?

You might be wondering why Federal Reserve notes (dollar bills) are a liability of the Fed. When bank notes were invented, they gave their owner a claim on the gold reserves of the issuing bank. These notes were *convertible paper money* and their holders could convert them into gold. So when a bank issued a note, it held itself liable to convert it into gold. The notes were "backed" by gold.

Federal Reserve notes are nonconvertible. A *nonconvertible note* is a bank note that is not convertible into gold and that obtains its value by government fiat— hence the term *fiat money*. These notes are the legal liability of the Fed, and they are "backed" by the Fed's assets. If everyone turned in their dollar bills and banks withdrew their reserves, the Fed would pay out by selling its assets.

### ■ How the Fed's Policy Tools Work: A Quick First Look

The next chapter explains how the Fed's policy tools work and how they change the quantity of money. Here, we'll take a quick first look at the basic ideas.

By increasing the required reserve ratio, the Fed can force the banks to hold a larger quantity of monetary base. By raising the discount rate, the Fed can make it more costly for the banks to borrow reserves—borrow monetary base. And by selling securities in the open market, the Fed can decrease the monetary base. All of these actions decrease the quantity of money, other things remaining the same.

Similarly, by decreasing the required reserve ratio, the Fed can permit the banks to hold a smaller quantity of monetary base. By lowering the discount rate, the Fed can make it less costly for the banks to borrow monetary base. And by buying securities in the open market, the Fed can increase the monetary base. All of these actions increase the quantity of money, other things remaining the same.

**Study Guide pp. 263–265**

**Practice Online 17.3**

**3** **Describe the functions of the Federal Reserve System.**

## Practice Problems 17.3

1. What is the Fed?
2. What is the FOMC?
3. What is the Fed's "power center"?
4. What are the Fed's main policy tools?
5. What is the monetary base?
6. Suppose that at the end of December 2005, the monetary base in the United States is $700 billion, Federal Reserve notes are $650 billion, and banks' reserves at the Fed are $20 billion. Calculate the quantity of coins.

## Exercises 17.3

1. What is a central bank?
2. What is the central bank in the United States?
3. Suppose that at the end of December 2004, the monetary base in the United States is $750 billion, Federal Reserve bills are $700 billion, and currency in circulation is $40 billion. What are the commercial banks' deposits at the Fed?
4. Suppose that at the end of December 2005, the monetary base in Canada is $85 billion, Bank of Canada bills are $75 billion, and there is $3 billion of currency in circulation. What are the deposits of the Canadian banks at the Bank of Canada?

## Solutions to Practice Problems 17.3

1. The Federal Reserve (Fed) is the central bank in the United States. The central bank in the United States is a public authority that provides banking services to banks and the U.S. government and that regulates the quantity of money and the monetary system.
2. The FOMC is the Federal Open Market Committee. The FOMC is the Fed's main policy-making committee.
3. The Fed's power center is the chairman of the Board of Governors. In 2003, that chairman is Alan Greenspan.
4. The Fed's main policy tools are required reserve ratios, the discount rate, and open market operations.
5. The monetary base is the sum of coins, Federal Reserve notes (dollar bills), and banks' reserves at the Fed.
6. To calculate the quantity of coins at the end of December 2005, we use the definition of the monetary base: coins plus Federal Reserve notes plus banks' reserves at the Fed. Coins equal the monetary base minus Federal Reserve notes minus banks' reserves at the Fed. If at the end of December 2005, the monetary base in the United States is $700 billion, Federal Reserve notes are $650 billion, and bank's reserves at the Fed are $20 billion, so the quantity of coins is $700 billion – $650 billion – $20 billion = $30 billion.

# CHAPTER CHECKPOINT

## Key Points

**1  Define money and describe its functions.**

- Money is anything that serves as a generally accepted means of payment.
- Money serves as a medium of exchange, a unit of account, and a store of value.
- M1 consists of currency, travelers' checks, and checkable deposits. M2 consists of M1 plus savings deposits, small time deposits, and money market funds.

**2  Describe the monetary system and explain the functions of banks and other monetary institutions.**

- Commercial banks, S&Ls, savings banks, credit unions, and money market funds are financial institutions whose deposits are money.
- Banks borrow short term and lend long term and make a profit on the spread between the interest rates that they pay and receive.
- Banks lend most of the funds they receive as deposits and hold only a small amount as reserves.
- Banks can borrow and lend reserves in the interbank federal funds market.

**3  Describe the functions of the Federal Reserve System.**

- The Federal Reserve is the central bank of the United States.
- The Fed influences the economy by setting the required reserve ratio for banks, by setting the discount rate, and by open market operations.

## Key Terms

Barter, 429
Central bank, 443
Commercial bank, 436
Credit union, 438
Currency, 430
Discount rate, 446
Electronic cash (e-cash), 432
Electronic check (e-check), 432
Excess reserves, 437
Federal funds rate, 437

Federal Open Market Committee, 444
Federal Reserve System, 443
Fiat money, 430
Liquid asset, 440
M1, 433
M2, 433
Means of payment, 428
Medium of exchange, 429
Monetary base, 446
Monetary policy, 443

Monetary system, 436
Money, 428
Money market fund, 438
Open market operation, 446
Required reserve ratio, 437
Reserves, 437
Savings and loan association, 438
Savings bank, 438
Store of value, 429
Unit of account, 429

## Exercises

1. What is money? Would you classify any of the following items as money?
   a. Store coupons for cat food
   b. A $100 Amazon.com gift certificate
   c. An S&L saving deposit
   d. Frequent Flier Miles
   e. Credit available on your Visa card
   f. The dollar coins that a coin collector owns
   g. Postage stamps issued to commemorate the 2002 Winter Olympic Games

2. What are the three vital functions that money performs? Which of the following items perform some but not all of these functions, and which perform all of these functions? Which of the items are money?
   a. A blank check
   b. A checkable deposit at the Bank of America
   c. A dime
   d. An antique clock
   e. Plastic sheets used to make Visa cards
   f. The coins in the Fed's museum
   g. Government bonds

3. Monica transfers $10,000 from her savings account at the Bank of Alaska to her money market fund. What is the immediate change in M1 and M2?

4. Naomi buys $1,000 worth of American Express travelers' checks and charges the purchase to her American Express card. What is the immediate change in M1 and M2?

5. Terry takes $100 from his checking account and deposits the $100 in his savings account. What is the immediate change in M1 and M2?

6. Vincenzo goes shopping. First, he visits an ATM, where he gets $200 from his savings account. Then he visits a clothing store, where he buys a shirt for $50 using his Visa card. At lunchtime, he meets Donna, his Italian girlfriend, who has just arrived from Rome and has only euros (the money of Italy) in her purse. Donna uses some of her euros to buy $100 from Vincenzo. Donna buys lunch and pays with the $100 that she got from Vincenzo. Did any of the transactions done by Vincenzo and Donna change the quantity of money?

7. In December 2002, banks in Australia had deposits of $500 billion, a required reserve ratio of 4 percent, and no excess reserves. The banks had $15 billion in currency. How much did the banks have in deposits at the Reserve Bank of Australia (the Australian central bank)?

8. In Canada in December 2005, the Bank of Canada (the central bank of Canada) had
   Gold and foreign exchange: $4 billion
   Banks' deposits: $3 billion
   Government securities: $10 billion
   Currency in circulation: $11 billion

The Canadian banks had
Checkable deposits: $400 billion
Savings deposits and time deposits: $600 billion
Currency inside the banks: $1 billion.
Calculate
  **a.** The banks' reserves
  **b.** The monetary base
  **c.** M1
  **d.** M2

9. In Mexico in January 2004, the Banco de México (the central bank of Mexico) reported that bills and coins outside the banks were 175 billion pesos. The Mexican banks had checkable deposits of 418 billion pesos and savings deposits and time deposits of 1782 billion pesos. Currency inside the banks was 28 billion pesos. The Mexican banks had deposits at the Banco de México of 186 billion pesos. Calculate
  **a.** The banks' reserves
  **b.** The monetary base
  **c.** M1
  **d.** M2

10. What are the main differences and similarities among commercial banks, thrift institutions, and money market funds? How do these institutions earn a profit? What are the main risks they face? How do they manage their exposure to risk?

11. List the policy tools of the Fed and sketch the way in which each tool works to change the quantity of money.

## Critical Thinking

12. The President of the United States has no formal authority over the Federal Reserve. In contrast, in some countries, the government directs the central bank and decides what its interest rate policy shall be. Provide some reasons why the central bank should be independent of the government as it is in the United States.

13. Suppose that e-cash issued by private online banks becomes so popular that it completely replaces physical cash and no one has any use for notes issued by the Fed and coins issued by the U.S. mint. What role do you think the Fed could play in such a world?

14. If banks are required to hold reserves at the Fed, doesn't that mean that the required reserves are not really reserves at all and that the only true reserves the banks hold are their excess reserves?

<u>Practice Online</u>   **Web Exercises**

**Use the links on your Foundations Web site to work the following exercises.**

15. Visit the Web site of the Federal Reserve. For the most recent week,
    a. What is M1?
    b. What is M2?
    c. What is the monetary base?
    d. What is the percentage increase in M1 over the past year?
    e. What is the percentage increase in M2 over the past year?
    f. What is the percentage increase in the monetary base over the past year?

16. Visit the page of the Federal Reserve Web site that provides data on the assets and liabilities of the commercial banks in the United States. For the most recent week and the same week a year earlier,
    a. What is the total amount of deposits?
    b. What is the total amount of cash assets?
    c. What is the total amount of loans?
    d. What is the percentage increase in deposits over the past year?
    e. What is the percentage increase in cash assets over the past year?
    f. What is the percentage increase in loans over the past year?

17. Visit the Web site of the Federal Reserve. For the most recent week,
    a. What is the total amount of reserves?
    b. What are the total borrowed reserves as a percentage of total reserves?
    c. What are excess reserves as a percentage of total reserves?

18. Visit the Open Market Operations page of the Federal Reserve Web site.
    a. What is the current target for the federal funds rate?
    b. How has the target for the federal funds rate changed over the past year?
    c. What do you think the Fed has been trying to do with the changes in the federal funds rate over the past year?

# Money Creation and Control

## CHAPTER CHECKLIST

**When you have completed your study of this chapter, you will be able to**

1  Explain how banks create money by making loans.

2  Explain how the Fed controls the quantity of money.

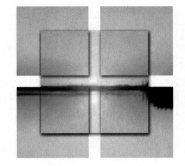

Making imitation dollar bills is a serious crime. But creating billions of dollars' worth of money is a perfectly legal activity that banks perform every day. In this chapter, you're going to learn how banks create money by making loans.

This chapter builds on what you learned in Chapter 17. There, you saw that most of the money in the United States today is deposits in commercial banks and thrift institutions. You also learned about the structure of the Fed and the tools it uses to control the quantity of money that circulates in the United States.

You're now going to see exactly how money gets created and how the Fed controls its quantity. Understanding these processes is crucial to understanding how inflation occurs and how it can be kept under control. It is also crucial to understanding how the Fed tries to smooth the business cycle.

First, we'll study the links between the banks' reserves, the quantity of loans that banks make, and the quantity of deposits that they create. Then we'll learn how the Fed uses open market operations and other tools to influence the quantity of money.

## 18.1 HOW BANKS CREATE MONEY

Banks* create money out of thin air! But this doesn't mean that they have smoke-filled back rooms in which counterfeiters are busily working. Remember, most money is bank deposits, not currency. Banks create deposits, and they do so by making loans. But they cannot create any amount of money they wish. The amount of deposits they can create is limited by their reserves.

### ■ Creating a Bank

The easiest way to see how banks create money is to work through the process of creating a bank. Suppose that you and your friends decide to create the Virtual College Bank, an Internet bank that specializes in banking services for college students. You will need to go through the following eight steps:

- Obtain a charter to operate a commercial bank
- Raise some financial capital
- Buy some equipment and computer programs
- Accept deposits
- Establish a reserve account at a Federal Reserve Bank
- Clear checks
- Buy government securities
- Make loans

#### Obtaining a Charter

Your first task is to obtain a charter to operate a commercial bank. You apply to the Comptroller of the Currency for this charter and establish a federally chartered bank. (If you wanted to establish a state commercial bank, you would apply to your state treasurer's office.)

#### Raising Financial Capital

**Balance sheet**
A statement that summarizes assets (amounts owned) and liabilities (amounts owed).

Your next task is to get some funds. You figure that you can open your bank with $200,000, so Virtual College Bank creates 2,000 shares, each worth $100, and sells these shares in your local community. Your bank now has a **balance sheet**—a statement that summarizes its assets and liabilities. The bank's assets are what it owns, and its liabilities are the claims against it, or what it owes, and its owners' equity. Table 18.1 shows your new bank's first balance sheet.

### ■ TABLE 18.1
Virtual College Bank's Balance Sheet #1

| Assets | | Liabilities | |
|---|---|---|---|
| Cash | $200,000 | Owners' equity | $200,000 |

You are now ready to take your third step.

---

*In this chapter, we'll use the term "bank" to include commercial banks and thrift institutions whose deposits are part of the money supply.

## Eye on the Past

### The "Invention" of Banking

Goldsmiths and their customers stumbled upon a brilliant idea that led to the creation of the first banks. You will gain useful insights into modern banks and the way they create money by looking at these early banks.

Because gold is valuable and easy to steal, the goldsmiths of sixteenth century Europe had well-guarded safes in which to keep their own gold. They also rented space in their safes to artisans and others who wanted to put their gold in safekeeping. The goldsmiths issued a receipt to the owners of the gold entitling them to reclaim their "deposits" on demand. These receipts were similar to the coat check token you get at a theater or museum.

Isabella has a gold receipt that shows that she has deposited 100 ounces of gold with Samuel Goldsmith. She is going to use her gold to buy some land from Henry. Isabella can make this transaction in one of two ways: She can visit Samuel, collect her gold, and hand the gold to Henry. Or she can give Henry her gold receipt, which will then enable Henry to claim the 100 ounces of gold from Samuel Goldsmith.

It is obviously much more convenient to pass the receipt to Henry. It is a simpler and safer transaction. When Henry wants to use the gold to buy something, he too can pass the receipt on to someone else.

So Samuel Goldsmith's gold receipt is circulating as a means of payment. It is money!

After some years, Samuel notices that the gold that people have placed in his safekeeping never leaves his vault. The receipts circulate, and the gold simply sits in the safe.

Samuel realizes that he can lend people gold receipts and charge them interest on the receipts. So he writes some receipts for gold that he doesn't have and lends these receipts.

After some further years, when many goldsmiths are doing what Samuel is doing, they begin to compete with each other for gold deposits, and instead of charging rent to gold owners, they start to pay interest on gold deposits.

Samuel and his fellow goldsmiths have made the transition from being goldsmiths to being bankers.

As long as they don't issue too many gold receipts, they will always be able to honor requests from depositors who wish to reclaim their gold.

### Buying Equipment

You buy some office equipment, a server, banking database software, and a high-speed Internet connection. These items cost you $200,000. Table 18.2 shows your bank's new balance sheet.

■ **TABLE 18.2**
Virtual College Bank's Balance Sheet #2

| Assets | | Liabilities | |
|---|---|---|---|
| Cash | $0 | | |
| Equipment | $200,000 | Owners' equity | $200,000 |

### Accepting Deposits

You are now ready to start accepting deposits. You pass the word around that you are offering the best terms available and the lowest charges on checkable deposits. Deposits begin to roll in. After a hectic day of business, you have accepted $120,000 of deposits. Table 18.3 shows Virtual College Bank's new balance sheet.

■ **TABLE 18.3**
Virtual College Bank's Balance Sheet #3

| Assets | | Liabilities | |
|---|---|---|---|
| Cash | $120,000 | Checkable deposits | $120,000 |
| Equipment | $200,000 | Owners' equity | $200,000 |

The deposits at Virtual College Bank are now part of the money supply. But the quantity of money in the economy has not increased. People have deposited either currency or checks drawn on other banks. To keep the story simple, we'll suppose that all these deposits are currency. So currency outside the banks has decreased by $120,000, and checkable deposits have increased by $120,000.

### Establishing a Reserve Account

Now that Virtual College Bank has deposits, it must establish a reserve account at its local Federal Reserve Bank. We'll suppose that your virtual bank is in College Station, Texas, in the Dallas Federal Reserve District. Virtual College Bank now opens an account at the Dallas Fed and deposits in that account all its cash. Table 18.4 shows Virtual College Bank's new balance sheet.

■ **TABLE 18.4**
Virtual College Bank's Balance Sheet #4

| Assets | | Liabilities | |
|---|---|---|---|
| Cash | $0 | | |
| Reserves at the Dallas Fed | $120,000 | Checkable deposits | $120,000 |
| Equipment | $200,000 | Owners' equity | $200,000 |

*Reserves: Actual and Required* You saw in Chapter 17 that banks don't keep $100 in bills for every $100 that people have deposited with them. In fact, a typical bank today has reserves of a bit less than $1 for every $100 of deposits. But there's no need for panic. These reserve levels are adequate for ordinary business needs.

The proportion of a bank's total deposits that are held in reserves is called the *reserve ratio*. Virtual College Bank's reserves are $120,000 and deposits are $120,000, so its reserve ratio is 100 percent.

The *required reserve ratio* is the ratio of reserves to deposits that banks are required, by regulation, to hold. We'll suppose that the required reserve ratio for virtual banks operated by college students is 25 percent, a much higher percentage than that for U.S. commercial banks (see Chapter 17, p. 446).

A bank's *required reserves* are equal to its deposits multiplied by the required reserve ratio. So Virtual College Bank's required reserves are

$$\text{Required reserves} = \$120{,}000 \times 25 \div 100 = \$30{,}000.$$

Actual reserves minus required reserves are *excess reserves*. Virtual College Bank's excess reserves are

$$\text{Excess reserves} = \$120,000 - \$30,000 = \$90,000.$$

Whenever banks have excess reserves, they are able to make loans. But before Virtual College Bank takes that step, it needs to learn how to clear checks.

## Clearing Checks

Virtual College Bank's depositors want to be able to make and receive payments by check. So when Virtual College depositor Jay writes a check for $20,000 to buy some computers from Hal's PCs, which has a checkable deposit at the First American Bank, funds must move from Jay's account at your bank to Hal's account at First American. In the process, Virtual College loses reserves and First American gains reserves. Figure 18.1 tracks the balance sheet changes that occur.

When Hal's PCs banks Jay's check, First American sends the check to the Dallas Fed for collection. The Dallas Fed increases First American's reserves and decreases Virtual College's reserves by $20,000—see Figure 18.1(a). First American now has an extra $20,000 in its reserves at the Dallas Fed, and it increases Hal's PCs' checkable deposit by $20,000. First American's assets and liabilities have both increased by $20,000 in Figure 18.1(b). The Dallas Fed returns the cleared check to Virtual College. Virtual College now has $20,000 less in its reserve account, and it decreases Jay's checkable deposit by $20,000. Virtual College's assets and liabilities have both decreased by $20,000 in Figure 18.1(c).

---

**FIGURE 18.1**

Clearing a Check

**Practice Online**

**Federal Reserve Bank of Dallas**

| Assets | Liabilities | |
|---|---|---|
| | First American reserves | +$20,000 |
| | Virtual College reserves | −$20,000 |

**(a) Change in Dallas Fed's balance sheet**

**First American Bank**

| Assets | | Liabilities | |
|---|---|---|---|
| Reserves at the Dallas Fed | +$20,000 | Checkable deposits | +$20,000 |

**(b) Change in First American Bank's balance sheet**

**Virtual College Bank**

| Assets | | Liabilities | |
|---|---|---|---|
| Reserves at the Dallas Fed | −$20,000 | Checkable deposits | −$20,000 |

**(c) Change in Virtual College Bank's balance sheet**

(a) First American sends a $20,000 check for collection to the Dallas Fed. The Dallas Fed increases First American's reserves by $20,000 and decreases Virtual College's reserves by $20,000.

(b) First American increases Hal's PCs' checkable deposit by $20,000. First American's assets and liabilities have both increased by $20,000.

(c) Virtual College decreases Jay's checkable deposit by $20,000. Virtual College's assets and liabilities have both decreased by $20,000.

The quantity of money is unaffected by these transactions. Checkable deposits have increased at First American and decreased at Virtual College, but total deposits are unchanged. Total bank reserves are also unaffected. First American's reserves have increased and Virtual College's reserves have decreased by the same amount.

Virtual College Bank is now ready to use some of its reserves to earn an income. It buys some government securities.

### Buying Government Securities

Government securities provide Virtual College with an income and a safe asset that is easily converted back into reserves when necessary. Suppose that Virtual College decides to buy $60,000 worth of government securities. On the same day, First American decides to sell $60,000 of government securities to Virtual College. In reality, a bond broker will match the First American sale with Virtual College's purchase.

Figure 18.2 tracks the effects of this transaction on the balance sheets of the two banks and the Dallas Fed. Virtual College gives First American a check for $60,000, and First American transfers the government bonds to Virtual College. First American sends the check to the Dallas Fed for collection. The Dallas Fed

---

### ■ FIGURE 18.2

**Practice Online**

Making Interbank Loans and Buying Government Securities

(a) Virtual College buys $60,000 worth of government securities from First American and pays by check. The Dallas Fed increases First American's reserves by $60,000 and decreases Virtual College's reserves by the same amount.

(b) First American's reserves have increased and its government securities have decreased by $60,000.

(c) Virtual College's reserves have decreased and its government securities have increased by the $60,000.

**Federal Reserve Bank of Dallas**

| Assets | Liabilities | |
|--------|-------------|---|
| | First American reserves | +$60,000 |
| | Virtual College reserves | −$60,000 |

**(a) Change in Dallas Fed's balance sheet**

**First American Bank**

| Assets | | Liabilities |
|--------|---|-------------|
| Reserves at the Dallas Fed | +$60,000 | |
| Government securities | −$60,000 | |

**(b) Change in First American Bank's balance sheet**

**Virtual College Bank**

| Assets | | Liabilities |
|--------|---|-------------|
| Reserves at the Dallas Fed | −$60,000 | |
| Government securities | +$60,000 | |

**(c) Change in Virtual College Bank's balance sheet**

increases First American's reserves by $60,000 and decreases Virtual College's reserves by the same amount in Figure 18.2(a).

First American's reserves have increased and its government securities have decreased by the same $60,000 in Figure 18.2(b). Virtual College's reserves have decreased and its government securities have increased by the same $60,000 in Figure 18.2(c).

After all the transactions we've just followed in Figures 18.1 and 18.2, Virtual College's balance sheet looks like that in Table 18.5.

■ **TABLE 18.5**

Virtual College Bank's Balance Sheet #5

| Assets | | Liabilities | |
| --- | --- | --- | --- |
| Reserves at the Dallas Fed | $40,000 | Checkable deposits | $100,000 |
| Government securities | $60,000 | Owners' equity | $200,000 |
| Equipment | $200,000 | | |
| Total assets | $300,000 | Total liabilities | $300,000 |

With deposits of $100,000 and a required reserve ratio of 25 percent, Virtual College must hold a minimum of $25,000 in reserves. Because it currently has $40,000 in reserves, Virtual College can make some loans.

## Making Loans

With reserves of $40,000 and required reserves of $25,000, Virtual College has excess reserves of $15,000. So the bank decides to make loans of this amount. Table 18.6 shows the bank's balance sheet on the day the bank makes these loans. Loans of $15,000 are added to the bank's assets. Loans are an asset to the bank because the borrower is committed to repaying the loan on an agreed-upon schedule. The bank places the $15,000 loaned in the checkable deposit accounts of the borrowers. So the bank's checkable deposits increase by $15,000 to $115,000.

■ **TABLE 18.6**

Virtual College Bank's Balance Sheet #6

| Assets | | Liabilities | |
| --- | --- | --- | --- |
| Reserves at the Dallas Fed | $40,000 | Checkable deposits | $115,000 |
| Government securities | $60,000 | Owners' equity | $200,000 |
| Loans | $15,000 | | |
| Equipment | $200,000 | | |
| Total assets | $315,000 | Total liabilities | $315,000 |

The bank has now created some money. Checkable deposits have increased by the amount of the loans, so the quantity of money has increased by $15,000. And although Virtual College has made loans equal to its excess reserves of $15,000, it still has those reserves! Because its deposits have increased, its required reserves have also increased. They are now 25 percent of $115,000, or $28,750. So the bank now has excess reserves of $11,250.

Before you get too excited and decide to lend another $11,250, let's see what happens when the borrowers of the $15,000 that you've just loaned start to spend their loans.

*Spending a Loan* To spend their loans, the borrowers write checks on their checkable deposits. Let's assume that they spend the entire $15,000. Most likely, the people to whom these checks are paid do not bank at Virtual College. That's what we'll assume. So when these checks are cleared, transactions like those that we described above take place. The receiving banks send the checks to the Dallas Fed for collection. The Fed increases the reserves of the receiving banks by $15,000 and decreases the reserves of Virtual College by $15,000. Virtual College's balance sheet now looks like that in Table 18.7.

**■ TABLE 18.7**

Virtual College Bank's Balance Sheet #7

| Assets | | Liabilities | |
|---|---|---|---|
| Reserves at the Dallas Fed | $25,000 | Checkable deposits | $100,000 |
| Government securities | $60,000 | Owners' equity | $200,000 |
| Loans | $15,000 | | |
| Equipment | $200,000 | | |
| Total assets | $300,000 | Total liabilities | $300,000 |

Both reserves and deposits have decreased by $15,000 because this amount has been paid to people with accounts in other banks. If some of the checks drawn were paid to customers of Virtual College, deposits and reserves would have fallen by less than the full $15,000 and the bank would still have some excess reserves. But in the situation shown in Table 18.7, the bank is fully loaned—its reserves are just sufficient to meet the required reserve ratio.

But the banks that received the deposits that Virtual College has lost have also received reserves. These banks now have excess reserves, so they can make some loans. And these loans will create some more money. Also, when Virtual College bought government securities from First American, the reserves of First American increased by $60,000. So other banks now have reserves of $75,000 that they didn't have before that they could now lend. So yet more money can be created.

If you told the loan officer at your own bank that she creates money, she wouldn't believe you. People who work in banks see themselves as lending the money they receive from others, but (unless they've studied economics) they don't see the entire process, so they don't realize that they create money. But in fact, even though each bank lends only what it receives, the banking system creates money. To see how, let's see what happens in the entire banking system when one bank receives some new reserves.

## ■ The Limits to Money Creation

Figure 18.3 is going to keep track of what is happening in the process of money creation by a banking system in which each bank has a required reserve ratio of 25 percent. We'll start the process off with every bank holding exactly its required reserves. Then Al Capone, after years of shady dealing, decides to go to school. He takes $100,000 of notes from under his mattress and deposits them at Virtual College Bank. Virtual College now has $100,000 of new deposits and $100,000 of new reserves. With a required reserve ratio of 25 percent, the bank's required reserves are $25,000. So the bank makes a loan of $75,000 to Amy. Then Amy writes a check for $75,000 to buy a copy-shop franchise from Barb. At this point,

Virtual College has a new deposit of $100,000, a new loan of $75,000, and new reserves of $25,000. You can see this situation in Figure 18.3.

For Virtual College, that is the end of the story. But it's not the end of the story for the banking system. Barb deposits her check for $75,000 in First American, where deposits and reserves increase by $75,000. First American puts 25 percent of its increase in deposits ($18,750) into reserves and lends $56,250 to Bob. And Bob writes a check to Carl to pay off a business loan.

Figure 18.3 shows the state of play at the end of round 2. Total bank reserves have increased by $43,750 ($25,000 plus $18,750), total loans have increased by $131,250 ($75,000 plus $56,250), and total deposits have increased by $175,000 ($100,000 plus $75,000).

When Carl takes his check to Fleet PC, its deposits and reserves increase by $56,250. Fleet PC keeps $14,063 in reserves and lends $42,187. This process continues until there are no excess reserves in the banking system. But the process

---

**FIGURE 18.3**

The Multiple Creation of Bank Deposits

Practice Online

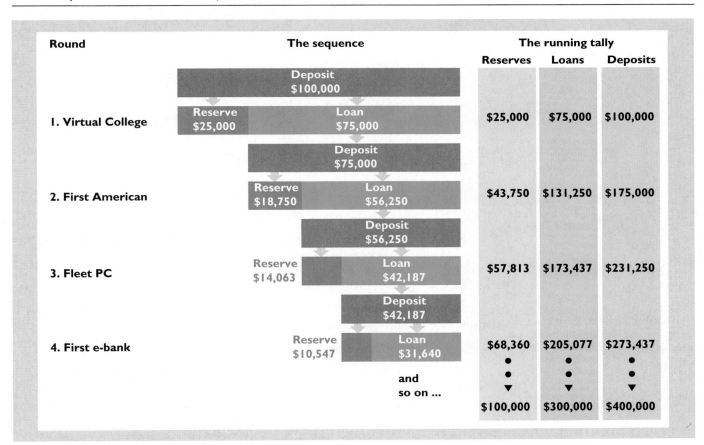

When a bank receives deposits, it keeps 25 percent in reserves and lends 75 percent. The amount loaned becomes a new deposit at another bank. The next bank in the sequence keeps 25 percent and lends 75 percent, and the process continues until the banking system has created enough deposits to eliminate its excess reserves. The running tally tells us the deposits and loans created at each stage. At the end of the process, an additional $100,000 of reserves creates an additional $400,000 of deposits.

takes a lot of further steps. Figure 18.3 shows one additional step. The figure also shows the final tallies: Reserves increase by $100,000, loans increase by $300,000, and deposits increase by $400,000.

The sequence in Figure 18.3 is the first four rounds of the process. To work out the entire process, look closely at the numbers in the figure. At each stage, the loan is 75 percent (0.75) of the previous loan and the deposit is 0.75 of the previous deposit. Let's call that proportion $L$ ($L = 0.75$). The complete sequence is

$$1 + L + L^2 + L^3 + L^4 + \ldots.$$

Remember, $L$ is a fraction, so at each stage in this sequence, the amount of new loans and new deposits gets smaller. The total increase in deposits when the process ends is the sum of the above sequence multiplied by the initial increase in reserves, which is

$$\frac{1}{1 - L} \times \text{Initial increase in reserves.}$$

If we use the numbers from the example, the total increase in deposits is

$$\$100,000 + 75,000 + 56,250 + 42,187 + \ldots$$

$$= \$100,000 \times (1 + 0.75 + 0.5625 + 0.42187 + \ldots)$$

$$= \$100,000 \times (1 + 0.75 + 0.75^2 + 0.75^3 + \ldots)$$

$$= \$100,000 \times \frac{1}{(1 - 0.75)}$$

$$= \$100,000 \times \frac{1}{0.25}$$

$$= \$100,000 \times 4.$$

$$= \$400,000.$$

So even though each bank lends only the money it receives, the banking system as a whole does create money by making loans.

### ■ The Deposit Multiplier

**Deposit multiplier**
The number by which an increase in bank reserves is multiplied to find the resulting increase in bank deposits.

The **deposit multiplier** is the number by which an increase in bank reserves is multiplied to find the resulting increase in bank deposits. That is,

Change in deposits = Deposit multiplier × Change in reserves.

In the example that we've just worked through, the deposit multiplier is 4. The $100,000 increase in reserves brought a $400,000 increase in deposits. The deposit multiplier is linked to the required reserve ratio by the following equation:

$$\text{Deposit multiplier} = \frac{1}{\text{Required reserve ratio}}.$$

In the example, the required reserve ratio is 25 percent, or 0.25. That is,

$$\text{Deposit multiplier} = \frac{1}{0.25} = 4.$$

## CHECKPOINT 18.1

**I** **Explain how banks create money by making loans.**

**Study Guide pp. 270–273**

**Practice Online 18.1**

## Practice Problems 18.1

1. How do banks create new deposits by making loans, and what factors limit the amount of deposits and loans they can create?

2. The required reserve ratio is 0.1, and banks have no excess reserves. Jamie deposits $100 in his bank. Calculate
   a. The bank's excess reserves as soon as Jamie makes the deposit.
   b. The maximum amount of loans that the banking system can make.
   c. The maximum amount of new money that the banking system can create.

## Exercises 18.1

1. Your bank manager tells you that he does not create money. He just lends the money that people deposit in the bank. Explain to him how he does create money.

2. If the banking system receives new deposits of $200 million, what determines the maximum amount of new money that the banks can create?

3. If a multibank system has a required reserve ratio of 0.05 and Erin deposits $50 in her bank, calculate
   a. The bank's excess reserves as soon as Erin makes her deposit.
   b. The maximum amount of loans that the banking system can make.
   c. The maximum amount of new money that the banking system can create.

## Solutions to Practice Problems 18.1

1. Banks can make loans when they have excess reserves—reserves in excess of those required. When a bank makes a loan, it creates a new deposit for the person who receives the loan. The bank uses its excess reserves to create new deposits. The amount of loans that the bank can make, and therefore the amount of new deposits that it can create, is limited by two things: the amount of excess reserves and the required reserve ratio.

2a. The bank's excess reserves are $90. When deposits increase by $100, the bank is required to keep 10 percent of the deposit as reserves. That is, required reserves increase by $10 and the bank has $90 of excess reserves.

2b. The maximum amount of loans that the banking system can make is $900. When reserves increase by $100, the deposit multiplier determines the maximum increase in deposits that the banking system can have. Deposits increase to make the bank's required reserves increase by $100. The deposit multiplier equals 1/Required reserve ratio, which is 1/0.1 or 10. With the $100 increase in reserves, deposits can increase to $1,000. Jamie deposited $100, so the banking system can create an additional $900 of deposits. It does so by making loans of $900.

2c. The maximum amount of new money that can be created is $900. When a bank makes loans, it creates new money. The maximum amount of new money created by the banking system equals the maximum amount of loans that it can make.

## 18.2  INFLUENCING THE QUANTITY OF MONEY

The Fed constantly monitors and adjusts the quantity of money in the economy. To change the quantity of money, the Fed can use any of its three tools:

- Required reserve ratios
- Discount rate
- Open market operations

Let's see how these three tools work.

### ■ How Required Reserve Ratios Work

If the Fed increases the required reserve ratio, the banks must increase their reserves and decrease their lending, which decreases the quantity of money. If the Fed decreases the required reserve ratio, the banks can decrease their reserves and increase their lending, which increases the quantity of money. The Fed changes the required reserve ratio infrequently because a small change in the ratio would have a drastic effect on bank lending and the Fed has more refined tools at its disposal.

### ■ How the Discount Rate Works

If the Fed increases the discount rate, the banks must pay a higher price for any reserves that they borrow from the Fed. Faced with higher cost of reserves, the banks are less willing to borrow reserves and prefer to decrease their lending. So when the discount rate increases, the quantity of money decreases. Similarly, if the Fed decreases the discount rate, the banks pay a lower price for reserves that they borrow from the Fed. Faced with a lower cost of reserves, the banks are more willing to borrow reserves and increase their lending. So when the discount rate decreases, the quantity of money increases. The discount rate has limited effect because the banks rarely borrow from the Fed.

### ■ How an Open Market Operation Works

Open market operations are the Fed's major policy tool. When the Fed buys securities in an open market operation, it pays for them with newly created bank reserves and money. With more reserves in the banking system, the supply of interbank loans increases, the demand for interbank loans decreases, and the federal funds rate—the interest rate in the interbank loans market—falls. Similarly, when the Fed sells securities in an open market operation, buyers pay for the securities with bank reserves and money. With smaller reserves in the banking system, the supply of interbank loans decreases, the demand for interbank loans increases, and the federal funds rate rises. The Fed sets a target for the federal funds rate and conducts open market operations on the scale needed to hit its target.

A change in the federal funds rate is only the first stage in an adjustment process that follows an open market operation. If banks' reserves increase, the banks can increase their lending and create even more money. If banks' reserves decrease, the banks must decrease their lending, which decreases the quantity of money. We'll study the effects of open market operations in some detail, beginning with an open market purchase.

## The Fed Buys Securities

Suppose the Fed buys $100 million of U.S. government securities in the open market. There are two cases to consider, depending on who sells the securities. A bank might sell some of its securities, or a person or business that is not a commercial bank—the general public—might sell. The outcome is essentially the same in the two cases, but you might need to be convinced of this fact. So we'll study the two cases, starting with the simpler case in which a commercial bank sells securities. (The seller will be someone who thinks the Fed is offering a good price for securities so that it is profitable to make the sale.)

**A Commercial Bank Sells** When the Fed buys $100 million of securities from the Manhattan Commercial Bank, two things happen:

1. The Manhattan Commercial Bank has $100 million less in securities, and the Fed has $100 million more in securities.
2. To pay for the securities, the Fed increases the Manhattan Commercial Bank's reserve account at the New York Fed by $100 million.

Figure 18.4 shows the effects of these actions on the balance sheets of the Fed and the Manhattan Commercial Bank. Ownership of the securities passes from the commercial bank to the Fed, so the bank's securities decrease by $100 million and the Fed's securities increase by $100 million, as shown by the red-to-blue arrow running from the Manhattan Commercial Bank to the Fed. The Fed increases the Manhattan Commercial Bank's reserves by $100 million, as shown by the green arrow running from the Fed to the Manhattan Commercial Bank. This action increases the monetary base and increases the reserves of the banking system.

The commercial bank's total assets remain constant, but their composition changes. Its holdings of government securities decrease by $100 million, and its reserves increase by $100 million. The bank can use these additional reserves to make loans. When the bank makes loans, the quantity of money increases by the process that we described in the previous section.

---

**FIGURE 18.4**                                          <u>**Practice Online**</u>
The Fed Buys Securities from a Commercial Bank

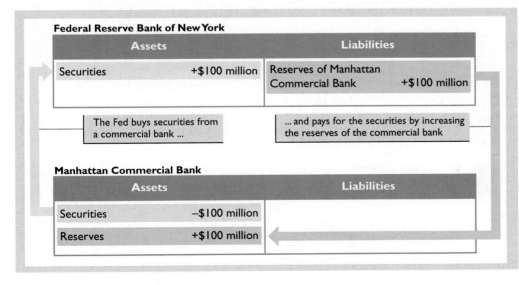

We've just seen that when the Fed buys government securities from a bank, the bank's reserves increase. What happens if the Fed buys government securities from the public—say, from Goldman Sachs, a financial services company?

**The Nonbank Public Sells** When the Fed buys $100 million of securities from Goldman Sachs, three things happen:

1. Goldman Sachs has $100 million less in securities, and the Fed has $100 million more in securities.

2. The Fed pays for the securities with a check for $100 million drawn on itself, which Goldman Sachs deposits in its account at the Manhattan Commercial Bank.

3. The Manhattan Commercial Bank collects payment of this check from the Fed, and the Manhattan Commercial Bank's reserves increase by $100 million.

Figure 18.5 shows the effects of these actions on the balance sheets of the Fed, Goldman Sachs, and the Manhattan Commercial Bank. Ownership of the securities passes from Goldman Sachs to the Fed, so Goldman Sachs's securities decrease by $100 million and the Fed's securities increase by $100 million (red-to-blue arrow). The Fed pays for the securities with a check payable to Goldman Sachs, which Goldman Sachs deposits in the Manhattan Commercial Bank. This payment increases Manhattan's reserves by $100 million (green arrow). It also

---

■ **FIGURE 18.5**

The Fed Buys Securities from the Public

**Practice Online**

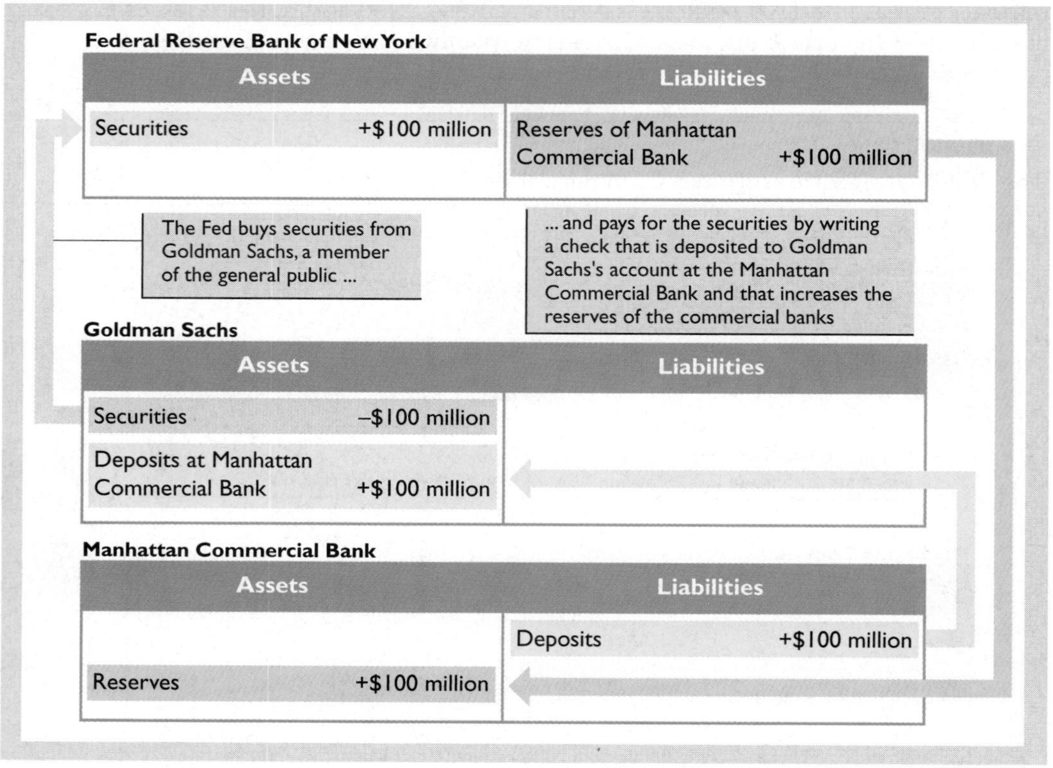

increases Goldman Sachs's deposit at the Manhattan Commercial Bank by $100 million (blue arrow). Just as when the Fed buys securities from a bank, this action increases the monetary base and increases the reserves of the banking system.

Goldman Sachs has the same total assets as before, but their composition has changed. It now has more money and fewer securities. The Manhattan Commercial Bank's reserves increase, and so do its deposits—both by $100 million. Because bank reserves and deposits have increased by the same amount, the bank has excess reserves, which it can use to make loans. When it makes loans, the quantity of money increases by the process that we described in the previous section.

We've worked through what happens when the Fed buys government securities from either a bank or the public. When the Fed sells securities, the transactions that we've just traced operate in reverse.

## The Fed Sells Securities

If the Fed sells $100 million of U.S. government securities in the open market, most likely a person or business other than a bank buys them. (A bank would buy them only if it had excess reserves and it couldn't find a better use of its funds.)

When the Fed sells $100 million of securities to Goldman Sachs, three things happen:

1. Goldman Sachs has $100 million more in securities, and the Fed has $100 million less in securities.

2. Goldman Sachs pays for the securities with a check for $100 million drawn on its deposit account at the Manhattan Commercial Bank.

3. The Fed collects payment of this check from the Manhattan Commercial Bank by decreasing its reserves by $100 million.

These actions decrease the monetary base and decrease the reserves of the banking system. The Manhattan Commercial Bank is now short of reserves and must borrow in the federal funds market to meet its required reserve ratio.

The changes in the balance sheets of the Fed and the banks that we've just described are not the end of the story about the effects of an open market operation; they are just the beginning. A multiplier effect on the quantity of money now begins. To study this multiplier effect of an open market operation on the quantity of money, we build on the link between bank reserves and bank deposits that you studied in the previous section.

## ■ The Multiplier Effect of an Open Market Operation

An open market purchase that increases bank reserves also increases the *monetary base*. The increase in the monetary base equals the amount of the open market purchase, and initially, it equals the increase in bank reserves. To see why, recall that the *monetary base is the sum of Federal Reserve notes, coins, and banks' reserves at the Fed*. An open market purchase increases the banks' reserves at the Fed by the amount of the open market purchase. Nothing else changes, so the monetary base increases by the amount of the open market purchase.

If the Fed buys securities from the banks, the quantity of deposits (and quantity of money) does not change. If the Fed buys securities from the public, the quantity of deposits (and quantity of money) increases by the same amount as the increase in bank reserves. Either way, the banks have excess reserves that they now start to lend.

Figure 18.6 illustrates the multiplier effect of an open market purchase of securities from the banks. The following sequence of events takes place:

- An open market purchase creates excess reserves.
- Banks lend excess reserves.
- Bank deposits increase.
- The quantity of money increases.
- New money is used to make payments.
- Some of the new money is held as currency—a currency drain.
- Some of the new money remains in deposits in banks.
- Banks' required reserves increase.
- Excess reserves decrease but remain positive.

**Currency drain**
An increase in currency held outside the banks.

This sequence is similar to the one you studied in the previous section of this chapter but with one addition: the currency drain. When banks use excess reserves to make loans, bank deposits increase but currency held outside the banks also increases. An increase in currency held outside the banks is called the **currency drain**. The currency drain does not change the monetary base. Bank reserves decrease, currency increases, and the monetary base remains the same. But a currency drain decreases the amount of money that banks can create from a given increase in the monetary base because currency drains from their reserves and decreases the excess reserves available.

The sequence of rounds described in Figure 18.6 repeats, but each round begins with a smaller quantity of excess reserves than did the previous one. The process ends when excess reserves have been eliminated.

---

**FIGURE 18.6**

A Round in the Multiplier Process Following an Open Market Operation

<u>**Practice Online**</u>

❶ An open market purchase increases bank reserves and ❷ creates excess reserves. ❸ Banks lend the excess reserves, ❹ new deposits are created, and ❺ the quantity of money increases. ❻ New money is used to make payments. ❼ Households and firms receiving payments keep some on deposit in banks and some in the form of currency—❽ a currency drain. The increase in bank deposits increases banks' reserves but also ❾ increases banks' required reserves. Required reserves increase by less than actual reserves, so the banks still have some excess reserves, though less than before. The process repeats until excess reserves have been eliminated.

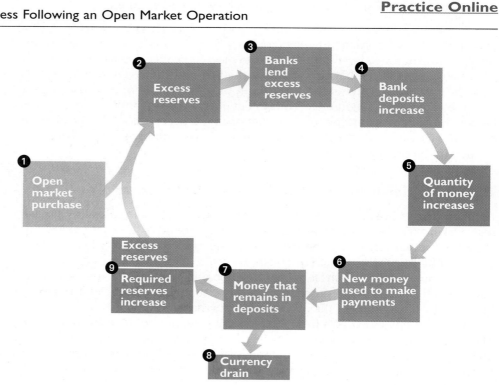

Figure 18.7 keeps track of the magnitudes of the increases in reserves, loans, deposits, currency, and money that result from an open market purchase of $100,000. In this figure, the currency drain is 33.33 percent of money and the required reserve ratio is 10 percent of deposits. These numbers are assumed to keep the arithmetic simple.

The Fed buys $100,000 of securities from the banks. The banks' reserves increase by this amount, but deposits do not change. The banks have excess reserves of $100,000, and they lend those reserves. When the banks lend $100,000 of excess reserves, $66,667 remains in the banks as deposits and $33,333 drains off and is held outside the banks as currency. The quantity of money has now increased by $100,000—the increase in deposits plus the increase in currency holdings.

The increased bank deposits of $66,667 generate an increase in required reserves of 10 percent of that amount, which is $6,667. Actual reserves have increased by the same amount as the increase in deposits—$66,667. So the banks now have excess reserves of $60,000. At this stage, we have gone around the circle shown in Figure 18.6 once. The process that we've just described repeats but begins with excess reserves of $60,000. Figure 18.7 shows the next two rounds. At the end of the process, the quantity of money has increased by a multiple of the increase in the monetary base. In this case, the increase is $250,000, which is 2.5 times the increase in the monetary base.

An open market *sale* works similarly to an open market *purchase*, but the sale *decreases* the quantity of money. (Trace the process again but with the Fed *selling* and the banks or public *buying* securities.)

**FIGURE 18.7**    **Practice Online**

The Multiplier Effect of an Open Market Operation

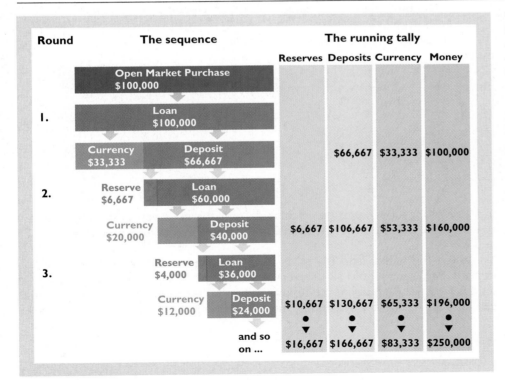

When the Fed provides the banks with $100,000 of additional reserves in an open market purchase, the banks lend those reserves. Of the amount loaned, $33,333 (33.33 percent) leaves the banks in a currency drain and $66,667 remains on deposit. With additional deposits, required reserves increase by $6,667 (10 percent required reserve ratio) and the banks lend $60,000. Of this amount, $20,000 leaves the banks in a currency drain and $40,000 remains on deposit. The process repeats until the banks have created enough deposits to eliminate their excess reserves. An additional $100,000 of reserves creates $250,000 of money.

### ■ The Money Multiplier

**Money multiplier**
The number by which a change in the monetary base is multiplied to find the resulting change in the quantity of money.

In the example we've just worked through, the quantity of money increases by 2.5 times the increase in the monetary base. The **money multiplier** is the number by which a change in the monetary base is multiplied to find the resulting change in the quantity of money. That is,

Change in quantity of money = Money multiplier × Change in monetary base.

In the example, the change in monetary base is the size of the open market purchase, which is $100,000, so

Change in quantity of money = 2.5 × $100,000 = $250,000.

The money multiplier is determined by the banks' required reserve ratio and by the currency drain. In the above example, the required reserve ratio is 10 percent of deposits and the currency drain is 33.33 percent of money. So when the banks lend their initial $100,000 of excess reserves, $33,333 drains off as currency and $66,667 remains in the banks as reserves and deposits.

With an additional $66,667 of deposits and a 10 percent required reserve ratio, the banks' required reserves increase by $6,667, so their excess reserves are $60,000. Notice that $60,000 is 0.6 of the original $100,000 of excess reserves. That is, in the second round of lending, the banks lend 0.6 of the amount they loaned in the first round. Call this proportion $L$ ($L = 0.6$). In the third round, the banks lend $0.6^2 = 0.36$ of the original amount ($36,000 in Figure 18.7).

Because $L$ is a fraction, at each stage in this sequence the amounts of new loans and new money created get smaller. The total amount of new money created at the end of the process is

$$\text{Quantity of money created} = \frac{1}{1 - L} \times \text{Open market purchase.}$$

If we use the numbers from the example, the total increase in the quantity of money is

$$\text{Quantity of money created} = \$100,000 \times \frac{1}{(1 - 0.6)}$$

$$= \$100,000 \times \frac{1}{0.4}$$

$$= \$100,000 \times 2.5$$

$$= \$250,000.$$

The proportion $L$ can be calculated from the currency drain and required reserve ratio. Call the currency drain $C$ and the required reserve ratio $R$. So $C = 0.33$ and $R = 0.1$.

When the banks lend $1, $C$ is held as currency and $(1 - C)$ remains on deposit. Banks must hold $R$ of reserves for each $1 of deposits, so they are free to lend $(1 - R)$ of each dollar on deposit. When $(1 - C)$ remains on deposit, banks can lend $(1 - C) \times (1 - R)$. That is, the proportion $L$ is

$$L = (1 - C) \times (1 - R).$$

## The Money Multiplier

We can measure the money multiplier in the United States by using the following formula:

Money multiplier = Quantity of money ÷ Monetary base.

Because there are two main definitions of money, M1 and M2, there are two money multipliers: the M1 multiplier and the M2 multiplier.

Also, there are two measures of the currency drain and bank reserve ratios. Part (a) shows the currency drain measures: the ratio of currency to M1 and the ratio of currency to M2.

Notice the increase in the ratio of currency to M1, which arises mainly from a surge in holdings of U.S. currency abroad.

In part (b), you can see that the reserve ratios have fallen as required reserve ratios have been decreased.

In part (c), you can see the two money multipliers. The M2 multiplier increased through the 1980s because required reserves decreased. This multiplier decreased during the 1990s because the currency drain increased. In 2002, this multiplier was about 8.

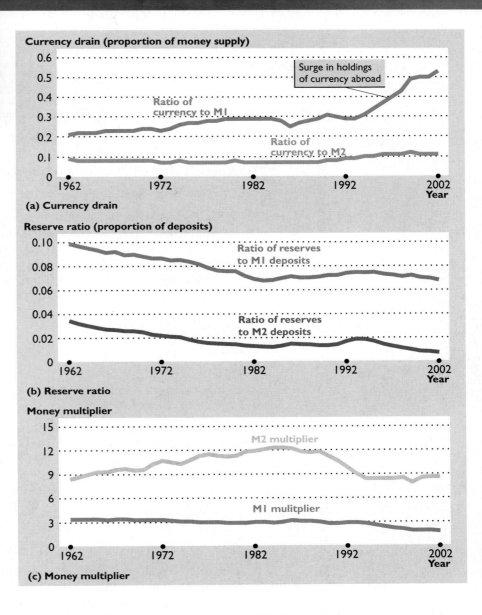

**(a) Currency drain**

**(b) Reserve ratio**

**(c) Money multiplier**

The M1 multiplier decreased from close to 4 in 1960 to about 2 in 2000.

The increasing currency drain is the main influence on this multiplier.

In terms of the numbers in our example,

$$L = (1 - 0.33) \times (1 - 0.1)$$

$$= (0.67) \times (0.9) = 0.6.$$

The larger the currency drain and the larger the required reserve ratio, the smaller is the money multiplier.

Study Guide pp. 273–277

Practice Online 18.2

**2** Explain how the Fed controls the quantity of money.

## Practice Problems 18.2

1. Which of the Fed's tools does it use most often?

2. What is the money multiplier? What determines its magnitude?

3. If the Fed makes an open market purchase of $1 million of securities,
   a. Who can sell the securities to the Fed in an open market operation? Does it matter from whom the Fed buys the securities?
   b. What initial changes occur in the economy if the Fed buys from a bank?
   c. What is the process by which the quantity of money changes?
   d. What factors determine how much the quantity of money changes?

## Exercises 18.2

1. What is an open market operation? How do open market operations influence the monetary base?

2. Explain how the banking system creates money when the Fed conducts an open market operation.

3. If the Fed makes an open market sale of $1 million of securities,
   a. What initial changes occur in the economy?
   b. What is the process by which the quantity of money in the economy changes?
   c. By how much does the quantity of money change?
   d. What is the magnitude of the money multiplier?

## Solutions to Practice Problems 18.2

1. The Fed's most used tool is the open market operation.

2. The money multiplier is the number by which a change in the monetary base is multiplied to find the resulting change in the quantity of money. The currency drain and the banks' required reserve ratio determine its magnitude.

3a. The Fed buys securities from banks or the public. The Fed does not buy securities from the government. It does not matter from whom the Fed buys the securities. The change in the monetary base is the same.

3b. The monetary base increases by $1 million. Ownership of the securities passes from the bank to the Fed. As a result, the Fed's assets increase by $1 million. When the Fed pays for the securities, it increases the bank's deposit with the Fed by $1 million. The Fed's liabilities increase by $1 million. The bank's assets are the same, but their composition has changed. The bank has $1 million more in reserves and $1 million less in securities.

3c. The bank's reserves have increased by $1 million and its deposits have not changed, so it has excess reserves of $1 million. The bank makes loans and creates new deposits. The new deposits are new money.

3d. The required reserve ratio and the currency drain determine the increase in the quantity of money. The larger the required reserve ratio or the currency drain, the smaller is the increase in the quantity of money.

# CHAPTER CHECKPOINT

## Key Points

### 1    Explain how banks create money by making loans.

- Banks create money by making loans.
- Banks hold a proportion of their deposits as reserves to meet the *required reserve ratio.*
- Reserves that exceed the required reserve ratio are *excess reserves,* which banks loan.
- The quantity of reserves and the required reserve ratio limit the total quantity of deposits that the banks can create.
- The deposit multiplier is the number by which an increase in bank reserves is multiplied to give the increase in bank deposits.
- The deposit multiplier equals one divided by the required reserve ratio.

### 2    Explain how the Fed controls the quantity of money.

- The Fed has three tools for controlling the quantity of money: required reserve ratios, the discount rate, and open market operations.
- An increase in the required reserve ratio forces the banks to hold more reserves and decreases the quantity of money that can be supported by a given amount of monetary base.
- An increase in the discount rate makes the banks pay a higher price for borrowed reserves, makes them less willing to borrow reserves, and decreases the quantity of money.
- When the Fed *buys* securities in an open market operation, it pays for them with newly created bank reserves. When the Fed *sells* securities in an open market operation, people pay for them with money and banks pay for them with reserves.
- An open market purchase increases the monetary base and creates the following sequence of events: banks lend excess reserves; the quantity of money increases; new money is used to make payments; some of the new money is held as currency—a currency drain; some of the new money remains on deposit in banks; banks' required reserves increase; excess reserves decrease. This sequence repeats until excess reserves are eliminated.
- The money multiplier determines the amount of money that banks can create from a given increase in the monetary base.
- The money multiplier is determined by the banks' required reserve ratio and by the currency drain.

## Key Terms

## Exercises

1. If the banking system receives new deposits of $2 million, the required reserve ratio is 0.1, and there is no currency drain, calculate
   a. The bank's excess reserves as soon as the deposit is made.
   b. The maximum amount of loans that the banking system can make.
   c. The maximum amount of new money that the banking system can create.

2. If the banking system loses deposits of $3 million, the required reserve ratio is 0.1, and there is no currency drain, calculate
   a. The bank's excess reserves as soon as the deposit withdrawal occurs.
   b. The amount of loans that the banking system must call in.
   c. The amount of money that the banking system must destroy.

3. The required reserve ratio is 5 percent and the currency drain is 20 percent. If the Fed makes an open market purchase of $1 million of securities,
   a. What is the change in the monetary base?
   b. Which components of the monetary base change?
   c. By how much does the quantity of money change?
   d. How much of the new money is currency and how much is bank deposits?

4. Initially, the banking system has $2 trillion of deposits and no excess reserves. If the Fed lowers the required reserve ratio from 0.1 to 0.05, calculate the change in
   a. Reserves.
   b. Deposits.
   c. The quantity of money.

5. The First Student Bank has the following balance sheet (in millions of dollars).

| Assets | | Liabilities | |
| --- | --- | --- | --- |
| Reserves at the Fed | 25 | Demand deposits | 90 |
| Cash in ATMs | 15 | Savings deposits | 110 |
| Government securities | 60 | | |
| Loans | 100 | | |

The required reserve ratio on all deposits is 5 percent.
   a. What, if any, are the bank's excess reserves?
   b. What is the bank's deposit multiplier?
   c. How much will the bank loan?
   d. If there is no currency drain and if all the funds loaned are deposited in the First Student Bank, what are the bank's excess reserves, if any, after the loans made in part c?
   e. If there is no currency drain and if all the funds loaned remain deposited in the First Student Bank, what is the quantity of loans and total deposits when the bank has no excess reserves?
   f. If the required reserve ratio is decreased to 2 percent and if there is no currency drain and all the funds loaned remain deposited in the First Student Bank, what is the quantity of loans and total deposits when the bank has no excess reserves?

6.  The Second Student Bank has the following balance sheet (in millions of dollars).

| Assets | | Liabilities | |
|---|---|---|---|
| Reserves at the Fed | 3 | Demand deposits | 90 |
| Cash in ATMs | 2 | Savings deposits | 110 |
| Government securities | 85 | | |
| Loans | 110 | | |

The required reserve ratio on all deposits is 5 percent.
   a. Does the bank have any excess reserves?
   b. Does the bank have a shortage of reserves?
   c. How much of the outstanding loans will the bank not renew?
   d. If there is no currency drain and if all the loans that are repaid are paid out of deposits in the Second Student Bank, what is the bank's shortage of reserves, if any, after the loans are repaid in part c?
   e. If there is no currency drain and if all the loans are repaid come from deposits in the Second Student Bank, what is the quantity of loans and total deposits when the bank has no excess reserves?

7.  If the Fed wants to decrease quantity of money, what type of open market operation might it undertake? Explain the process by which the quantity of money decreases.

8.  Suppose that the currency drain is 10 percent and the required reserve ratio is 1 percent. If the Fed sells $100,000 of securities on the open market, calculate the first round changes in
   a. Excess reserves.
   b. Deposits.
   c. Currency in circulation.

9.  What can the Fed do to increase the quantity of money and keep the monetary base constant? Explain why the Fed would or would not do each of the following:
   a. Change the currency drain
   b. Change the required reserve ratio
   c. Change the discount rate
   d. Conduct an open market operation

10. The commercial banks have the following balance sheet (in billions of dollars).

| Assets | | Liabilities | |
|---|---|---|---|
| Reserves | 10 | Deposits | 210 |
| Government securities | 50 | | |
| Loans | 150 | | |

The required reserve ratio is 5 percent, there is no currency drain, and the Fed conducts an open market purchase of securities of $1 billion.
   a. What is the initial change in the reserves of the banks?
   b. By how much do loans increase?
   c. By how much do deposits increase?

## Critical Thinking

11. An early goldsmith banker earned a profit (and sometimes a large profit) simply by writing notes to certify that a person had deposited a certain amount of gold in his vault. By writing more notes than the amount of gold held, the goldsmith could lend the notes and charge interest on them.
    a. Did the goldsmith bankers make money out of thin air in a form of legal theft?
    b. Should the goldsmith bankers have been regulated to ensure that the amount of gold in their vaults equaled the value of the notes they created?
    c. What were the main benefits from the activities of the goldsmith bankers?

12. In the United States today, the Federal Reserve is the only bank that is permitted to create bank notes.
    a. Do you think that Citigroup and JP Morgan Chase should be permitted to issue their own private bank notes in competition with the Fed?
    b. Do you think the Fed should be the only bank that is permitted to issue e-cash?

13. Bank deposits are insured against the risk of bank failure. Can you think of any bad side effects of this arrangement?

**Practice Online**  ## Web Exercises

**Use the links on your Foundations Web site to work the following exercises.**

14. Visit the Web site of JP Morgan Chase and obtain the most recent balance sheet data for this bank.
    a. What is the total amount of deposits?
    b. What is the total amount of loans?
    c. What is the total amount of reserves held?
    d. What is the reserve ratio?
    e. Why can't you determine from the published balance sheet the deposits that are part of M1 and the deposits that are part of M2?

15. Visit the Web sites of JP Morgan Chase and Citigroup and obtain the most recent earnings data for these large banks.
    a. What are their profits during the most recent year?
    b. Explain how these banks earn such large profits.

16. Visit the Web site of the Federal Reserve and obtain the most recent data on the monetary base, M1, M2, and the composition of money and calculate for the most recent month
    a. The currency drain (using both M1 and M2).
    b. The banks' reserve ratio (using both the M1 deposits and the M2 deposits).
    c. The money multiplier (for both M1 and M2).

17. Visit the Web site of the Federal Reserve and obtain the most recent information on "Factors Affecting Reserve Balances of Depository Institutions."
    a. Have the reserves of depository institutions increased or decreased?
    b. Has the Fed increased or decreased the amount that it has loaned to depository institutions?

# CHAPTER 19

# Money, Interest, and Inflation

**When you have completed your study of this chapter,
you will be able to**

1. Explain what determines the demand for money and how the demand for money and the supply of money determine the *nominal* interest rate.

2. Explain how in the long run, the quantity of money determines the price level and money growth brings inflation.

3. Identify the costs of inflation and the benefits of a stable value of money.

You know what money is, how banks create it, and how the Fed controls its quantity. In this chapter, you are going to learn about the effects of money on the economy.

First, you'll see how, on any given day, the quantity of money determines the interest rate. The effect of money on the interest rate is one of the channels through which the Fed influences expenditure plans and the business cycle. You'll learn more about these aspects of money in subsequent chapters.

Second, you'll see how, when we smooth out the influence of the business cycle and look at the long-term trends, the quantity of money determines the price level and money growth in excess of potential GDP growth brings inflation.

Finally, you'll see why inflation—ongoing *changes* in the price level—can have a big influence on people's lives.

# WHERE WE ARE AND WHERE WE'RE HEADING

Before we explore the effects of money on the interest rate and the inflation rate, let's take stock of what we've learned and preview where we are heading.

## ■ The Real Economy and the Standard of Living

To understand why real GDP per person in the United States is almost 20 times that in Nigeria, or why real GDP per person in the United States in 2003 is twice what it was in 1963, we need to consider differences in the quantities of labor and capital and their productivity. These *real* factors are the source of differences in living standards across regions and countries and over time (Chapter 16). These real factors are independent of the price level. That is, to explain differences in real GDP across countries and over long time periods, we can ignore differences in the cost of living. In the long term, the forces that determine the standard of living are independent of those that determine the cost of living.

## ■ The Money Economy, the Cost of Living, and the Business Cycle

Money—the economy's means of payment—consists of currency and bank deposits (Chapter 17). Banks create deposits by making loans, and the Fed controls the quantity of money through its open market operations, which determine the monetary base and the federal funds—interbank loans—interest rate (Chapter 18).

The effects of money on the economy, which we explore in this chapter, are complex and to explain and understand them, we proceed in three steps. We take these steps in an order that might seem strange but that turns out to be the most effective.

Step one looks at the immediate effect of the Fed's actions. This effect is on the short-term nominal interest rate. The Fed raises and lowers the short-term nominal interest rate by changing the quantity of money.

Step two looks at the long-term effects of the Fed's actions. These effects are on the price level and the inflation rate—on the cost of living and its rate of change. The Fed lowers or raises the price level by decreasing or increasing the quantity of money. And the Fed lowers or raises the inflation rate by slowing down or speeding up the rate at which the quantity of money grows. We take these two steps in the current chapter.

Step three provides the blow-by-blow story of how the Fed's actions ripple through the economy and ultimately change the price level and the inflation rate. This story is a long one that needs to be broken down into manageable bites, and we explore it in Chapters 20 and 21 with the help of a model of the economy that enables us to understand the business cycle and the possibility of moderating the cycle by adjusting the quantity of money and the interest rate.

Some people approach a novel in this order: first, read the introduction, then the conclusion, and then the steps in between. Try it. It sometimes helps to keep track of where you are if you know where you are going to end up!

## 19.1 MONEY AND THE INTEREST RATE

To understand the Fed's short-run influence on the interest rate, we must understand what determines the demand for money, the supply of money, and the forces that bring equilibrium in the market for money. We'll begin by studying the demand for money.

### ■ The Demand for Money

The amount of money that households and firms choose to hold is the **quantity of money demanded**. What determines the quantity of money demanded? The answer is a benefit–opportunity cost calculation. The quantity of money that households and firms choose to hold is the quantity that balances the benefit of holding an additional dollar of money against the opportunity cost of doing so. But just what are the benefit and opportunity cost of holding money?

**Quantity of money demanded**
The amount of money that households and firms choose to hold.

#### Benefit of Holding Money

You've seen that money is the means of payment and that it serves as a medium of exchange, unit of account, and store of value (Chapter 17, pp. 428–429). You don't need any money to use it as a unit of account. You can keep financial records in dollars and cents even if you don't have any money. You don't need money to store your wealth. You can store it in the form of bonds, stocks, and mutual funds. Money and other financial assets are substitute stores of value. But you do need money to make payments and do transactions. These two features of money are the sources of benefit from holding money. The more money you hold, the easier it is for you to make payments and transactions.

The marginal benefit of holding money is the change in total benefit that results from holding one more dollar as money. The marginal benefit of holding money diminishes as the quantity of money held increases. If you hold only a few dollars in money, holding one more dollar brings large benefits—you can buy a cup of coffee, take a bus ride, or use a pay phone. If you hold enough money to make your normal weekly payments, holding one more dollar brings only a small benefit because you're not very likely to want to spend it. Holding even more money brings only a small additional benefit. You barely notice the difference in the benefit of having $1,000 versus $1,001 in your bank account.

To get the most out of your assets, you hold money only up to the point at which its marginal benefit equals its opportunity cost. But what is the opportunity cost of holding money?

#### Opportunity Cost of Holding Money

The opportunity cost of holding money is the interest rate forgone on an alternative asset. If you can earn 8 percent a year on a mutual fund account, then holding an additional $100 in money costs you $8 a year. Your opportunity cost of holding $100 in money is the goods and services worth $8 that you must forgo.

A fundamental principle of economics is that if the opportunity cost of something increases, people seek substitutes for it. Money is no exception. Other assets such as a mutual fund account are substitutes for money. And the higher the opportunity cost of holding money—the higher the interest income forgone by not holding other assets—the smaller is the quantity of money demanded.

### Opportunity Cost: *Nominal* Interest Is a *Real* Cost

The opportunity cost of holding money is the nominal interest rate. In Chapter 14, (p. 367), you learned the distinction between the *nominal* interest rate and the *real* interest rate and that

$$\text{Nominal interest rate} = \text{Real interest rate} + \text{Inflation rate.}$$

We can use this equation to find the real interest rate for a given nominal interest rate and inflation rate. For example, if the nominal interest rate on a mutual fund account is 8 percent a year and the inflation rate is 2 percent a year, the real interest rate is 6 percent a year. Why isn't the real interest rate of 6 percent a year the opportunity cost of holding money? That is, why isn't the opportunity cost of holding $100 in money only $6 worth of goods and services forgone?

The answer is that if you hold $100 in money rather than in a mutual fund, your buying power decreases by $8, not by $6. With inflation running at 2 percent a year, on each $100 that you hold as money and that earns no interest, you lose $2 worth of buying power a year. On each $100 that you put into your mutual fund account, you gain $6 worth of buying power a year. So if you hold money rather than a mutual fund, you lose the buying power of $6 plus $2, or $8—equivalent to the nominal interest rate on the mutual fund, not the real interest rate.

Because the opportunity cost of holding money is the nominal interest rate on an alternative asset,

> **Other things remaining the same, the higher the nominal interest rate, the smaller is the quantity of money demanded.**

This relationship describes the money holding decisions of individuals and firms. It also describes money holding decisions for the economy—the sum of the decisions of every individual and firm.

We summarize the influence of the nominal interest rate on money holding decisions in a demand for money schedule and curve.

### The Demand for Money Schedule and Curve

**Demand for money**
The relationship between the quantity of money demanded and the nominal interest rate, when all other influences on the amount of money that people wish to hold remain the same.

The **demand for money** is the relationship between the quantity of money demanded and the nominal interest rate, when all other influences on the amount of money that people wish to hold remain the same. We illustrate the demand for money with a demand for money schedule and a demand for money curve, such as those in Figure 19.1. If the interest rate is 5 percent a year, the quantity of money demanded is $1 trillion. The quantity of money demanded decreases to $0.98 trillion if the interest rate rises to 6 percent a year and increases to $1.02 trillion if the interest rate falls to 4 percent a year.

The demand for money curve is *MD*. When the interest rate rises, everything else remaining the same, the opportunity cost of holding money rises and the quantity of money demanded decreases—there is a movement up along the demand for money curve. When the interest rate falls, the opportunity cost of holding money falls and the quantity of money demanded increases—there is a movement down along the demand for money curve.

■ **FIGURE 19.1**
The Demand for Money

**Practice Online**

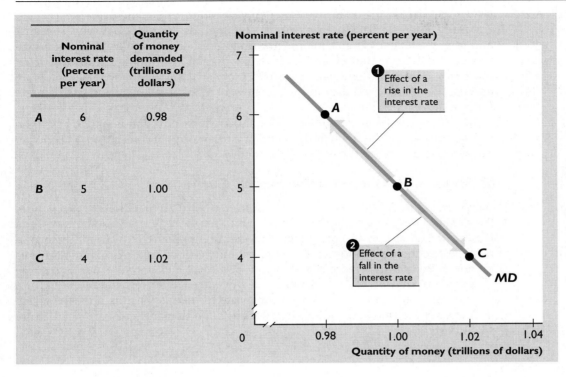

| | Nominal interest rate (percent per year) | Quantity of money demanded (trillions of dollars) |
|---|---|---|
| **A** | 6 | 0.98 |
| **B** | 5 | 1.00 |
| **C** | 4 | 1.02 |

The demand for money schedule is graphed as the demand for money curve, MD. Rows A, B, and C in the table correspond to points A, B, and C on the curve. The nominal interest rate is the opportunity cost of holding money.

❶ Other things remaining the same, an increase in the nominal interest rate decreases the quantity of money demanded, and ❷ a decrease in the nominal interest rate increases the quantity of money demanded.

■ **Changes in the Demand for Money**

A change in the nominal interest rate brings a change in the quantity of money demanded and a movement along the demand for money curve. A change in any other influence on money holding changes the demand for money. The three main influences on the demand for money are

- The price level
- Real GDP
- Financial technology

**The Price Level**

The demand for money is proportional to the price level—an $x$ percent rise in the price level brings an $x$ percent increase in the quantity of money demanded at each nominal interest rate. The reason is that we hold money to make payments: If the price level changes, the quantity of dollars that we need to make payments changes in the same proportion.

**Real GDP**

The demand for money increases as real GDP increases. The reason is that expenditures and incomes increase when real GDP increases. So households and firms must hold larger average inventories of money to make the increased expenditures and income payments.

### Financial Technology

Changes in financial technology change the demand for money. Most changes in financial technology come from advances in computing and record keeping. Some advances increase the quantity of money demanded, and some decrease it.

Daily interest checking deposits and automatic transfers between checking and savings deposits enable people to earn interest on money, lower the opportunity cost of holding money, and increase the demand for money. Automatic teller machines, debit cards, and smart cards, which have made money easier to obtain and use, have increased the marginal benefit of money and increased the demand for money.

Credit cards have made it easier for people to buy goods and services on credit and pay for them when their credit card account becomes due. This development has decreased the demand for money.

## ■ Shifts in the Demand for Money Curve

A change in any influence on money holdings other than the interest rate changes the demand for money and shifts the demand for money curve, as you can see in Figure 19.2. A rise in the price level, an increase in real GDP, or an advance in financial technology that lowers the opportunity cost of holding money or makes money more useful increases the demand for money and shifts the demand curve rightward from $MD_0$ to $MD_1$. A fall in the price level, a decrease in real GDP, or a technological advance that creates a substitute for money has the opposite effect. It decreases the demand for money and shifts the demand curve leftward from $MD_0$ to $MD_2$.

---

**■ FIGURE 19.2**

Changes in the Demand for Money

**Practice Online**

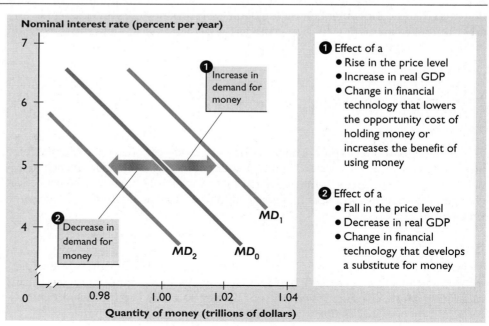

## ■ The Nominal Interest Rate

People hold some of their financial wealth as money and some in the form of other financial assets. You have seen that the amount that people hold as money depends on the nominal interest rate that they can earn on other financial assets. Demand and supply determine the nominal interest rate. We can study the forces of demand and supply in either the market for financial assets or the market for money. Because the Fed influences the quantity of money, we focus on the market for money.

Figure 19.3 shows the market for money. The quantity of money supplied is determined by the actions of the banking system and the Fed. On any given day, there is a fixed quantity of money supplied. In Figure 19.3, that quantity is $1 trillion. The **supply of money**, which is the relationship between the quantity of money supplied and the nominal interest rate, is shown by the vertical line *MS*.

Also, on any given day, the price level, real GDP, and the state of financial technology are fixed. Because these influences on the demand for money are fixed, the demand for money curve is given and is the curve *MD* in Figure 19.3.

The interest rate is the only influence on the quantity of money demanded that is free to fluctuate. And every day, the interest rate adjusts to make the quantity of money demanded equal the quantity of money supplied—to achieve money market equilibrium. In Figure 19.3, the equilibrium interest rate is 5 percent a year. At any interest rate above 5 percent a year, the quantity of money demanded is less than the quantity of money supplied. At any interest rate below 5 percent a year, the quantity of money demanded exceeds the quantity of money supplied.

**Supply of money**
The relationship between the quantity of money supplied and the nominal interest rate.

---

■ **FIGURE 19.3**
Money Market Equilibrium

Practice Online

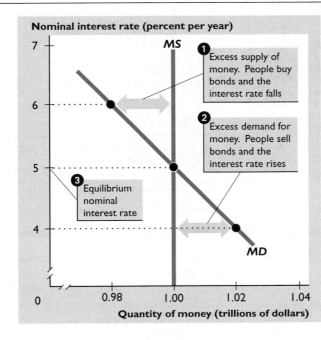

The supply of money curve is *MS*, and the demand for money curve is *MD*.

❶ If the interest rate is 6 percent a year, the quantity of money held exceeds the quantity demanded. People buy bonds, the price of a bond rises, and the interest rate falls.

❷ If the interest rate is 4 percent a year, the quantity of money held falls short of the quantity demanded. People sell bonds, the price of a bond falls, and the interest rate rises.

❸ If the interest rate is 5 percent a year, the quantity of money held equals the quantity demanded. The money market is in equilibrium.

# Eye on the U.S. Economy

## Money and Credit Cards

The quantity of M1 money has decreased as a percentage of GDP. Part (a) of the figure shows that M1 fell from 20 percent of GDP in 1970 to less than 12 percent in 2002.

In sharp contrast to the use of M1 money, credit card ownership and use has expanded strongly. Part (b) of the figure shows the upward trend. In 1970, 16 percent (one in six) of families had a credit card. By 1999, 72 percent of families had a credit card. And by 2005, it is projected that 80 percent of families will use a credit card.

Most people use their credit card account as a substitute for money. When they buy goods or services, they use their credit card. And when the monthly bill arrives, many people pay off some of the outstanding balance, but not all of it. In 1998, 42 percent of credit card holders had an outstanding balance after making their most recent payment, and the average card balance was $4,000.

The changing financial technology has led to a steady decrease in the demand for money and a leftward shift of the demand for money curve. Part (c) of the figure shows the shifts in the demand curve for M1. Here, we're measuring the quantity of M1 as a percentage of GDP so that you can see the influence of the interest rate and financial technology on the demand for money.

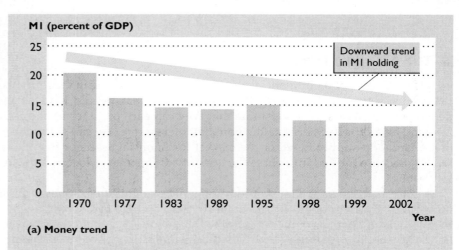

(a) Money trend

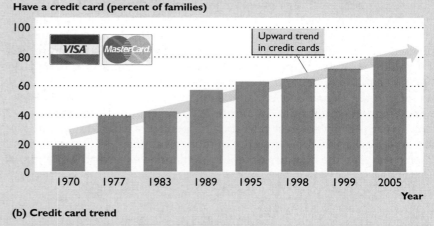

(b) Credit card trend

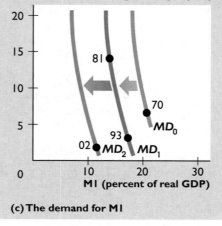

(c) The demand for M1

SOURCE: The Federal Reserve.

**The Interest Rate and Bond Price Move in Opposite Directions** When the government issues a bond, it specifies the dollar amount of interest that it will pay each year on the bond. Suppose that the government issues a bond that pays $100 of interest a year. The interest *rate* that you receive on this bond depends on the price that you pay for it. If the price is $1,000, the interest rate is 10 percent a year—$100 is 10 percent of $1,000.

If the price of the bond *falls* to $500, the interest rate *rises* to 20 percent a year. The reason is that you still receive an interest payment of $100, but this amount is 20 percent of the $500 price of the bond. If the price of the bond *rises* to $2,000, the interest rate *falls* to 5 percent a year. Again, you still receive an interest payment of $100, but this amount is 5 percent of the $2,000 price of the bond.

***Interest Rate Adjustment***    If the interest rate is above its equilibrium level, people would like to hold less money than they are actually holding. So they try to get rid of money by buying other financial assets such as bonds. The demand for financial assets increases, the prices of these assets rise, and the interest rate falls. The interest rate keeps falling until the quantity of money that people want to hold increases to equal the quantity of money supplied.

Conversely, when the interest rate is below its equilibrium level, people are holding less money than they would like to hold. So they try to get more money by selling other financial assets. The demand for financial assets decreases, the prices of these assets fall, and the interest rate rises. The interest rate keeps rising until the quantity of money that people want to hold decreases to equal the quantity of money supplied.

## ■ Changing the Interest Rate

To change the interest rate, the Fed changes the quantity of money. Figure 19.4 illustrates two changes. The demand for money curve is *MD*. If the Fed increases the quantity of money to $1.02 trillion, the supply of money curve shifts rightward from $MS_0$ to $MS_1$ and the interest rate falls to 4 percent a year. If the Fed decreases the quantity of money to $0.98 trillion, the supply of money curve shifts leftward from $MS_0$ to $MS_2$ and the interest rate rises to 6 percent a year.

■ **FIGURE 19.4**

Interest Rate Changes

Practice Online

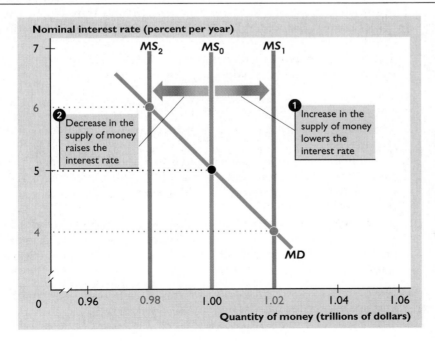

The demand for money is *MD*, and initially, the supply of money is $MS_0$. The interest rate is 5 percent a year.

❶ The Fed increases the quantity of money and the supply of money curve shifts to $MS_1$. The interest rate falls to 4 percent a year.

❷ The Fed decreases the quantity of money and the supply of money curve shifts to $MS_2$. The interest rate rises to 6 percent a year.